Managing Depression, Growing Older

Even when he's grey around the muzzle, the black dog of depression can still deliver a ferocious bite.

Depression can strike at any age, and it may appear for the first time as we get older, as a result of life circumstances or our genetic makeup. While older people face the same kinds of mental health issues as younger people, they can find it more difficult to deal with them owing to the stressors which accumulate with age. There is also a high incidence of undiagnosed depression in older age, presenting extra challenges for carers.

Managing Depression, Growing Older offers a systematic guide to identifying depression in older people, supporting them at home or in an aged care setting, and the importance of diet, exercise and attitude in recovery. It is essential reading for anyone who works with the elderly.

Kerrie Eyers is a psychologist, teacher and editor with many years' experience in mental health, based at the Black Dog Institute, Sydney, Australia.

Gordon Parker is Scientia Professor of Psychiatry at the University of New South Wales and Executive Director of the Black Dog Institute, Sydney, Australia. He is a renowned researcher with over 30 years' experience with mood disorders.

Henry Brodaty is Professor of Psychogeriatrics at the University of New South Wales and Director of the Academic Department for Old Age Psychiatry at the Prince of Wales and Prince Henry Hospitals.

Managing Dep
Growing Older

A guide for professionals and carers

Kerrie
Henry

Routledge
Taylor & Franci

LONDON AND NEV

First published in Australia 2012
By Allen & Unwin
Sydney, Melbourne, Auckland, London

First published in the United Kingdom 2012
by Routledge
27 Church Road, Hove, East Sussex BN3 2FA

Simultaneously published in the USA and Canada
by Routledge
711 Third Avenue, New York NY 10017

Routledge is an imprint of the Taylor & Francis Group, an informa business

British Library Cataloguing in Publication Data
A catalogue record for this book is available from the British Library

Library of Congress Cataloging in Publication Data
A Catalog record for this title has been requested

ISBN: 978-0-415-52150-5 (hbk)
ISBN: 978-0-415-52151-2 (pbk)

Typeset by Midland Typesetters, Australia

MIX
Paper from
responsible sources
FSC
www.fsc.org   **FSC® C004839**

Printed and bound by CPI Group (UK) Ltd, Croydon, CR0 4YY

Contents

Foreword

This book on depression and ageing is timely. The world is getting older. Life expectancy is increasing a year each decade, and baby girls born today in Western countries have a 50 per cent chance of reaching 100. Currently, centenarians are the fastest growing demographic group. The baby boomers born after 1945 are starting to turn 65, and are planning or already enjoying retirement. In countries such as Japan, Sweden and the United Kingdom, 20 per cent of the population are already aged over 65, and this percentage is expected to climb further (to 25–30 per cent) in the next 30 years. Other Western countries are less than a generation behind. China, India and many developing countries will achieve similar rates of ageing within one or two generations.

Age catches us by surprise. Something happens and we realise that we are not young. It may be a change in our physical ability, earning capacity or mental agility. It may be the realisation that the attractive young colleague whom we think of as an equal regards us as parental or, worse, does not even notice us. It may be the shop attendant who talks to our adult child or grandchild and overlooks the wise person (us) standing in front of them. Or it may be illness that makes us grasp all too concretely the fact of our mortality. Perhaps it is a growing feeling that we are a burden on others or that we are no longer making a contribution. Grief over losses and loneliness may add to the toll.

Depression is no stranger to old age. Surprisingly, perhaps, rates are said to be no higher in the elderly, except for particular groups. Older people afflicted by pain, a physical illness (especially heart disease), or any condition affecting the brain such as stroke,

Alzheimer's or Parkinson's disease have high rates of 'clinical' depression. Older people in residential care and carers of people with dementia are also prone to depression.

However, growing old is not a diagnosis and becoming depressed is not a normal accompaniment of ageing. When depression does affect an older person, it is more likely to be melancholic, which means that it is coloured by symptoms such as loss of appetite and weight, disturbed sleep, agitation, slowing of movements and thinking—or in severe cases, delusions of poverty, persecution or disease. Suicidal risk also climbs steeply with older age—especially in men—but signs of depression should be taken seriously at any age. Such a melancholic pattern may reflect reversible chemical changes and/or structural brain changes, as detailed later.

This book presents 'inside out' views from people with depression and those who care for them, and their strategies for dealing with it, gleaned from accounts sent to the annual Black Dog Institute writing competition. It also offers 'outside in' views from clinicians who are international experts in psychogeriatrics, sharing their experiences of helping people with depression. We aim to bring the 'invisible people'—that is, older people with depression—out of the shadows and give them and their carers a voice. We hope to reduce the double stigma of ageism—discrimination just for being old—and mental illness.

Older people themselves have strong prejudices against both psychiatry and seeking treatment for depression. After all, they grew up in an era when seeing a psychiatrist was equivalent to being crazy, when psychiatrists were called 'alienists' by their medical colleagues, when drugs for treatment of mental illness had not been developed and when admission to a psychiatric hospital—the 'lunatic asylum' or 'bin'—meant you might be committed there for years, or even for life. The current generation of older people have gone through life believing you do not talk about depression or ever admit to not coping.

The stories and case notes presented here (all identifying details have been changed) demonstrate the varied presentations of depression, and the many different approaches used to overcome it and to resume growing older with grace and contentment. Contributors to this book—comprising people with depression, their loved ones and specialist clinicians—have been honest and revealing. The clinicians discuss their successes and failures and the lessons they have learnt.

We hope this book contributes to the better understanding of aspects of growing older and increases compassion and wisdom in dealing with the 'black dog', depression.

We warmly thank the authors who have generously given their time and shared their experiences.

The Editors,
Kerrie Eyers, Gordon Parker and Henry Brodaty
(average age 67)

1

And now we are 65

Why are our days numbered and not, say, lettered?

Woody Allen

This book is intended for professionals and carers involved with those who are growing older. There are perspectives from both sides of the clinician's desk: stories from those growing older and from the people involved in their support. We wish to present ageing in a positive context, tackling some of the myths, fears and prejudice that surround this phase of our life, and consider some solutions to age-related difficulties.

We ask your indulgence for the span of the material. It ranges in complexity from the everyday experience of people with depression and what they have found helpful, carers and their perspective, and more complicated material from specialist clinicians. Where terminology becomes technical, equivalent words are provided in brackets to assist the lay reader's better understanding.

We also explore the differences in the causes, presentations and management of depression that may arise as people grow older, and the influence of age, biology and psychological and social factors on mental health. Increased understanding and empathy help destigmatise mood disorders and may encourage those affected to more readily seek diagnosis and treatment.

The material presented here is about ageing and related issues in Western industrialised countries. It affirms and emphasises that clinical depression is not a 'normal' response to ageing, and attempts to trace a path through the maze, from diagnosis through to weighing up the factors that contribute to the onset and maintenance of a depressive episode and to its successful reversal. We emphasise that, when the black dog comes sniffing at the door, there are effective treatments and strategies to enable older people to banish or master depression and to re-engage with their life.

THE EMERGING CLAIMS OF AGE

I don't do alcohol anymore—I get the same effect just standing up fast.

Anon

With advancing age, we are called upon to shape our lives in a way that has not been expected of us before. The freedoms and disengagements of older age bring a more diffuse range of options than we may be used to. Previous stages—our younger lives—were shaped and codified, with clear roles: from birth to teens, the structure was provided by family and educational institutions; then 40 years of workplace obligations; the 'mating game', the search for a partner, a suitable match, maybe forming a family; the intensity of the child-rearing years; and then perhaps (sometimes to tide over a mid-life crisis) a final run up the career ladder and/or the start of a new intimate relationship.

By the age of 65, some of this involvement has waned and we have time to contemplate with pleasure, apprehension or a mixture of both what we can see is the shortening time remaining and our plans for what to do with it.

Many on the verge of leaving the accustomed routine of the middle years don't really have strategies, other than financial, for this disengagement. We presume that we'll be glad to be 'free' and to have more time to ourselves, perhaps take up golf, bridge, bowls, a foreign language, a community involvement—pursuits we've never had the time for previously. It is wise (but not usual) for us to anticipate such a change and to weigh up our options when younger in order to better understand our preferences and possibilities for this next stage of life.

EXTERNAL CIRCUMSTANCES INTERVENE

Inside every older person is a younger person wondering what happened.

Jennifer Yane

Many of us assume that as we grow older we will be able to continue much as before, but with engagement in the paid or voluntary workforce more on our own terms—'dying in the saddle', as it were. Instead, we may be faced with more limited choices than we had envisaged. While those who transition from the workforce into part-time, self-employed or temporary employment often remain healthier and more engaged,[1] older workers are seen as lacking the energy, speed and technological know-how that internationally competitive organisations require. Despite rhetoric to the contrary, analyses of companies' recruitment behaviour and workforce composition demonstrate the reason that many senior would-be workers have given up seeking employment: organisations are just not interested in employing an older person.

The following account from 'Alex', a 73-year-old man formerly working in top executive roles, illustrates how unprepared we are for stepping away from the workplace where many of us, for four decades, have spent more than a third of our waking hours. In a reversal of Lord Kitchener's British World War I recruitment poster 'Your Country Needs YOU', Alex has been shown that he is inessential.

My depression emerged suddenly

 My depression emerged suddenly, upon retirement, and I fear black moods will stay with me for the rest of my life . . .

I'm not sure how high I rate on the 'depression scale', as it has never been assessed professionally. Identifying the severity of one's depression is elusive. Obviously, there are few outward symptoms: nothing showing on your body, no ache or pain or anything indicated by x-ray. How much of my problem is just 'old age' is hard to evaluate, but it is pretty clear that these depressive cycles are debilitating and have changed my character.

My confidence in dealing with other people has reduced. I am often asocial and dread leaving the house. I don't want to meet new people. I stress over minor issues and irritations—hiring a tradesman for house repairs or having the car serviced can be very disturbing. I spend most of my days at home alone. When I make the bed, it's hard to stop myself getting back into it. My daily shower has become less than that and I have let my hair grow rather long.

After three score and ten years of life (plus a couple more), I fear being consumed by my own anxiety and anger. I worry about the appalling performance of parliamentarians; teenage girls' binge drinking; obesity; climate change; 'shock jocks' inciting racial hatred on the radio; young lads with massive bank balances from sport not knowing how to avoid trouble. Somehow, I feel responsible that things are not better.

My previous high-profile working life was successful by most standards. There were disappointments, but none seemed to drive me down. I held senior positions in both the public and the corporate sectors, rubbing shoulders with politicians and leading businessmen. Large numbers of people reported to me. I made decisions that impacted on people's lives and I mentored the young and inexperienced. In the 1990s, I was the CEO at a retirement village and hostel. It is to my deep regret that I never initiated any programs to handle depression. In retrospect I realise that many residents would have been suffering from it, usually in silence.

The onset of retirement and the removal from regular interaction with others seems to be one shortcut to depression. For some of us elderly, that depression will become a constant. Irrelevance and invisibility take over. The phone hardly ever rings, extended families have too much on their plates to worry about you. Even ex-workmates, some still employed, are often too busy to meet for a drink. You are 'yesterday's man', somewhat alone and certainly forgotten. It is likely you will spend a lot of time in a chair, staring into space and wondering what happens now. You are not valued anymore. Years of experience, survival of hard times, wars, tragedy and success don't count.

In older age, you had expected to be revered; sought after to scatter pearls of wisdom and dispense sage advice; have the satisfaction of a grandchild on your knee attentively absorbing your knowledge and adventures. Such dreams are nothing but fantasy. The only reality is that you are being sucked into a vortex of introspection, loneliness, even despair. Previously, you had never felt irrelevant in your life. Now, it's there every day.

That irrelevance and invisibility brings on intolerance and impatience. (Everything seems to start with 'I'.) You show intolerance in many ways. You become angry with people who express a contrary point of view. You cancel the newspapers because the writers get it wrong. If you ask for something, you seem to be low down on the priority list. Your blood boils while you wait. But nobody notices. After all, you are invisible.

So what to do? Perhaps seek professional medical advice. What if you tell your doctor that nobody seems to be listening anymore and your stressed-out GP doesn't have time to listen either? Anyway, most men will only visit the doctor for an obvious problem or to get a script renewed! For my age (they say), my health is good. I don't feel inclined to share moods of anger, loneliness and despair. I don't want to be prescribed medication to be taken for the rest of what is left of my life.

The catastrophic results of people giving up these medications or forgetting to take them are well documented—not a danger that an older person needs.

I sleep pretty well, although the dreams are often quite horrendous and almost always relate to past events and people. I go to bed as late as possible. I have no debt, and a working wife, so money is not an issue. We've had the overseas trips, holidays and cruises. When the holidays end, I am usually back into moods of despondency almost before the unpacking is completed. My only regular activities are a commitment to crosswords to activate the brain, and a weekly class to exercise the body. There has been some urging that I should take on volunteer work. Frankly, I fear being useless should my mood turn sullen, and the depressing fact that you are probably dealing with people whose needs are real and greater than yours. I have never felt suicidal—at my age, death is a companion who doesn't need any help.

So, where to from here?

That I recognise where I am now is obviously a good thing. Writing this has been somewhat therapeutic. But the reality is that only by finding something bright and inspiring will I be sure of being able to fight the times of darkness. Religion can be uplifting, but having lived as an atheist I expect to die as one. People often ask somebody they've just met: 'And what do you do?' Retirement translates as 'Nothing' and they are inclined to move on. You are often judged by what you do rather than what you are.

But I firmly believe my problems, depression and anguish, would diminish with any sort of a job, just something I could talk about to strangers and be proud about. Not often does a 73-year-old get a second chance, but what a great antidote to depression if you can pull it off.

Dream on? Alex

This scenario—though stingingly fresh to Alex—is commonplace and sanctioned. Those growing older move (or are moved) aside to make room for the energy and innovation of the young. The remedy for people so displaced is less obvious, however, and requires some 'bespoke' tailoring of capacities to opportunities.

What should Alex do, how does he regroup, where does he invest his energy and sense of self now? Because of the contrast with his previous effectiveness, does one judge that his present dark outlook is 'depression', or is it the shock of a role change that's not yet absorbed? Is he describing 'clinical depression', or is this normal sadness?

Assessment might weigh the following concerns. Are his current feelings impairing him substantially? Enough to warrant some sort of intervention? Does Alex seem likely to self-regulate, and eventually bounce back and adjust to his circumstances and find new opportunities for re-engagement? In his present mood, his negativity and feelings of hopelessness are eroding his capacity to function effectively. Intervention that addresses factors involved in his present 'dis-ease' might usefully act as a circuit-breaker.

We have become increasingly 'psychologically minded' in the last decades. Depression is more readily diagnosed and treated—some would say too readily—but consulting an astute mental health professional during a transition of this kind can help address risk factors and foster a more positive resolution.

PERSONAL CIRCUMSTANCES INTERVENE

A further account of leaving the workplace—in this case a 'forced' retirement of a different sort—comes from the daughter of a man who had to step away from his work when vulnerabilities from his earlier life suddenly assailed him.

This Is Your Life

I warmly welcomed over thirty people into my home to host my dad's recent birthday party. Mum had spent the previous days preparing a wonderful selection of foods. My husband and children had excelled and had the house spotless. The day was full of laughs and funny stories as we celebrated Dad's achievements with a special presentation of 'This Is Your Life'.

Dad's sense of humour and 'gift of the gab' have been with him for as long as I remember. This milestone celebration helped us show him how very much loved he is by all who were present. His hearty laugh rang out often during the afternoon and it always made me smile broadly—it was such a pleasure to hear.

Dad was brought up with a strong work ethic and an even stronger commitment to his wife and children. As a child I remember the physically demanding work he put into the farming industry. He was also a superb craftsman and everything in his workshop was in order. I most admire the beauty of his cursive writing, a reflection of that inner peace that is evident in his warm and ready smile when we need it the most.

Dad was employed as a counsellor at an emergency shelter—a tough job. For eight years he had been working with displaced and disadvantaged people. No two days were the same, as he managed clients with varying degrees and types of problems, from substance abuse, domestic violence and the financially destitute to the many varieties of mental illness. His job had always been extremely demanding but he still managed that smile, even in his weariest hours.

Then one day the smile disappeared. There was a phone call from Mum telling me Dad had suffered a 'breakdown' and that he was now on 'stress leave' from work. I couldn't comprehend the picture—my dad! Never had I seen a hint of weakness. He was always the backbone of the family, he expressed love and acceptance to all those around him, and now Mum was telling me he couldn't even accept himself.

How, why, did this happen? What could we do to make this go away?

The following days overflowed with confusion, denial, apprehension and a huge feeling of loss. If these were our feelings, how much worse were Dad's feelings, or did he even know what he was feeling? I think not. Mum was the splint for his broken spirit. This was not something that was ever anticipated.

Were there warning signs? Dad had no history of depression, so had we missed something? What had triggered this breakdown? I had to accept the situation as fact and not dwell on the 'whys' that were wasting my emotional energy— there might never be answers to these questions. We were in unknown territory and required all the strength and energy we could muster.

Dad's recovery was dictated by him. For one so experienced in counselling, he was often stubborn and difficult when it came to suggestions. He chose to avoid medications for depression. The stigma attached to a medical record showing that you have been treated for depression was still something that was not socially accepted at the time.

He'd agreed to see a therapist, though she often felt like the 'patient' herself, as Dad put the questioning back onto her! She assessed him as suffering a 'situational depression' that had been aggravated by working in the environment at the emergency shelter. I imagine feelings of failure were strong for Dad at this time, but he made the right choice to resign. His lifelong ability to isolate his inward emotions to protect himself had come from a traumatic childhood. This shut-down mechanism kicked in with a force that put him into a total protective state, making it extremely hard for those closest to care for him, and he still struggled to make sense of daily life.

Mum was magnificent. She saw and dealt with more hardship than we will ever know. After nearly forty years of marriage she had to give herself permission to take over the decision-making for everything. She took charge of a man who had always been the head of the house. Depression had taken away Dad's independence and his ability to make the easiest of decisions. This was a vital time for Mum to use the support from family and friends to enable her to voice her feelings and share her grief. Choosing who to share with was crucial, because many people who haven't experienced depression first hand as a carer or sufferer simply don't understand the condition. 'Can't he just snap out of it?' or 'He should find a less stressful job' was unhelpful and sapped our energy.

At first, I was frightened to visit Dad. He was at home. What would I say? How would he react to me being there? Would we just pretend that nothing had happened? How tolerant would he be of the children, his grandkids whom he loves very much? But, like Mum, I had to put my insecurities aside and remind myself that Dad needed me to visit and not to stay away.

It hurt to see my dad in the grip of depression, but grieving can be done in private and appearing strong and supportive in his presence was an important part of his healing. I didn't need him to feel guilty that he was causing such heartache for his own family. I began to know that I would see him smile again.

Dad is himself again now. His journey with depression and his recovery have added to his life experiences. Never could we have imagined that at his birthday we would add 'surviving depression' to his list of achievements.

Dad's smile is back and we have all 'survived'. We are all much more aware of this illness and it has strengthened us. We speak openly about it when the subject comes up and I admire Dad for this, as I expect others who have journeyed through depression would struggle with such a conversation. We cannot change what has happened in our lives but we can acknowledge it and know that there is exceptional support available. We all need a willingness to accept our vulnerabilities and reach out for help.

Congratulations Dad, 'This Is Your Life'—and we are proud to celebrate it! Alisha

Alisha's story about her father illustrates how, as we age, personal vulnerabilities can become more insistent, more difficult to keep at bay, and how they can interact with stressors to crack open psychological 'fault lines' that are often outside our awareness. However, also demonstrated is that with family and professional support, such rifts can be healed—not just cemented over—and that an individual can use this new awareness to learn and employ fresh and effective ways of managing stressors and emotional pain.

Scaling down work or leaving the workforce entirely represents just one consequence of becoming older. Many other aspects and challenges will be examined in the following chapters, in which we also list strategies people employ to help them age with grace. Such individuals have anticipated the changes and have planned in advance—as mentioned, a key strategy for success.

DEPRESSION IS NOT A NORMAL PART OF AGEING—SEEK HELP

For those encountering a depressive illness—either a recurrence of the illness from earlier in life, or newly occurring—early recognition and intervention are paramount. This leads, for most, to successful recovery and a return to capacity and enjoyment.

One danger, illustrated in many of the stories that follow, lies in the perverse nature of depressive illness. Though 'clinical' depression—depression that is present every day, hasn't lifted after a fortnight, and is severe and impairing—is a physical disorder, it has a psychological manifestation. Depression 'talks'. Its effect is evident in the individual's profoundly negative attitudes about self-worth and purpose, and pervading feelings of hopelessness and helplessness. Those in its grip have difficulty understanding that these are 'abnormal' feelings. The condition can also rob a person of the will to seek help—and, at its most serious, of the desire to continue living.

Compounding this as people grow older is the expectation that the ageing process itself is inherently depressing—and so the ageing individual, and his or her family and health care professionals too, may come to think that it is 'normal' to be depressed in the face of encroaching age. But it is essential to reiterate that depression is not a 'normal' aspect of ageing.

NOTEWORTHY

A more optimistic outlook on ageing

In spite of illness, in spite even of the arch enemy sorrow, one can remain alive long past the usual date of disintegration if one is unafraid of change, insatiable in intellectual curiosity, interested in big things, and happy in a small way.

Edith Wharton

Positive psychology—focusing on strengths, not deficits
'Positive psychology' focuses on the individual's strengths, encouraging affirmative characteristics and aiming to increase resilience. One technique is to practise mental exercises that help a person mimic happiness until a more positive frame of

mind becomes ingrained. While some of our natural psychological setting is genetic, there is increasing optimism that even neural 'hard wiring' responds to such repeated training and discipline.

What makes people 'flourishers' or 'languishers'?
Flourishers are naturally positive, vibrant and curious and 'seize the day'.

Languishers are cautious, negative, hesitant, see the glass as 'half-empty' and fail to grasp opportunities.

(A general overview of this area is provided by Wikipedia.[2])

The Character Strengths and Virtues (CSV) test provides a measure of positive human qualities that consistently emerge as effective across history and culture. These include:

- wisdom (embodied in creativity, curiosity, open-mindedness, love of learning, positive perspective on life)
- courage (including persistence and integrity)
- humanity (characterised as love, kindness and social intelligence)
- justice (citizenship, fairness and leadership)
- temperance (modesty, prudence and self-regulation)
- transcendence (appreciation of beauty, excellence, gratitude, hope, humour and spirituality).[3]

Neurogenesis—the rejuvenating brain
There is now credible evidence that the adult human brain can create new neurons (brain cells), many of which integrate themselves into the working brain. In contrast to earlier belief, the mature brain continues to develop with experience—and especially with practice—well into older age.

Some facts about neurogenesis
- Neurogenesis still occurs in the later decades of life.
- The most active area for the production of new neurons is the hippocampus, a region involved in learning and memory.
- To become incorporated into the working brain, a new neuron needs connections with other neurons, or it withers and dies.
- Animal studies have shown a correlation between learning and the survival of new neurons in the hippocampus; the more the animal learnt, the better the neurons survived.
- Coupled with new learning, physical exercise improved the new neurons' survival rates further.
- Studies have suggested that antidepressant therapy may stimulate the production of new neurons in adult animals, while excess stress seems to work against the production of new cells.

These findings suggest new avenues for research into ways of healing the brain after traumatic injury, diseases like dementia, and age-related cognitive decline.

2

On growing older

> I don't feel old. I don't feel anything till noon. That's when it's
> time for my nap.
>
> Bob Hope

When does 'older age' begin? There is fortunately no universal indicator of senescence—biology vies with demography, employment is not an indicator, and labels of 'young' and 'old' are influenced by life expectancy and culture. Individuals age at different rates. For administrative purposes and statistical analyses, however, older age is usually defined as starting around our 65th year.

Ageing is not a disease, and over the last century life expectancy has increased and health has improved. So age itself is not a prescription for lurching decline, even for those less blessed in the genetic lottery of longevity—though increasing age is a risk factor for many diseases. Research, however, indicates how large a role both self-efficacy levels and good management play in the ability to continue effective engagement with family, friends and community, and in finding meaning in life as the years slip by.

STAGES OF MATURITY

> Wisdom doesn't necessarily come with age. Sometimes age just
> shows up all by itself.
>
> Tom Wilson

Psychologist Erik Erikson framed our lives as a sequence of eight stages of development.

The first, during infancy, is when a baby learns whether or not people are dependable and able to satisfy its basic needs, thereby nurturing trust and hope. As the toddler develops will and confidence—the second stage—he/she benefits from carers who can strike a balance between support and autonomy. Next, during the preschool years, the child becomes more able to exercise initiative and judgement.

Ages seven to twelve see a growing sense of individuality and self-confidence, a quest to learn and eagerness to complete tasks. Next, the transition from childhood to adulthood (around ages thirteen to nineteen) involves the adolescent bringing his/her inner and outer identity into alignment and establishing boundaries.

In young adulthood—say, years 20–34—the individual shifts from wanting to 'merge' with friends and peer group to a desire for intimacy and commitment to another. During 'middle age', years 35–65, the maturing individual hopefully experiences a sense of mastery and pride derived from his/her contribution in a number of areas—family, work, society.

The eighth stage of development, 65 years and onwards, sees the individual assessing whether life goals have been achieved—with the attendant feelings of accomplishment and contentment, or discontent. Ideally, this is a stage where the elder is able to provide wisdom and support to the broader 'tribe' of family and community.

As the individual reaches later years—Erikson later added a ninth stage that encompasses extreme older age—a sense of accomplishment may offer a steady compass for reaching a calm harbour; alternatively, a lingering feeling that there is 'unfinished business' may lead to renewed efforts to rectify what's missing—with varying degrees of success.[1]

THE CHANGING PROFILE OF OLDER AGE

I'm not 70, I'm eighteen with 52 years' experience.

Anon

The recent and rapid 'greying' of the population, the burgeoning cost of health care and increasing pressure on the shrinking family unit have tended to cast a shadow over growing older—a process that in previous decades was a rather short time at the end of a person's working life. Now, on average, life expectancy at 65 years has increased from ten more years (1950) to eighteen more years of life (2003).[2]

Over the same decades in Western countries, fewer births and increased life years have meant that 'support ratios' have diminished significantly—that is, the number of persons of working age per person aged 65 and older has decreased from six in the 1950s to around four in the year 2000.[3]

This changing demographic pattern has seen the emergence of the 'sandwiched' generation—it is common for both partners to be engaged in the workforce (often facing increased work demands), while also juggling the needs of their children and those of their ageing parents.

In the following account, an adult son observes these pressures.

Life cycles

 From nappies to knickers, from kindy to uni, from sandals to stilettos—these are some of the many transitions human beings make as we mature.

Early on we build our core beliefs, thoughts, experiences, feelings and character, and during this time our parents put their lives on hold, work hard and make sacrifices to ensure that we children have the best education, the best set of morals and values, the best occupation. And the list goes on. Over the years, mostly, the children grow into happy and healthy young adults, study hard, reach their goals and enter the workforce to become successful professionals.

Well, so it is thought . . .

Seven a.m. starts, twelve-hour work days, increased responsibility. We enter the rat race.

In this increasingly fast-paced world, our ageing parents and relatives can often feel like a burden on their families and all who care for them. The varying amounts of support they need and the inclusion in their grown families' activities, they feel, has become a 'duty' for those younger. Their sons and daughters may feel like there are simply not enough hours in the day.

Dad telephones. Not being able to comfortably talk in an intense workplace, I whisper, 'What's wrong?' He tells me he just wanted to see how I was going. I say I'll phone him back in a minute for a quick chat.

Ten hours later I return the call but Mum says Dad's fast asleep. Etan

LONGER LIFE SPAN, NEW EXPECTATIONS

You can't turn back the clock. But you can wind it up again.

Bonnie Prudden

Along with increased years of life and better health come increasing expectations. Now as we grow older we are seeking new ways to engage with our families, the community and the workplace.

Though there are the predictable challenges that occur with age—changing roles, feelings of irrelevance, loneliness, health and financial problems—self-awareness and the support of others helps to chart a course through these shoals. Unless restricted by disease or poverty, most older people have more choices than did any previous generation.

Active people aged 65 years or older are no longer as enticed by the notion of 'retirement'. When given the option, many decide to continue at work, take up part-time work or start a small enterprise. Voluntary work is also popular, both for altruistic reasons and for structuring time—though both the volunteer and the not-for-profit organisation need guidance to help make this commitment satisfying for all.

So older age, for the majority, does not involve increasing invisibility, followed by bleak years in institutional care. In fact, final residence in a nursing home involves only a small, albeit visible, number of the oldest old; the vast majority of older people are hale, though variably affected by the vicissitudes of age. A North American national nursing home survey reported that two out of three people who turned 65 in 1990 will either never spend any time in a nursing home, or will spend less than three months in one.[4] Presently, of those aged 65–84 in Australia, 94 per cent live in the community, and of those aged 85 and older, 74 per cent still continue to live independently with varying degrees of assistance.[5]

While there will be a marked increase in older people—by 2050, the population aged 65 years and over is projected to be at least double its present size—the vast majority of people under 80 years of age are predicted to continue to live in their own dwellings with spouse or family. This option is less costly; nursing home and hostel care are expensive alternatives to being supported at home, and innovative strategies are being trialled to maintain even the frailer aged in their family home. People aged 80 and over are the group most likely to require nursing home or hostel accommodation or other forms of support.

ATTITUDES TO AGEING—THE INFLUENCE OF THE BIRTH COHORT

> The first forty years of life give us the text; the next thirty supply the commentary on it.
>
> Arthur Schopenhauer

What we feel about growing older is influenced by the broader expectations and attitudes inherent in each birth generation. Those now in their eighth decade—the golden oldies—have shown remarkable resilience, surviving the Great Depression, two world wars and local upheavals, together with limited opportunities and education. Their acceptance and endurance were forged in a time when people were less 'psychologically minded' and more stoic. Fewer opportunities to relocate meant tighter communities, less freedom and a greater sense of duty. The life of one 81-year-old woman, celebrated by her adopted daughter in the following passage, illustrates some of the features of this generation. It is a generation that is less likely to recognise depressive illness and doubtful about psychiatric treatment.

A mother, my mother

Her hallmark has always been loyalty and selflessness. A life beginning in 1929, a world war, the Depression and a time where women were not encouraged to reach their potential academically; her legacy is one of sheer human kindness and unswerving devotion to others.

She left school prematurely due to bad eyesight and was required as a carer for her younger siblings to enable her parents to work. Her employment options were limited; however, later she was given the opportunity to work as a nursing assistant; she was well suited to this and pleasure filled her life.

She married an Italian immigrant and moved to the outskirts of the city, to a bushy area that was slowly becoming urbanised. Her days were spent helping her husband, a builder, complete their home. While labouring hard and long hours to help, she was injured in some way from the strain and was later unable to have her own children, a great sadness to her—perhaps her first creeping sadness.

But good fortune came to her in 1957 when she was able to adopt a son and shortly thereafter a daughter. They were the delight of her life ... although there was still sadness within and a sense of low self-worth. However, she was contented and loving, tirelessly helping and caring for her family and working part time at the local greengrocer to help out financially. She joined the informal community made up of the many other stay-at-home mums.

The children grew and left the nest to study and commence employment. She had a sense of loss common to all new stages of life. Her husband, due to a heart condition, prematurely retired—and insisted on returning to the town he had first migrated to, so she found herself once again having to re-establish herself, although this time much older and without many activities to link her to the new community. The climate was hot, the distance to loved ones far, and her husband happy with time spent in his own interests. She felt the beginnings of isolation.

She masked her pain with alcohol—socially acceptable amounts—and with a constant stream of cigarettes, as if willing the minutes on to the next shopping outing or meal to prepare or chance to be needed. Sadness was creeping back—you could see it in her face—the pain of a life without much current fulfilment. Though still serving others and giving solace when the need arose, she now lacked purpose or motivation to change her own circumstances.

The days became years; her husband died. She gave up alcohol and cigarettes, her once constant friends. She moved again, this time to help her ageing mother, granting her mother dignity and the chance to avoid an aged cared facility. Selflessness again.

However, her mother had been unabated in her criticism over the years and her daughter's care and loyalty went mostly unrecognised, never acknowledged or encouraged. Day after day her mother's bitter words flowed over her, yet her character remained resilient and forgiving in the harsh environment. We watched silently. We discussed options, helplessly, among ourselves. After many more years her mother moved to a nursing home. Faithfully, Mum visited and cared for her until her mother's death at 99 years.

Another move, finances running down but a new opportunity provided by her son-in-law, relocating to the outskirts of New South Wales to join the community her daughter lives in. The move seems good, other widows aplenty. New life opens up and there is a special neighbour who becomes a friend to enjoy and share life with. Country music and walking to town, eating out, night concerts; the happiness comes back into her face, the deep lines soften. She is filled with a new-found zest, involvement, activity, grandchildren close by and, especially, a new baby. She is needed once again, meals, babysitting, overnight visits, school drop-offs and afternoon tea with the youngest grandchild—all such a delight. Joy fills her life like pulsing oxygen.

But another setback, macular degeneration—her sight is fading, slowly taking away the joys of reading and some of her independence. Meals on Wheels is now her new friend. Again life contracts. And another sadness: her neighbour, her greatest friend, dies from a cancer denied for some time. The days pass, she struggles with her loss and grief and acknowledges it. There is no denying sadness, now that it is recognised: she decides to talk to the doctor. Her failing eyesight pervades so much, even misting the beloved face of her youngest grandchild; disappointment threatens to envelop her.

Some plaintiveness is noticed by family members, even a suggestion she is looking for death to come. This nagging sadness engulfs her at times. But she once again finds renewal, moves incrementally forward and tries to embrace the next thing. Eventually, she steps out again in friendship with other widows and new outings. The effort is more difficult this time and less motivated, but it is there.

An idea emerges, a plan for a holiday, albeit alone, with an organised tour; now the pleasure of anticipation. Past sadness retreats into a corner of the room, hides, though self-deprecation rolls too easily off her tongue, fuelled by unachieved dreams maybe. These last years she takes what is on offer—the many opportunities. She finds joy for her grandchildren's hopes and vocations, marvels at the lucky country—so different now, so many possibilities—and nurtures her hopes for those she loves—her children and their children.

She learns to live with her sadness—maybe it is normal to have it as a companion. Though it is at times too hard to shoulder and its depth can be frightening, maybe it is there, she thinks, to remind us of our humanity, to remind us to feel and to notice and to live with compassion and embrace inter-dependence with others who love us. Sophia

The next account, 'What is a snowflake?', sets out some of the challenges peculiar to older migrants, some of whom were not literate in their first language. Years of hard work—to provide for themselves and to settle their children into the adopted country—can deplete older people born in another time and culture. Growing older, they may find themselves isolated by lack of language, robbed of purpose when hard physical work is no longer possible or necessary, and at sea with the increasingly alien values of their children and grandchildren. Ironically, it is because of this older generation's remarkable effort that the succeeding generations have assimilated so well into the adoptive culture.

Zora is faced not only with the challenge of persuading her mother to seek help for mental distress, but also with trying to do this from a distance—from another city—and within the tight time frame dictated by her full-time job.

What is a snowflake?

My cousin, who has started with the children in our family a tradition of decorating gingerbread shapes, told her mother about a snowflake cookie-cutter she had bought.

'What is a snowflake?' asked her highly intelligent mother (whose first language is not English).

'You know, like a piece of snow—a flake of snow—a snowflake!'

Her mother remained perplexed: 'What does it look like?'

'Like a star, sort of...' began the tortured explanation, 'like a crystal ... it's meant to look like a piece of snow.'

'But snow doesn't look like that.'

She was right. Snowflakes, as we see them, do not look like their cookie-cutter or tree ornament equivalents.

My cousin and I have a long-running commentary on trying to explain or translate concepts to our parents. 'If I cannot explain this, what can I explain?' she asks. This gulf in understanding is caused by English not being our parents' first language and because they never had the opportunity to be educated in their home countries, let alone in their adopted one.

My cousin's struggle to explain a simple cookie-cutter shape got me thinking. Depression—as a clinical illness— has finally become understood (somewhat) in my family. It is present in many branches of the family tree. Its roots are deep and invasive. But try explaining the term 'carer' as it is used by clinicians or defined by the government for the purposes of getting a 'carer's allowance'. It's getting into snowflake territory.

My father is a carer. He is also ageing. But who will care for him, when the time comes? My father is the only one of eleven children who came to this country after World War II. After escaping from the communist republic of Yugoslavia, he spent time in a refugee camp in Italy. When I asked him why he chose to come here, he answered, 'There was a boat. I got on it.'

His first home on migration was his cousin's garage. Since then, he has married and raised a family of three children, worked hard, established his own successful cleaning business, and owns his home. Any extra money always goes towards supporting family, including his four grandchildren, and anyone else in need.

Where is my mother in all this? The way I see it—through the distorting lens of childhood and the mother–daughter relationship—she gradually lost her ability to work, to take care of herself and her family. At the time I was resentful. Angry. Confused.

Now, as a mother myself, struggling to balance work, self and family, I see it differently. She is a woman of individuality and humour, clever but frustrated, loyal and loving, steadfastly refusing to accept any 'diagnosis' presented to her and any 'medication' that might come with it. It was as an adult that I came to understand that she had a mental illness. And it was as an adult that I experienced mental illness myself. So did my brother. And my sister.

We all tried to get her the help that we had found for ourselves. But she wouldn't have it. 'Mental illness' was not in her vocabulary. Any intervention she thought was meddlesome, invasive and downright rude. None of it made sense to her—she had worked, raised a family, given everything she had until there was nothing left. We were the mad ones!

Factors contributing to depression in older people include the impact of experiences such as war, migration or suicide in the family.[6] My mother has experienced all of these. So have many other migrants and refugees. Due to large-scale immigration after World War II, it is predicted that by 2011 one in every five people in this country aged 80 or older will be from a culturally and linguistically diverse background, and that, by 2026, this proportion will increase to one in every four people.[7] Who will take care of them? The largest group of primary carers is women of middle age. But more women are working—their participation in the labour force has risen from 44 per cent in 1978 to 57 per cent in 2005,[8] and the majority of women with dependent children now work. I have two children, I work full time and my capacity to support my parents when they most need me has been depleted. I live in a different city and I am less available than ever.

My husband, who works part time, visits my parents more than I do. He helps ensure that my parents' relationship with their grandchildren is strong and a source of joy. My daughters delight in their grandmother's capacity for child-like foolishness and fun. They love helping my father fix things. His capacity for hard physical work, especially when it comes to maintaining our old house, is only slightly diminished by age. I remember him picking up an enormous top-loading washing machine and walking it down our back stairs to our laundry. My husband and I looked at each other in wonder, then laughed.

My father is a man of both enormous physical and emotional strength. He believes that 'you got to talk about things', but sometimes I see him get tired, reticent and dumbly accepting. He is a support to many in his family and community, but I see that it also takes its toll. A few years ago, he believed he was having a heart attack, which saw my sister rushing from a hair salon with half a haircut to drive my father to the hospital. The initial diagnosis of angina turned out to be anxiety. Not a heart attack but a panic attack! My father had the wisdom to know that if he did not take care of himself, everyone's health and welfare would be at risk. He did as the doctor ordered: rested more, talked about what was troubling him, took medication and now has physical checks with his GP every six to twelve months. He bought a bike. He went to the gym. He ate healthy food. But a series of losses had made him vulnerable: the cousin he lived with when he first came to this country died of cancer; his dearest sister died; his youngest sister took her own life; a close friend and neighbour also died of cancer.

The process of migration means enduring loss. To revisit this type of experience later in life is not easy and is often cause for depression among older people.[9] Waves of migrants are experiencing the same things as my parents. Some are refugees; some have endured torture, trauma and unspeakable horrors in their homelands. These stories are not uncommon. And they will be even less uncommon as the population ages.

We all need to be taken care of. As we age, this need becomes greater. It's hard to face for those who are ageing and those with the responsibility of supporting ageing parents or relatives. As my dad says, 'You got to talk'—to friends, family, partners or whoever can provide support. Take care of yourself or you sure won't be able to take care of anyone else. Take a break. Stay active. Maintain social contacts. How can the simple things be so hard? 'You got to talk.' Silence breeds misery and loneliness and is the harbinger of depression. 'You got to talk' not just about the bad stuff but the good stuff, too.

My mother has lots of good memories. I listen to them now, when once they frustrated me. 'But what about now?' I would shriek. 'Stop living in the past!' I'm more accepting of what makes her happy, now. I try to affirm what is good in our relationship instead of focusing on the bad. She is a person in her own right, not just my 'mother', a role which I now understand is primal, yet tightly socially constructed ... so that we can easily feel like failures. My exposure to feminism, education and working mothers as the norm allows me the privilege to contemplate and change my situation if I wish. My mother didn't have these choices. Maturity has allowed me to develop a greater respect and understanding for people who grew up in a different generation. This is what I wish to receive from others as I age.

Just as a cookie-cutter will never represent a snowflake as we see it, no cookie-cutter will ever represent the experience of real people. Looking beyond templates to understand the behaviour and experience of individuals and their relationship to any broad group—whether it's carers, migrants, refugees, people with a mental illness or the aged—is worth striving for. If we can achieve this as individuals, we might be able to achieve it as a community or as a government or as a nation.

Then, step by step, we might just get somewhere. Zora

NEW APPROACHES TO GROWING OLDER

My wife said, 'What are you doing today?'
I told her, 'Nothing.'
She said, 'You did that yesterday.'
I said, 'I wasn't finished.'

Anon

Part of the ability to continue with meaningful activity and engage with community, family and friends as we age comes from vitality, either inherent or cultivated. The saying 'use it or lose it' is accurate: when body machinery is disused or abused there is atrophy and creeping impairment. The ageing body may be likened to a vintage engine; a distinction can be made between what is 'broken' and the parts that are showing wear and tear—hence the importance of 'maintenance'. Regular physical exercise benefits body and mind, and can be readily tailored to avoid exacerbating nagging injuries and to maximise functioning.

The view that the processes of ageing are pre-set by a biological self-destruct mechanism has recently been replaced with the notion that ageing is caused by a gradual build-up of faults in our body's cells. This has fostered a new perception. The focus is now on improving the prospects for healthy ageing, and seeking insights into the relationship between ageing and disease. This new approach is refreshing and circumvents the fatalism and ageism that can prejudice us about growing old. The deterioration automatically associated with age is something of a self-fulfilling prophecy. Research in this area yields the following observation:

> Surprisingly, the age-related decline in physical fitness appears to be more related to expectation than to biology. As we age, we expect to be less fit so we exercise less, worry less about weight gain and attempt less demanding roles.[10]

AGEING GRACEFULLY

> Youth is the gift of nature, but age is a work of art.
>
> Stanislaw Jerzy Lec

In his book The Art of Ageing, Dr Sherwin Nuland considers what is involved in ageing well. A physician who is now in his early 80s, he found he needed to make ongoing adjustments to play to his strengths. He notes that as we age we are called on to become keen observers of our body's needs and abilities, and to adapt to them as horizons draw closer.

Those whose calling is to work with an older population know that the ability to adapt, to learn and then accept one's limitations, is a determinant of what the professional literature of geriatrics calls 'successful ageing'. Adapting is not mere reconciling. Adapting brings with it the opportunity for far greater benisons and for brightening the later decades with a light not yet visible to the young. Even the word itself is insufficiently specific to convey what is required. In the subtle but nevertheless enormously significant shades of meaning that characterise the English language, 'attune' may, in fact, better describe the process than 'adapt': 'attune' in the sense of being newly receptive to signals welcome and unwelcome and to a variety of experiences previously not within range, while achieving a kind of harmony with the real circumstances of our lives.[11]

Dr Nuland's case studies demonstrate that growing older doesn't have to presage unseemly decline. In the West we are heirs to longer, healthier and wealthier lives, and most of us have the time, skills and education to enable us to find renewed place and purpose in our older years. Illness does become more common, but generally (barring extreme factors) our choices are shaped, rather than dictated, by our health, 'connectedness' to others, finances and maintaining our vigour.

The observations from Trevor, the next writer, come from his vantage point of selling retirement village housing. He thinks that those who seek out or continue with their interests and cherish their independence—despite some constraints—are the people who experience a positive older age.

Adjusting to age: some observations

As each generation moves on into older age, wouldn't we hope that the generation following is focused a little more on learning from our experiences—and making us feel as important as we should feel? We will all grow old.

Older age can be all about loss: losing loved ones, friends and relatives, control of our bodies, losing rights and being given ambiguous privileges like concession cards...these happen naturally as we get older.

But getting older need not only be about losses, being pushed to one side and becoming invisible. Many of the choices we have during our life shape the pathway that leads to where we end up, and adapting to this endpoint can have a big influence on our state of mind. Attitudes are critical to determining our stance in older age, as with any challenge.

I met Gerry when I was selling retirement village units at a coastal town. In younger days, with a clear vision of who he would become and what he would do with his life, Gerry, then 83, remembered how he felt walking tall down the church aisle to marry his one true love at the age of 22. 'She passed away nine years ago,' he explained softly to me. 'God I loved her! She was everything to me. Our family grew up and for years my children and their families used to visit our home, until I fell in the garden and broke my hip. Then they said I needed more help and they got me to sell up and I moved here. I like it here because there are other people to talk to and everything is done for you. All of the meals are provided, our beds are made and they have carers who look after all of us all the time.'

But I could tell Gerry was unhappy.

Within six months of moving in, he was dead. That seemed to happen a lot. Some folks just didn't know how to deal with getting old, with being alone or with retirement village living. I could almost tell from the first meeting which ones would live long and happy lives and which ones were going to hang on as long as they could, despite the fact that 'getting old' was making them more miserable every day.

Many who passed away quickly said that they were 'happy', that everything was okay. I personally felt that they were masking their feelings, probably the same way they had throughout much of their lives. Many were miserable a lot of the time, because they realised they were coming close to the end of their stay on this planet. And being 'happy'? Well, that was common courtesy—the right thing to do, not to complain or become any more of a burden on their families and others than they already were!

That older people battle the blues is not widely publicised. For this reason, awareness of the symptoms and causes, and the potential remedies and 'permission' to use them, is seriously lacking. Such feelings are handled differently by older people because of what they have grown through and the stigma they attach to not coping. If, as Albert Einstein once said, 'Commonsense is the collection of prejudices acquired by age eighteen', it stands to reason that an older man or lady who has never experienced feeling 'low' before may react differently to the concept of being 'depressed' than, say, a person born in the past twenty years.

Of course, not all of the people who moved into the retirement village were unhappy. It always seemed to be the ones who were not being babied by their children—who were already being treated with respect and who preserved their own independence—lived longer, fuller lives. One lady in particular (and still a redhead!), who arrived on her own, looked at the first-floor units and not those on the ground floor because she wanted to make sure she stayed active and healthy. Without doubt it was the people who purchased a unit at the top of those stairs who lived longer. Yes, they had to carry their bags up and down the stairs, but if they wanted their shopping delivered then that was their choice too. Purposeful and intelligent in the selection of their environments, some older people make decisions that allow them more life. Likewise, the people who had an interest in life were always there to meet the new neighbours. Perhaps they make these decisions where others do not because they are more 'hungry' for life than the others?

Lance was a favourite of mine. He liked me to drop in. A keen fisherman, he was fortunate to pick up a resale that backed onto a creek connecting with a coastal inlet. He would spend his mornings fishing for bream and his afternoons re-rigging his lines or cleaning the reels with WD-40, ready for the next day. Lance was older than any of the other men or ladies who I sold accommodation to during those three years, and yet he was perhaps the happiest! Something about his attitude and disposition, his 'view' of life and what getting old was all about, was different. The way his children talked to him and the way they allowed him to make final decisions was also evident.

Even in respite care you could see clearly the same patterns in people and the way that they lived their lives. Some formed groups and fostered new and vibrant friendships. Others would prefer to complain from their beds about the quality of the care, their selfish children or the pain. Still others would move freely about, reading books or doing crosswords without a murmur. I would play the piano for anyone who was around when I was in the common room and I'd get a dinky-di high from their enjoyment.

Getting 'down' in older age could be the result of any of many things, but irrespective of whether it is related to loss, fear, ineptitude, lack of interest in life or a change of environment, what is essential is to get people talking about it! Awareness and discussion allow an individual to explore their own feelings, no matter how old they are. The key to this is accessibility and acknowledgement by the individual of the choice to have someone listen, and being open to advice or suggestions about ways to counter such feelings.

A fable: three old men in a common room within their retirement village are talking about their aches, pains and bodily functions. The youngest of the group, a 72-year-old man, says: 'I have this problem. I wake up every morning at seven and it takes me twenty minutes to pee.'

The 80-year-old man says, 'My case is worse, mate. I get up at eight and I sit there and grunt and groan for half an hour before I finally have a bowel movement.'

The 96-year-old man says, 'Boys, at seven I pee like a horse and at eight I crap like a cow.'

'So what's your problem?' ask the others.

'Well, I don't wake up until nine.'

Let's try to be less like the 96-year-old. As long as we are 'awake' enough to realise we're too 'down' and that there are choices to help manage it, then these feelings are something that we can work through and teach others about, even if it takes us time. Getting old is as much about growing and learning as it is for a young schoolchild. There are amazing opportunities that our mind, body and wisdom can afford us. Learning the best way to manage feelings of depression will turn life back from monochrome to colour. Trevor

Of course, as retirement villages gather people of the same age group together in high concentrations and effectively isolate them from everyday interaction with people of other ages and stages, this carries messages and consequences. However, as the population ages, advances in 'gerontechnology' (see the 'Noteworthy' box at the end of this chapter) will enable many more ageing people to remain independent and to follow a widely expressed preference to remain 'at home' in a less institutional setting.

Hopefully, when the very end of the road is reached, such technology advances (for instance, on-call home-visit palliative care nurses) will enable the individual to die with dignity in familiar surroundings, rather than in greater distress—and certainly at greater cost—in the sterile surroundings of the local hospital's intensive care unit.

NOTEWORTHY

Combating some myths about ageing

Myth: Ageing means illness, pain and incapacity . . .
Truth: Two out of three people aged 65 years and over rate their health as good to excellent. During older age chronic diseases may be a problem, but each decade brings earlier and more effective interventions to lessen disability and damage. Older people also understand that attitude, engagement and exercise contribute to 'successful' ageing.

Myth: Depression is a normal response to ageing . . .
Truth: Depression is not a normal response to growing older. Feeling so persistently 'down' as to be unable to carry on normal activities with enjoyment could be the sign of a depressive illness. Seek help; there is effective treatment!

Myth: Older people are a burden . . .
Truth: The vast majority of older people live independently, contribute significantly to their communities (especially via voluntary work), give more than they receive and are valued members of their family and community.

Myth: Older people are no good at learning anything new . . .
Truth: The fastest growing group of internet users is people over 55. More than 50 per cent of the people under 75 use computers in their homes. Older people can successfully—though usually more slowly—integrate new material into their existing skills and knowledge. There is increasing awareness, too, that physical exercise confers mental benefits.

Myth: Mature-age workers take more time off . . .
Truth: Older people continuing in the workforce have fewer accidents at work than younger colleagues, and absenteeism rates are similar for older and younger workers.[12]

Myth: Age equals dementia . . .
Truth: Only a small minority of people experience dementia as they age: 2 per cent between ages 65 and 74; 6 per cent of those aged 75–84; and around one in five people aged 85 and older.[13]

'Gerontechnology'

The use of technology to help older people remain healthy, safe and supported is known as gerontechnology.

Maintaining older people in their homes for as long as possible is realistic and cost-efficient compared to the cost of institutional care. The use of 'suites' of services tailored to individual needs can also relieve some of the burden on the carers involved. Advances in technology will both assist and somewhat circumvent the shortage of health care professionals and carers needed to support the increased number of frail elderly.

Gerontechnology will help older people remain:
- In their home—architectural design can make the home more liveable, well lit, safe, warm/cool and navigable. The use of simple dials instead of complex buttons as well as monitoring alarms (such as smoke and water-level detectors) will combine with electronically coordinated home help, respite care, day care and night sitting to foster a balance of self-care and support. Touch screens, home computing services (e.g. for ordering groceries) and multimedia entertainment facilities may help the housebound. The addition of 'motes' (information

sensors) will show the use patterns of household utilities (such as number of meals cooked, loads of washing done), provide checks on basic needs and suggest when to replace ingredients and what to cook for meals. Additionally, alarms and sensors can be set to automatically activate when the house is unattended.

- Content—scooters and other mobility aids can combat isolation and help maintain friendships; electronic reminders may help with maintaining pets and community engagement; and maybe sociable robots will add to support. Also, affordable aids for hearing, seeing and walking will be better designed and more widely available.

- Well—technology can aid early diagnosis: for instance, a drainage system that analyses human waste for early warning signs, and sensor motes on a pill bottle to signal whether a person has taken their medication. Monitors of movement, heartbeat and breathing rate of those at home, telemedicine link-up for access to experts, and help with medication compliance via electronic reminders are all under development. Minimally invasive nanomedicine will be more commonly used, and technology-assisted symptom recording will help create accurate records that may enhance partnerships with medical professionals in the management of chronic diseases such as arthritis, diabetes and depression.

- Supported during rehabilitation—effective treatment and rehabilitation can occur at home, and mobile phone-based programs may encourage engagement and compliance with rehab programs.

- Safe in public places—disability-friendly design, good lighting, handrails, seating, ramps, smooth surfaces and CCTV will all help in making public places more accessible and safer.
- Connected—devices such as mobile phones, video and email can be used to coordinate community support services, facilitate safety, link older people to family and carers, and are invaluable for communication and entertainment, enhancing social opportunities ('sofalising') and education—especially services that can be delivered remotely. Their 'reach' can also provide effective links for rural and remote communities.
- Stigma-free—accorded dignity and time, via organisational programs and technological support that allow opportunities for continuing social and community participation and promote positive images of ageing.
- Mobile—able to access suitable transport. Other options include assisted driving (such as the use of satellite guidance programs for motorised scooters), with warning systems for older drivers, together with safer transport vehicles.
- Linked in—technology aids include memory-reminder devices for appointments and medications; devices that monitor blood pressure and blood sugar levels at home and electronically forward results to medical providers; sensors in clothes and furniture that detect unusual patterns of movements; and the use of 'live' aids—for example, dogs that can be trained to alert their owner to an impending epileptic seizure, or alert carers to falls in the elderly.[14]

3

Untreated depression
in older age

Start every day with a smile and get it over with.

W.C. Fields

When depression has become so severe that it impairs our capacity to function—so-called 'clinical' depression—it has become an illness. However, treatment of depression is generally highly effective, and with counselling and/or medication and support, complete recovery is the norm.

While there seem to be grim statistics about the prevalence of depression in older age, rates are in fact reported to be lower than in younger age groups. However, this lower rate is in dispute. It may reflect older people not presenting and/or not being referred so readily for treatment; some sub-populations of older adults do have much higher rates of depression. But depression is not an inevitable companion of older age: an estimated 85 per cent of older people in the Western world continue to lead reasonably healthy, independent and contented lives.

A PERSISTENT 'DOWN' MOOD IS NOT 'TO BE EXPECTED'

As noted earlier, it is a common trap for health professionals to view depressive disorders as a normal part of ageing and as a reasonable response in the face of losses, illness and social and financial constraints. This is a belief shared by the depressed elderly themselves. However, while sadness, grief and 'blue moods' are normal, as they are in younger people, persistent depression that impairs the ability to function is not.[1]

It is estimated that at least 5 per cent of those 65 years and older experience such clinical depression. This rises to around 11 per cent in elderly hospitalised patients, and to around 13 per cent in those needing health care at home.[2] In older people with medical illnesses—especially neurological disorders such as stroke,

Parkinson's disease and Alzheimer's disease—rates are much higher.

Additionally, an unknown number of seniors with depressive illness do not seek help. Rates of depression may also be higher than estimated because of lack of recognition, silence due to stigma and/or stoicism, and even the way that statistics are gathered—for instance, the mental health of residents in aged care and hospitals is often not assessed. Additionally, there is also a group with 'sub-syndromal' depression; that is, symptoms that are quite distressing but not of sufficient severity or duration to qualify as clinical depression. While over-treatment is to be discouraged, this group may be quite impaired and is at increased risk of developing clinical depression.[3] Follow-up of such at-risk individuals is warranted.

DEPRESSION'S PRESENTATION IN OLDER AGE

Depression reflects a range of biological and social factors, and may be difficult to diagnose as its presentation in older people bears different hallmarks from depression in those who are younger. We return to this in more detail throughout the following pages.

Some of the biological wear and tear of age can influence both the development of depression and the types of treatment needed to combat it. Depression in the older age group often presents via physical symptoms. The illness itself seems to amplify aches and pains, often leading to a fruitless slew of investigations in the quest to track down the 'dis-ease'. Troubling physical symptoms should, of course, be investigated at any age, but when there is a constellation of vague somatic (bodily) symptoms with no obvious physical cause, particularly neck and back pain, the health professional might begin to suspect depression as a root cause.

DEPRESSION IS VERY TREATABLE

Clinical depression is an illness—and sometimes a disease—not a character weakness. Our continual emphasis is that better (and earlier) recognition of depression, and encouragement to seek help and effective treatment interventions, can restore an older person to good health. Other illnesses are treated because they cause pain and distress, but the same rationale doesn't seem to apply to depression.

Additional burdens arising from untreated depression—apart from increased suicide risk—include the increased risk of contracting other diseases (conversely, other diseases also predispose the older person to depressive illness), and a subsequent slower and less certain recovery. Heart disease is a case in point in that depression increases the chance of serious cardiac events (such as heart attack) and worsens the outcome after any such serious cardiac event.[4]

DEPRESSION: WEIGHING UP THE SYMPTOMS

A mood disorder—at any age—is often a tangle of many threads: genetic, psychological, physical and situational. Additionally, depressive states, despite causing considerable disablement and distress, may persist unrecognised for years. In later years, physical health impairments characteristic of ageing may contribute and also obscure the diagnosis. For instance, symptoms of depression, even unusual ones such as constipation, may be attributed to physical illness, and vice versa.

Non-melancholic depression is the most common type of depression in older age. Often, common depressive symptoms—such as a loss of interest in life, lack of enjoyment in normal activities, apprehension, anxiety, poor sleep, persistent thoughts of death or chronic unexplained pain—are incorrectly attributed to old age, dementia or poor health. Non-melancholic depression reflects the impact of stressful life events on the individual's personality style, and can be viewed as more 'psychosocially' based, rather than due to primary biological (i.e. physically caused) origins.

Melancholic depression is the other type of depression. It is characterised by anhedonia (loss of pleasure and interest), mood non-reactivity (an inability to be cheered up), diurnal mood variation (mood generally worse in the morning), and psychomotor changes (distinctly impaired concentration, slowing or retardation of thought, speech and movement and/or distinctive bursts of motor restlessness or agitation). Melancholic depression is primarily biological, and while it may have been triggered by a stressor, the depressive response is usually disproportionately severe and persistent. Features of depression are further explored in Chapter 5.

A PICTURE OF HOW DEPRESSION FEELS

Here is an account of an episode of clinical depression as it actually feels to someone experiencing it. While some presentations of depression are masked, paradoxically, by an inability to feel (dubbed 'non-dysphoric' depression), Jessie displays what we have come to recognise as the classic symptoms of severe depression. She becomes raw and isolated and very close to ending it all. Her depression— most likely non-melancholic—resolves once the stressors abate.

The deep dark well

 After eighteen sad years of marriage we realised that the relationship just wasn't working anymore. We had spent many months judging, criticising, analysing and blaming. The day came when we sold the property, a beautiful rural homestead with magnificent views. I had been putting on a very brave face to friends, family and work colleagues, but most especially to myself . . . It was all going to be okay . . . Wasn't it?

Next, not only did I cut my ties to everything familiar at home, but I also handed in my resignation at work. My boss persuaded me not to actually resign but to apply for six months' unpaid leave, thus leaving the door open should things not work out for me. To top off my madness, I bought a little house in the country, 400 kilometres away in a tiny village I had once visited while on holidays. I knew no-one there. What was I thinking?

But all I wanted to do was to run away—as far as I could from the sadness and misery which had engulfed my life. I was going to start anew, meet new people, change my career and throw myself into new hobbies. I had high hopes and expectations for myself and my new world. But dreams and reality were chasms apart.

As I tried to settle into my new house, I busied myself in repairs and alterations to overcome the immediate loneliness and isolation. I applied for every suitable job advertised in the local papers, but it soon became apparent that not only was I not going to find a job at my age, but I was also not going to find companions. The locals seemed to have 'closed ranks'. I went for days without seeing or speaking to another human being.

I started to panic as a sort of blackness began to envelop me. Fear took the reins and galloped my anxiety into raging terror. I became terrified of everything. Was I now losing my mind? I feared going to the letterbox in case another bill had arrived, or looking at people in case they could see my fear, or shopping in case I had insufficient money at the check-out, or noises, big and small. I feared Fear itself—the worst of all fears. My thoughts became irrational. I remember that I could no longer calculate my bank balance, although figures were bombarding my brain from all sides. Time became warped. Colours were too vivid, flavours too sharp, textures too coarse, sounds too loud. Days, weeks and seasons were blurred.

I reacted by shutting the doors: the house doors, the car doors, the garage doors, the fridge, the grocery cupboards and the bank accounts. The days had become endlessly long, so I frantically painted all the rooms and fixed every little thing I could find. I cleared the garden, slashed creepers, clipped hedges, pruned bushes, scattered seeds, planted seedlings, propagated and weeded with an obsessive vengeance.

I kept telling myself that if I kept very busy I would survive.

But a new fear crept up on me. As I walked my two dogs along the creek each morning, I began to imagine myself falling down a deep dark well. If I fell down, down, I would disappear forever and no-one would know where to find me. My family was a long way away and busy with their own lives, friends presumed I must be busy settling in, and work colleagues had all but forgotten who I was. In my mounting anxiety and terror, to gain some sort of control, I stopped eating. 'That will save me money till I find a job,' I reasoned. And, combined with the house renovations, I very quickly lost weight. I barely noticed.

After a few weeks, a friend phoned me, but all I could do was cry. She rang again and I cried every time she rang. She must have told other friends because they, too, tried calling me, but again I just cried. Over those nightmare months I cried enough tears to fill my terrifying deep dark well. In the end, friends stopped calling me; they had no idea what to do about my sad state. Nor did I. My mother thought her phone calls were making me sad, so she, too, stopped calling me.

The only thing that stopped me putting an end to my dreadful, self-inflicted months of sadness was my dogs. If I died, they would be taken to the pound and destroyed, or turn feral. They were the only reason I had to live. And I hung on to that notion every waking minute of every day. Those two dogs sensed my sadness, staying close to me, licking my hands as my tears poured onto their glossy black coats. They knew me better than I knew myself—they tried so hard to console me.

I could not claim to be religious in any sense, but during that time I prayed so hard to anyone who would hear me. Who would hear my desperate prayers for help? Who would help me—and how? God? The spirits? Old souls? My long-departed father or grandfather? Sleep was a temporary relief if only I could find it. Yet I dreaded the mornings when I would wake and have to start my inner wars again. I truly believed things could get no worse and when I resigned myself to this tormenting madness whirling around me, hour upon hour, day after day, I tried to take stock of myself and to think rationally. But nothing came into focus.

Snap! Out of the blue, my boss phoned me. Could I return to the office to fill a temporary vacancy? In an instant I put on my calmest voice, varnished with false self-confidence which I hoped he wouldn't detect. I told him I would be available within the week. Then, tragically, another friend phoned to give me heart-breaking news—her son had been killed in a car accident. Would I come back for the funeral?

Suddenly the doors had opened; I could be of use, involved in something larger than myself. The house was good enough to put on the market and in two days I had everything packed, ready to go. Hope stared at me and I stared back. I told my dogs we were going home. They wagged their tails and grinned, sensing my change of heart and lifting spirits.

Soon I found accommodation for my pets and me back in my own town. I fled the scene of the greatest sadness I had ever experienced. I gradually soothed my soul, talking kindly to myself, pushing away self-blame and mental obstacles by playing Mozart till I could sleep without fear. Books lay abandoned in the corner. Reading was a hurdle for another day. The office provided welcome relief: familiar people, surroundings and routine. My first pay cheque was spent buying nourishing food for my body, which, in turn, began to heal my mind and soul.

Five years on and my two pets have passed over to their doggie Heaven and have left me to deal with the one remaining—my 'black dog'. I am still acutely aware of how close I can get to the edge of that dark well, and how easily I can slip down. But when I sense darkness closing in, I turn up the music and hurl myself into a new hobby. It's still very painful to talk about my sadness; it forces aching memories to the top. Better I leave it alone and ignore it, my black dog, my deep dark well, and get busy with my next project. Will it be a puppy, I wonder? Jessie

Jessie's account brings to mind the adage: 'When it is not necessary to make a decision, it is necessary not to make a decision'. There can be temptation to completely change our circumstances in the face of bereavement or loss—sell the house, take that overseas trip, remarry, leave familiar routines and surroundings—but the accepted wisdom is to allow a settling period, time to catch up with oneself, before instigating major changes.

THE COSTS OF UNTREATED DEPRESSION

The next piece, by Dr Jan Orman, tells her father's story. The mood disorder that he developed removed him from his family and ultimately destroyed what had once been an effective and productive man. Jan, now a doctor who treats and educates general practitioners about this illness, hopes that others can be saved from the consequences of unrecognised and untreated depression.

For my father, and for all of us

We lost my father long before he died. He disappeared slowly and inexorably into himself. All that was left was the steel-blue emptiness in his eyes and a hollow shell.

Dad had been a young man full of enthusiasm. A good cricketer, a keen tennis player, a handsome and articulate man-about-town who'd swept my gentle mother off her feet like a romantic hero from one of her favourite 'penny dreadfuls'. She ran away from home with him in the middle of the night to be married in secret in a town 50 miles away. It was a daring thing indeed for a shy, sweet, obedient youngest daughter of a good-living country family.

He was the eldest child in a 'pioneering family'. They'd opened up a part of the ranges for grazing that had never been worked before. They'd worked hard, depending on their wits and physical endurance. They'd done it at a time when bushrangers were only one of the dangers of life in the bush. My grandmother told me there was more than one occasion when my dad was a baby that the notorious bushranger Thunderbolt had popped in for tea.

Dad left school at thirteen. The family saw no need for education beyond what was necessary to learn to read and write. In his young adult years his family left the property they'd pioneered and bought the general store in town. Dad was the only one schooled enough to run the store—and he did it well. He was street smart, good with people, friendly, always ready to help, and learnt very quickly whatever he needed to learn. As time went on these characteristics drove what he would do with the rest of his life—and they were all part of what was noticeably absent in the end.

Others tell me that Dad was often the life of the party. He was a great one for spinning a yarn and no-one ever knew whether to believe him or not! The job he took after he sold the general store saw him away from home all week and when he returned at the weekends he regaled family and friends over dinner with stories of the places he'd been and the people he'd met. Many say my dad was a terrific bloke, full of mischief and surprises, but more often than not he had my mother tearing her hair out over his enthusiasms. He would take an idea and run with it. He might arrive home with a dozen or so pure-bred canaries or 50 standard roses to plant along the driveway but he could just as easily lose his enthusiasm for a project and leave Mum to clean up in his wake. He never drank. The rumours of other women were put down to the small-mindedness of country towns. His biggest fault was that he smoked 60 cigarettes or more a day and had done since he was about thirteen. It made him smell bad, but no worse than a lot of other men.

He did pretty well with his life, all things considered. He made enough money (though not a lot), climbed up the ladder at work, moved to a big country town, had a few friends, caught a few fish (though not many), paid some attention to his kids (though not too much) and was generally pretty pleased with himself and his life.

I am the youngest child by far in my family. My siblings remember this man, but it is not the man I remember at all. When I was nine, something happened. I never really knew what it was. I'm not sure that my mother did either. Something scandalous happened that meant he was demoted in his job and we had to move again, this time to another small town—a very small one. Grey-suited men came from head office and solemnly gave him the news. We have all wondered since if it was about money but that is unlikely: a self-respecting insurance company would have simply sacked him if there had been any financial funny business. We were told that he had 'acted inappropriately', but there were no more details. Nothing more was ever said.

We settled into our new life and for a year or so things seemed okay. Dad didn't go away during the week anymore. He spent most of his leisure time in front of our newly acquired television, watching whatever happened to be on at the time and smoking continuously. The television reception was lousy but it didn't matter. Mum was on edge and watchful and Dad was increasingly unenthusiastic but I was having too much fun to notice much of what was going on in their lives or to have it affect me.

The men in grey visited again just after my tenth birthday. They said Dad had been unproductive and there had been several complaints about his behaviour. They said they were sorry it had to come to this after such a long and successful career with the company but they insisted that he retire on medical grounds. This was the mid-1960s. Things like that seem to have happened then. We quietly packed our bags and moved back to the town he'd left all those years before.

Dad went to bed when we got there. At 59 he went to bed and stayed there for a very long time. Sometimes he got up to watch TV, sometimes he just stayed in bed for days or weeks on end. Sometimes he'd get up to go to the doctor to get some pills for his blood pressure, sometimes he wouldn't bother. Mum wouldn't let him smoke in bed and a lot of the time he couldn't be bothered to get up even if it meant he could have a cigarette. Once, a few months after his retirement began, he got out of bed, had a shower, spruced himself up and went fishing. He didn't catch anything but he met a bloke who sold him a good many boxes of a fancy new-fangled toilet-cleaning device that turned the water blue as it cleaned the toilet. The bloke promised Dad it was the next big thing in household products and that he was sure to make a killing from it. For two or three weeks Dad got up every morning, drove to the neighbouring towns and villages and tried to sell the stuff to the local general stores but there was little interest. General stores didn't buy supplies from travelling salesmen anymore. It became clear he'd spent most of his superannuation on a dead duck, so he came home and went back to bed.

Dad's state slowly worsened over the next seven years. He went to the doctor for his blood pressure pills but no mention was ever made of his psychological state or his obvious deterioration. At 66, when Mum died, he was deemed incapable of looking after himself and nursing home care was the only option. He had moved almost imperceptibly from untreated depression into dementia.

It was a mystery then but it is clear to me now, 40 years later, what it was that happened to my father. At the time I was a child, my family had no medical knowledge, and mood disorders were not something people spoke about.

Could anything have been done differently back then? Would he have responded to the treatments available at the time if anyone had thought to offer them? Would he have responded to the treatments available now?

I tell my father's story partly in the hope that it is no longer possible for that sort of thing to happen. Dr Jan Orman

Here is another account of a life lost to untreated depression. In this case, Brian tries to come to terms with the damage—through uncontrolled rage and frustration—wrought by his father on their family.

The black dog is unluckier than black cats

 Imagine if every day of your life began with the utter isolation of untreated depression: the constant frustration, unrelenting

anxiety and the enveloping loneliness of a disease that you do not understand. Imagine how this would affect your well-being, your day-to-day activities, your relationship with your spouse, your children, your family and friends. Imagine the effort it takes in these circumstances to try to live a happy, normal life, to succeed in your daily endeavours and to maintain healthy relationships, all the while desperately trying to keep your private battles within yourself and taking whatever measures necessary to ensure that nobody knows what you are dealing with.

My father passed away two weeks before my 40th birthday. For each of those 40 years I watched him try to unsuccessfully deal with a depression that slowly ate away at him from the inside out. It was some time after his death that I came to fully understand what was happening to him. The frustration and anxiety caused by his depression manifested itself in extreme fits of anger that were directed at whoever and whatever was near enough to feel his vengeance. My mother, my siblings and I constantly found ourselves being held responsible for something that we had taken no part in. We were simply targets close enough at hand to receive his wrath. For the most part we considered him to be a monstrous man with no self-control or real feelings for those who should have been closest to him.

Over each consecutive decade my father's depression grew, his anger increased and his self-control became non-existent, until he had reached a stage where he couldn't undertake the simplest of tasks without being overtaken by a rage that would leave him incapable of functioning on any level. The unfortunate side effects of his actions only further alienated him from his family. In his later years when family would return home to visit, he would sit alone in the lounge while we saw my mother in the kitchen. At best, family members would put their head in the door and say hello and little more. Such are the long-term effects of misunderstood and untreated depression.

While I have not, even after all these years, found it within myself to totally forgive my father for the way that he treated my mother and his children, I now understand a little what he was dealing with and the internal battle that he fought on a daily basis. I am saddened by the fact that his illness was left untreated throughout his life, as I believe that if appropriate treatment was available to him he could have lived an entirely different and rewarding life that would have included love and respect towards and from his family.

I know from conversations I had with him in his later years that he dearly wished for the love and friendship that was missing from his life; however, too many bridges had been burnt, so his frustration and loneliness was with him to the end. At the time of his death his body was riddled with cancer which, in my belief at least, was the result of his struggle throughout his life.

I am, however, my father's son, so my understanding of his battles is not accidental but through personal experience. I now know first hand what he had lived with for a lifetime and the devastating effect that it can have on your personal health and your relationships, and the never-ending battle to keep the black dog at bay. In the years between my 20th and 40th birthdays, my bouts of depression and the side effects that ensued cost me two marriages and two businesses. Finally, I found myself at a crossroad in life where I was forced to make the most important decision of my life. I chose at that defining moment to step back and ask for help. The journey from there to where I am today has been long and difficult, but every day becomes easier. I will be eternally grateful to a small group of friends and professional people who have assisted me along that pathway. Brian

AVOIDING THE DIAGNOSIS OF DEPRESSION

In the following account, Alastair acknowledges that something is awry, but his defences and pride stand in the way of seeking help—until his illness has nearly robbed him of the capacity to manage it. Those closest to him are aware, but have a dilemma—unless he becomes a danger to himself or others, they are unable to intervene. An individual with depression, as typified by this story, may be very sensitive and guarded, shoring himself up and mounting defences because he feels that he is losing his footing.

Please don't pat the dog

 The Black Dog comes to you. Never whistled, never welcome and never leaving until good and ready. What kind of reward is that for someone finishing nearly 50 years in the workforce?

You've taken the retirement package and made the pledge to shift down a gear. The stress is gone and your time, your life, is no longer a possession of others. You tell yourself that you can live easily in this different space. There's an endless list of new things to do and more than enough time to catch up on projects put aside for so long. The first twelve months is a blur as you tick the list, but although the second year is more leisurely, you now feel it's there that something—an intangible something—began. Its nascence remains unmarked, but you sense that there must have been a signal that was simply disregarded and dismissed. After all, you were a captive to other things, matters that meant more in your new life.

The cur comes. Your life changes.

At first, there is a subdued hum of anxiety that distracts you. The days seem a little darker, your hopes a little weaker. Strengthening doubt seems to lock out calm consideration. Your thoughts are scattered, skidding in all directions. Disquiet and Doubt. That makes you smile. The myth-makers of old had Scylla and Charybdis and now you have your own twin perils: Disquiet and Doubt.

To those you can add Denial.

You say you're just moody. That's a better way to put it, you insist. And you're perhaps a little bored. But the others— the ones you love and by whom you're loved—prefer to say grumpy or out of sorts. Not wanting to offend the old bloke, they use the words softly, with humour. What do you expect, you remind them, you're getting old . . . it's just a phase, sure to pass soon enough. They nod in response to your answer, but the question lingers in their eyes.

You're starting to sit a lot. By yourself. No, that's not quite accurate; it's more like sitting 'inside' yourself. Or you're simply beside yourself. You joke and try to lower the temperature by saying you're thinking things through. Surely they can see that.

It's a long time before someone uses the word 'depression' and—after a wrenching reaction—an even longer time before it's used again.

You feel better, you lie. That's one thing at which you're getting better. That's what you tell them, but what you tell yourself is that you've embraced a dark indulgence. You don't know what it is, either in shape or intent. It sits like a stone in your belly. Self-absorption shifts up to self-obsession. You want to know what that feeling of dread is. That's why you're distracted. There's nothing more important. If you dissect this feeling, you may be released. You'll say it again: surely the others can see that. The problem-solver appears to have a problem, one says in return.

They shouldn't use the word 'depression', that's one thing you're pretty sure about. It's become too much 'flavour of the month'. There seems to be a lot of it going around. Not that this means you are suffering from the same illness. Something similar, perhaps. If anything. Probably nothing, really. Some are calling it a crisis. If you were the media, you could look serious and call it an epidemic. And at the centre of this is the almost daily ritual of public confessions from familiar figures, 'outing' themselves as unable to continue with their duties and diversions because of ... well, you know, the 'D' word. How could you number yourself among them? Who'd want to be a part of that abasement? Have a little dignity, please. There's a world of difference between feeling just a little more anxious than usual and thinking you should expose yourself on that bandwagon!

Still, it'd be good to tidy up matters by putting a label on the malaise. Something succinct to denote these sudden, surprising plunges into nagging despair. Maybe if they plumbed a little deeper they'd learn why there's not much laughter these days. And why the others say your moods are darker and your silences longer, and when those intervals end there's a destructive edge to your words. You dispute that. Of course. Just as you dispute much, most—practically all—judgements of your condition.

Condition? You most certainly dispute that as an appropriate description. Especially while it's still possible to maintain that you might be just fussing too much about an adjunct in the process of ageing. But your case is shaky.

Take a look at yourself, they say. We do, we see ...

You see what you want to see, you say.

There's no need to snap, they say.

I didn't, you say.

Every conversation is a loop, taking you back to where you don't want to be.

The Dog bides its time. It's an uneven attendant. Its absences are welcomed but you know it'll be back. Often now, its return catches you by surprise and the creeping suspicion grows that the visits will never end. Lighten up, you urge yourself; manage this! Management is the key, you emphasise, almost believing it. You're sure your family have their own Management 101 approach: deal with the matter by not dealing with it. You resent that. You see they're receding from you and you want them to stay in the fight. Not that you want to appear to need them, but if they bow out you'll be alone out there on the fringe. Just you and the Dog.

Lighten up, you tell them, but they seem to have stopped listening.

You have to give more ground to them. You could bear the gloom and the dark meditations but it's all the other tangled emotions that are bringing you undone. Do you really believe that, you ask yourself. Hopelessness and regret are the norm in your existence now. Your confidence has drained away. There is dislocation. Foreboding. The only decision you can make is not to make any more decisions. One morning, you wake and instantly know the Dog is with you, as it was when you went to sleep the night before. You pull up the sheet and curl under it. Before, there was limited refuge in staying still, but this is different. This is the beginning of a new phase. Now you seem paralysed. There's so much to do and you've not the will to begin. It's better to stay where you are.

You should see someone, you're told.

That rankles. Don't they think you can get on top of the situation? It's better to wait—you figure—things always change. This will stabilise. You'll soon have the measure of matters. You'll shake off this lethargy, this torpor, and whatever else has such a tight grip on you.

You should see someone, you're told again.

You've always taken care of yourself, made decisions and lived by them and you'll do so in this case. You just need some separation—some time out—from the problem. With that time, you'll steal back the day from the Dog. The choices are limited. Let things roll over you ... but where would that end? Besides, it's not your way. Try focusing further ahead, beyond the nearest hurdle? The Dog drags you back. Ignore it? That merits no response. Seize on something that someone says and distract yourself by expanding it? Let their thinking become yours?

There's a new voice now, a repetitive one, saying simply that you're no use to yourself. Or anyone else.

You should see someone, the others say.

I should see someone, you say.

For now, the Black Dog comes. Never whistled, never welcome. Alastair

Families, when faced with a member who is so obviously distressed and impaired, may decide to present a united front, emphasise their worry and insist that the individual see a doctor. Sometimes the presence of physical symptoms such as lethargy and broken sleep can provide a useful entry point for insisting that the older person have a medical assessment.

Once an appointment is made, it may be possible to speak with the family GP ahead of the visit, and also to reach agreement with the older person that a family member can attend the appointment too. However, even if the diagnosis of 'depression' is reached and accepted, adherence to any medication prescribed may be resisted, especially as side effects often occur before benefits are felt. Regular appointments with a doctor and a counsellor (if a counsellor has been found and tolerated) can help to consolidate improvements and compliance.

In the stories so far, the protagonists have been affected by depression of varying severity and differing causes. However, depression from any cause can freeze and diminish the person, destroy the family, exacerbate existing disease and pave the way for onset of other disorders. The longer the individual lives with untreated depression, the more it can take hold biologically and psychologically. Apart from the biological changes that are wrought—which are mostly reversible—the illness can have a powerful effect on a person's view of themself.

NOTEWORTHY

Recognising and managing older-age depression

Depression in adults aged over 65 years can be difficult to recognise, as the symptoms are often similar to the vicissitudes of ageing.

- Symptoms can include unexplained physical symptoms, memory loss, anxiety and behavioural changes.
- Presenting symptoms of depression may be atypical, making diagnosis more difficult—for example, paranoid delusions, loss of appetite and weight, or severe anxiety.
- Sometimes, paradoxically, the individual may feel numb or 'frozen' or unable to feel any emotion.
- When depression causes loss of concentration and poor memory it mimics dementia, and the older person's illness may be misdiagnosed and untreated.
- While it is important to address related factors that may be contributing to lowered mood (for instance, psychosocial problems, loneliness and isolation, stressful life events), clinical depression in an older person should be treated separately to issues of age.
- A message for carers: seek an assessment from a professional who is accustomed to dealing with those who are older.

- Older age does not diminish the effectiveness of treatment. Improvement and recovery is seen in the majority of people after the right treatment and management.[5]

Depressive signs and symptoms are discussed further throughout the following chapters.

4
Reaching a diagnosis

> Life would be infinitely happier if we could only be born at the age of 80 and gradually approach eighteen.
>
> Mark Twain

Stories in earlier chapters have underlined depression's toxic effects. The benefits in successfully diagnosing and treating depression, at any age, include alleviating misery, improving health and reducing the costs of continuing medical interventions.

PATTERNS OF ONSET

The onset of clinical depression in older age can broadly be divided into two types. First, there are those with 'depression grown older'— people who have had previous episodes of depression during their earlier years and are at risk of recurrence. When the onset of depression first occurs in earlier life, it is probable that genetic factors, personality and life experiences have contributed.

The second type comprises those who experience 'late-onset depression'—people who develop depression for the first time in their later years, usually after age 60. Late-onset depression is less likely to have a genetic contribution and is more commonly associated with the biological changes that accompany ageing. Also, experiences more common in older age, such as bereavement, illness, nursing home admission and loss of role in life, can be linked to late-onset depression.

RECOGNISING AND ACCEPTING DEPRESSIVE ILLNESS

> A psychiatrist is a fellow who asks you a lot of expensive questions that your wife asks for nothing.
>
> Joey Adams

The road to diagnosis can be fraught and difficult to negotiate. As mentioned earlier, one common presentation of depression in an older person is via physical symptoms ('somatisation'), and this may provide the rationale for seeking help.

In the following account, from Professor Brian Draper, 'Bill' comes to his GP's notice because of a host of physical symptoms that have no obvious foundation. An older person may be acutely tuned in to body signals that become amplified by the presence of depression—these symptoms act as a sort of 'proxy' for emotional distress. A cluster of research findings indicate that depression and pain may share common pathogenic (disease-associated) pathways.

CASE NOTES

'But I am not depressed'

How would you react if your GP asserts that 'you are depressed' when your main symptoms are muscle pain, tiredness and weight loss? Despite numerous blood tests and x-rays over the previous few months, there has been no progress into working out the cause of these physical symptoms. To top it all off, now your GP is suggesting that you should see a psychiatrist to check if you are depressed!

'But I am not depressed—just tired and irritable about not feeling well. I am not the type to get depressed and I haven't suffered any nervous complaints over my 75 years of life.'

This is how Bill described his reaction to his GP's suggestion that he should see me—a psychogeriatrician—about his persistent vague somatic complaints. My greatest surprise was that he was here at all given his adamant rejection of his GP's advice but it was clear that despite his scepticism about the referral, Bill trusted his GP implicitly and was prepared to suspend judgement, albeit temporarily—especially since his wife thought that it was a good idea too.

My challenge was to gain sufficient respect and trust from Bill to allow him to provide me with the history to determine if his GP was right, and to build therapeutic rapport. Fortunately Bill was more than willing to describe his symptoms—some patients in this situation clam up and refuse to cooperate, and of course many simply will not see a psychiatrist at all. I find that it is important to initially focus on the patient's somatic symptoms in some detail before enquiring about the psychological ones, which I tend to frame as 'How are you coping with these problems?'

Bill told me that his symptoms started about three months before, without any clear precipitant. He just noticed increasing fatigue and vague muscular aches and pains that were all over his body. As a result he had stopped his normal weekly lawn bowls and twice-weekly visits to the club with his mates, and no longer helped his wife with the housework. He felt he was no longer enjoying anything, including his food, and was concerned that he was losing so much weight—about five kilograms at last count. Indeed he was worrying so much about all of this that he was having trouble sleeping, waking up at 4 a.m. every morning. He was starting to think that if this was what old age had in store for him, what was the point of living? But he quickly denied that he would ever harm himself—his wife and family meant too much to him for that to happen.

Of course I asked Bill if these problems were getting him down at all, if he was feeling at all depressed or sad or worthless. He replied in a somewhat irritated manner that he had been over this with his GP, and had already told him that he wasn't feeling at all depressed but was certainly frustrated with his lack of progress.

I backed off and asked Bill to tell me more about himself and his health. His history was unremarkable—born here, uneventful childhood, happy marriage of over 50 years, three children and five grandchildren, retired banker, contented retirement. Health-wise there had been a few issues—longstanding hypertension, coronary artery bypass surgery, type 2 diabetes, high cholesterol and gastro-oesophageal reflux disease—but he had been taking his antihypertensives, a statin and metformin for years and had a regular check-up with his GP. There was no personal or family history of depression. I also did a brief cognitive assessment that included frontal lobe tasks, informing Bill that this was standard for all my examinations. No significant abnormality was detected.

Of course, in this situation, and indeed in all cases of first-episode late-life major depression, it is absolutely essential to exclude a physical cause. Apart from a normal physical exam, his GP had thoroughly investigated Bill for diverse conditions such as polymyalgia rheumatica, thyroid dysfunction, anaemia and vitamin B12 deficiency, and considered the possibility of occult malignancy by including a chest x-ray and a review by a gastroenterologist, who had 'scoped' him top and bottom without finding anything.

With this information to hand I had little doubt that Bill was suffering from depression. One of the myths about clinical depression is that feelings of depression are an essential feature. It has long been known that this is not the case, and that loss of interests or pleasure in life can be equivalent clinical features. These symptoms often seem to the patient to be secondary to the somatic complaints. Who wouldn't lose pleasure in life when vague muscular pains, tiredness, loss of appetite and inability to sleep at night persist for weeks on end? The criteria used to diagnose depression, however, do not vary with the predominance of physical symptoms or the person's age, but the way that the criteria are applied often requires an understanding of the nuances of symptom interpretation that comes from good history-taking. At times, the patient's preoccupation with their physical symptoms, despite appropriate reassurance, may be due to the depression having a psychotic intensity with hypochondriacal delusions.

This type of depression has been described in many different ways over the years—masked depression, atypical depression and non-dysphoric depression are just a few of the terms used. It is more likely to occur in older people than younger adults, and for many sufferers it is their first episode of depression. For some older people, symptoms of sadness or depression may be present, but in an attenuated form that is under-reported. The extent to which this tendency is either an age-related effect, or a cohort effect—reflecting a stoic generation that was raised during the world wars and Great Depression—is not known. Symptoms usually are incorrectly attributed by patient, family, friends and doctors to old age or physical ill-health, with the result that depression may go undetected and untreated for a long time.

The initial recognition and diagnosis of the depression is the first of many challenges facing clinicians. I knew that I somehow had to convince Bill that depression was the correct diagnosis. 'But I am not depressed' remained the hurdle to overcome. The approach I took was to provide an explanation of late-life depression that acknowledged that the term 'depression' did not accurately describe his symptoms, but happens, perhaps unfortunately, to be the medical term used for his condition. I then focused on a very 'physical' explanation for late-life depression that drew on issues related to ageing brain changes in general, and cerebrovascular disease in particular (aware he had a significant vascular history). [Cerebrovascular disease refers to disease of the blood vessels, especially arteries, that supply the brain.]

At this point I noted that Bill had not had a brain scan, and suggested that this was worthwhile to see if there were any signs of cerebrovascular disease or other neurological explanations for his symptoms. I usually do a CT scan rather than an MRI scan, as in most circumstances it is sufficient to detect significant abnormality. One common reason that older people develop depression for the first time in late life is that cerebrovascular disease has damaged parts of the brain felt to be critical to mood control, especially in the frontal and subcortical regions—so-called vascular depression.

Apathy, poor motivation and generally slowed cognitive processes are key features here.

I didn't ignore the psychosocial aspects of Bill's symptoms; I simply reframed them in terms of how he was coping with his distressing symptoms. This general approach worked sufficiently well to develop enough rapport with Bill to enable him to agree to a trial of antidepressant therapy. I used a very physical 'neurotransmitter' explanation that drew on an analogy with the treatment of other disorders such as Parkinson's disease. Bill had a few questions about all of this and I could tell that he retained a healthy scepticism, but at the same time he was appreciative that at last someone was able to provide an explanation of his symptoms, along with a treatment.

I chose an antidepressant that I thought Bill could tolerate, in his case a short half-life SSRI [selective serotonin reuptake inhibitor], and made sure he commenced at low dose for a week to minimise side effects before titrating to a therapeutic dose. I informed him that he might not start to improve for two to four weeks, and that it might take up to eight weeks to really feel a lot better. Too often antidepressants are discontinued prematurely because either the patient or the clinician has unrealistic expectations. I scheduled a review two weeks later to see how he was travelling and to discuss the results of his CT scan.

At that review, Bill was tolerating the antidepressant but had not noticed any change. His CT scan showed some mild age-related brain changes and I discussed this finding with him. Two weeks later he was starting to improve; a month later he was getting back to his old self, and in these sessions I was able to further assist in his understanding of his condition and impressed upon him that he needed to remain on the antidepressant for at least a year.

Bill was fortunate. Perhaps a third or more of patients, especially those with 'vascular' depression (disruptions in brain systems associated with age), do not respond to the first course of antidepressants. This can be a crucial point in the therapeutic process. 'I told you that I wasn't depressed' may well be the response—if the patient returns for their appointment! To minimise the risk of this latter development, it is important for the clinician to map out a plan of action with the patient and their family that encompasses a change of antidepressants as a potential back-up strategy if the first treatment doesn't work. During this phase, it is essential for the clinician to retain therapeutic optimism, conveyed by word and manner, to the patient.

Despite recovering from his depression, Bill was never entirely convinced that this was his problem—but at the same time he was insightful enough to realise that the treatment worked and that it was best to follow his doctors' advice.

Professor Brian Draper

NON-DEPRESSIVE ILLNESS CAN HAVE SIMILAR SYMPTOMS

Ill-defined or slow-onset diseases (for example, multiple sclerosis) may take years to develop and have diffuse and variable symptoms. Such disorders may initially be misdiagnosed as arising from psychological causes and the real underlying disease missed, as in this example from editor Brodaty.

CASE NOTES

Context helps diagnosis
An 84-year-old woman presented with similar symptoms to 'Bill' (see previous account): specifically, muscle weakness, tiredness, decreased energy and declining ability to carry out household tasks. She had been diagnosed with depression by her doctor . . . understandably, as she was upset about having these symptoms.

When I saw her, she had an unfilled prescription for anti-depressants. I was impressed, however, by how specific her symptoms were, for instance, 'inability to hang out the washing'; by how localised her weakness was—to the upper muscles of her arms; and by her lack of sadness.

Blood tests confirmed a diagnosis of polymyalgia rheumatica —an autoimmune disease more common with ageing, which causes inflammation of the muscles and which leads to these very symptoms.

She recovered quickly after a course of steroids to suppress her immune system's attack on her own muscles.

Professor Henry Brodaty

EXPLORING THE 'DEPRESSIVE EQUIVALENT'

The skill in reaching a correct diagnosis is highlighted by the converse: where physical symptoms, or somatising disorders such as headache and other chronic pain, 'mask' or take the place of emotional distress—a presentation known as the 'depressive equivalent'.

The next report explores this presentation further. As Professor Max Kamien indicates, it is not unusual for medical investigation of diffuse symptoms to continue for years before psychological explanations are explored. He suggests that it would be preferable if all doctors included the possibility of a psychiatric cause as part of their initial diagnostic problem-solving.

CASE NOTES

'Psychiatry' is not spoken here

Queen's University in Belfast was particularly proud of its state-of-the-art video set-up for monitoring student consultations. I suggested they should provide more analytical feedback to students. With typical Northern Irish charm and cunning, they asked me to demonstrate. I could see I was being set up, but was always one for a challenge. The resulting scene was a consulting room, containing a medical student and a patient unknown to the student and to me. Together with some local medical teachers, I observed the student consultation.

The patient was in fact an Australian—an older woman who had lived in Ireland for 50 years. She had developed hydatid cysts in her lungs and liver, and had become something of a celebrity patient. The knighted doyen of surgery had successfully removed the hydatid cysts but the patient still complained of persistent, severe abdominal pain. She had seen no fewer than 31 different consultants and had had all the tests then known to medical science, including six barium meals and an exploratory laparotomy. No pathology could be found.

The student was having some difficulty getting beyond hypotheses about hydatid or Crohn's disease. I coaxed him to think more holistically. But there was still no diagnostic progress. I then changed places with him and set up rapport by saying 'G'day'. We chatted about her home town in Australia, its dogs and diseased sheep. Her eyes were incredibly sad and something in my subconscious mind made me say: 'Tell me, what sits on your heart like a rock?'

I had never used that question before. It produced a flood of tears and an abreaction [release of repressed emotions] that went on for the next half-hour. She had married an Irish landed baronet but she had been unable to produce an heir. She also had other symptoms that led me to a diagnosis of depression. The patient, medical student and watching doctors were not so sure. But all agreed that a trial of antidepressant medication was a reasonable approach.

One year later her GP wrote to me, saying: 'She improved immensely on the antidepressant and has never once produced a further organic symptom resulting in needless investigation. She is delighted and has become a much brighter and more extroverted person.' I asked if he had fed this information back to the 31 specialists who had treated her. He had not. 'If I were to tell the referring specialist that he was wrong he would never admit another of my patients to his hospital,' he said.

But, in my view, failure to give feedback is educationally unethical, and an inability to accept it professionally stupid. So I wrote to the specialist concerned. He replied, graciously thanking me for contributing to his education and assuring me he would present the 'completed case' at a Grand Rounds with his colleagues and staff, 'who might also need to learn to speak psychiatry'.

Lessons learnt

All medical doctors have blind spots in their knowledge and attitudes. This situation has been well described by a former US Secretary of Defense, the much-lampooned Donald Rumsfeld. 'There are known knowns. There are things we know we know. We also know there are known unknowns; that is to say we know there are some things we know we do not know. But there are also unknown unknowns—the ones we don't know we don't know.' And a common manifestation of this last position is a failure of doctors, of all medical disciplines, to consider the possibility that a patient's difficult-to-diagnose pain may be a manifestation of an underlying psychiatric disorder.

Sometimes doctors think about a psychiatric diagnosis as a last resort. 'I have done every test known to man. It must be a psychiatric problem.' It would be preferable if all doctors included the possibility of a psychiatric cause as part of their original diagnostic problem-solving.

In his textbook General Practice, widely regarded as the 'bible' on general practice, Professor John Murtagh rates depression as one of the seven most common 'diagnostic masquerades'. A depressed patient may present with bodily symptoms such as persistent pain. This used to be called a 'depressive equivalent'—a 'forme fruste' or partial manifestation of a depressive disorder. It doesn't take extraordinary communication skills to unearth a strong underlying, persistent feeling of sadness. But in such cases the doctor does have to think about depression as a possible diagnosis and, empathically, ask about it.

Professor Max Kamien

Depression creeping up in older age can be camouflaged by physical symptoms—'niggling health issues'. These symptoms are real, they are not faked. In fact, they are so real to the person affected that he or she may worry that they are dying of an undiagnosed disease.

Riding the black dog: an excerpt . . .

Over the next few weeks the world started to look grey and strangely unreal. I began to feel an overwhelming physical urge to curl up in a dark corner as if I was a hibernating animal. Things that I previously did spontaneously made me extremely anxious.

Noise, any noise, overwhelmed me. I cried as if I was grieving but I could not explain why. It occurred to me that I might be losing my mind and I became very frightened and tried to hide it from everyone, including myself. I had always believed I could do anything if I tried hard enough so I tried to talk myself out of what I was experiencing. It didn't work. I could not think properly; I felt confused and so indecisive that whether to have coffee or juice for breakfast, use the stairs or the lift, became excruciating decisions of immense importance.

After a while I felt so unwell I worried whether I actually had a malignant illness and was slowly dying. I was ashamed at how dependent I became, frightened of being alone, but not comfortable being with people. Daphne

FAMILY HISTORY CAN PROVIDE INDICATIONS

Depression often has a strong genetic loading. Some families are more prone to mood disorders—just as other families tend to high blood pressure or types of cancer. This doesn't make depression inevitable, but it is helpful to know the family history when evaluating the possibility of clinical depression.

In the following account, Lena recognises that she is at risk of depression because of her awareness that the illness is a recurring motif in both sides of her family. Sharing this history with a health care professional is very important, as is information about any previous episodes of depression or anxiety.

You were not invited

 Every morning it was there—a dull black fog in my head, fuzzing up my brain, lowering my energy. Take a shower. Shake my head, still there. Sit quietly, eat breakfast, drink water, read the paper. Why won't it go away? The fog lingers heavily, invading my person. Who am I? What is my plan for today? Household chores—too many and what are they?

The morning passes somehow, the washing hanging on the line blows with the breeze. Is the kitchen tidy? What time is it? Morning tea? Yes, where's that coffee? Try reading, persist with the fog. Finally, a clearing appears, doors open and the sun enters with a nod and a wink and beckons me into the garden.

So, is this how retirement works, so many foggy mornings to push through. When the clouds clear it might be a fine day. Sometimes the weather is bleak and too cold to make a start. Try some chores. The house is clean! Aimless, tired, can't settle. Oh for heaven's sake, lighten up! Let it go, make a hot drink, gather a rug and into the big chair, warm and cosy, read a book.

Another day, the sun is shining, our morning is leisurely and we drive to the art gallery. The beauty of art surrounds my senses, relax and chat, take a walk beside the lake. Everything is fine, there is no fog in sight today and my mind is active and alert.

A weekend away comes up for me as a member of a team. Supporting people to develop and enhance communication skills. No worries . . . have been on this team before; assisting people through their thoughts and feelings, so empowering and rewarding. But the first morning, I crash. I can't focus. What's my task? Oh no! The fog descends insidiously and without permission. My mind becomes a muddle of vague thoughts and actions. I'm pushing away the fog, trying to forge a clearing and find a path that leads away from this hell. Maybe I can go home, but the team is small. Who would take over my tasks? Another night and day before me and I struggle on, make it through and arrive home, unsettled, embarrassed, tearful.

Realisation dawns, a doctor's appointment is made. Days later, my head clears and only a little fog rolls in occasionally. My sexual feelings begin to return, although I'm not so sure I noticed them leaving. Thanks, doctor, for your listening and prescription.

How did this happen? I am over 60, happily married, with a son, a daughter, their partners and two grandchildren in each family. We share family celebrations together and my time spent with the grandchildren is regular and enjoyable. I ponder the WHY? of these depression issues. They have been an unspoken feature of my mother's family for many years. My mother and brother have both had psychotic periods and now keep well with medication. I recall my younger days and my mother being a happy person who loved gardening and caring for our family. She refuses to talk about her depression and the psychosis that descended when she was in her 70s and living in a retirement village. My brother was not so lucky and was in his early 30s when he encountered his first psychosis.

As an adult, my interest and research into my paternal and maternal family histories uncovered the dark secrets of depression in my mother's family. Her father was in his early twenties when severe depression affected him. Her father's father took his own life in his 40s (although this story was well hidden until my gleaning produced a death certificate one could not ignore). I saw my grandfather as a happy, kind, gentle man. We had a great rapport and he taught me all I know about football. His depression was hidden from the family for many years.

In his 70s and 80s, my father too suffered from depression. He was not as debilitated as my mother and his medication allowed him to remain active and healthy. My son and daughter have also recovered from occasions of depression following stressors in their lives. It seems our genes for coping with stress are fragile and we are more susceptible to glitches in wellbeing.

Like many others, my life has had its ups and downs. My first marriage disintegrated after twenty years. My second husband was a wonderful, sane man, but died of cancer a month before we could celebrate our tenth wedding anniversary. I was depressed during his illness and for a time following his death.

Some years later and closer to retirement, I marry again. My life is happy and fulfilling, with many pleasures and activities. The local University of the Third Age (U3A) has a wide range of special-interest groups. We have joined our favourites, on occasions together. With careful budgeting we are planning an overseas holiday.

However, one day at a time, they say. When the days are clear and fine and the 'fog' is nowhere in view, I treasure the clarity and peace around me: maybe a little gardening, a little reading, some conversation with others and quiet moments enjoying the opportunity to be free from the intrusion of the black dog. To redefine this 'new' self—incorporating these episodic 'blue' patches—has been a time of reflection and introspection for me. A closer awareness of mind and body, exercise and friendship, has replaced quick and impulsive decisions. Daily meditations before dinner have become a new pattern.

A less anxious and more aware 'me' has allowed time to reflect and consider the future. Although the late arrival of depression in my life was a complete surprise, at 62 I have become a keen observer of my new situation. A life ambition to write about a family history event has come to the fore more strongly. The challenge of this task has led to me joining up with others who write, an established group of U3A women.

So, although uninvited, that black dog has given me the opportunity to review my life and reconsider my priorities. With a strong family network, goals to maintain focus and important friends around me, my journey through the third age is sure to hold many surprises and hopefully rewards. Lena

When relevant family medical history is withheld, there is the potential for over-investigation and for treatment to take a completely wrong path, with attendant complications. This next account tells of Professor Tom Arie's ministrations to an elderly and very sick woman. All information is potentially relevant and can shape and improve the outcome of treatment, but in this instance Ms W's family withheld a crucial piece of the puzzle from the clinician.

CASE NOTES

A key withheld

Some patients are never forgotten. I draw here on recollections of 40 years ago.

Ms W was 82, a spinster, and she lived alone. Referred on account of unexplained recent general deterioration, she was seen as usual at home. There were no obvious physical signs but she was befuddled, probably mildly delirious, with no spontaneous talk; she was unresponsive to questions, slow, dishevelled, incontinent of urine, refusing food and drink and dehydrated. She looked, in short, decrepit and unwell. Neighbours were unforthcoming but yes, they hadn't lately seen her around. I admitted her to the joint medical and psychiatric unit for older people which we, 'the two Toms' [doctors Tom Dunn and Tom Arie], had set up.

There was family, but only distant, and they said they were unaware of any possible causes of the change in Ms W, or any 'loss events' in her recent life. No, they said, they knew of no history of psychiatric illness in the patient or in her family. The patient's doctor was clear that a few weeks previously she had seemed well and he too had found nothing specific on physical examination.

In hospital, hydration and blood chemistry were attended to, and other tests were negative. The nurses were asked to observe her carefully and to record whatever little she might say. They reported that she often looked sad and that occasionally, under her breath when she thought she was unobserved, she made what seemed to be self-deprecating and 'hopeless' utterances.

In view of these observations and in the absence of an obvious physical cause for the recent change in her, such as a stroke or an infection, it seemed reasonable to suspect a depressive illness. It was decided to make a tentative trial of electroconvulsive therapy (ECT; more readily embarked on in those days). Improvement came almost at once. She started accepting food and drink, but still at first spoke little; spontaneous talk returned after more treatments, and after six treatments she was well.

It was only at this point that the family 'confessed' that about twenty years earlier she had had a depressive illness but without the physical deterioration, and that she had likewise recovered with ECT. The patient confirmed that this was so. But the family 'hadn't liked to mention it' when originally asked, 'in case it made you think she was mental'.

Lessons learnt

Pretty obvious, I suppose—but a few may be worth spelling out even so: that in very old people depression can have a primarily physical presentation (it may be the consequence or the cause of the physical illness). And the patient may be 'confused'.

A history of a fairly abrupt recent change without evident physical cause raises the question of depression. And recurrent depression may look quite different when it recurs in late life. A history from others can be decisive; a previous history or a family history of depression can raise the odds. Here that history was withheld.

However, careful observation can yield great dividends. The recent change in Ms W and the absence of an apparent physical cause, along with the observed 'furtive' sadness, suggested depression. A bonus would have been to have learnt of a precipitating life event but there seemed to be none—which is not unusual. (In another instance which presented in similar fashion at about that time, it transpired that the change in the patient began after a much-loved dog had been run over.)

Crucial were the observations made by the nurses who, unlike doctors, are there around-the-clock. Despite the likely psychiatric nature of the illness, medical measures are crucial too. And of severely depressed very old people, probably many more die of dehydration and derangements of blood chemistry than of suicide.

So the case is strong for close collaboration between psychiatric and medical teams in the care of old people—a style of working which was later consolidated in our joint teaching department of psychiatrists and physicians in Nottingham.

Incidentally: 40 years ago, 82 was 'very old'. Not usually so these days!

Professor Tom Arie

INDIVIDUAL 'DIAL SETTINGS' IN RELATION TO WELLBEING

Just as there can be a family loading that confers vulnerability to depression, bipolar disorder or anxiety, research also indicates that an individual's feeling of wellbeing is a genetically based and stable personality trait. The 'setting' for wellbeing and happiness is considered to be at least 50 per cent inherited. Each individual has a 'set point' of happiness (the 'hedonic' set point), with a small range on either side. For instance, even after a lottery win, the euphoria is only temporary and then we return to our set point. Similarly with unhappiness: a person suffering a loss will be temporarily unhappy and then revert to his or her general disposition. A further 40 per cent of our setting is attributed to intentional activity—actions under our voluntary control. Life circumstances, possessions and income are estimated to contribute a further 10 per cent.

One of the markers of depression is that the individual becomes 'stuck' in their down mood and does not spontaneously revert to their set point. Professor Max Kamien illustrates this as he tells of Harry and his 'dark brown' outlook, and how antidepressant medication boosted his set point to positive. These medications, especially the SSRIs, can be helpful in muting ruminations, worry and negative preoccupations. While Harry's diagnosis is unclear—though more likely non-melancholic depression and with a personality contribution—medical intervention successfully dissipated his chronic low mood.

CASE NOTES

When someone is chronically depressed

'Harry' was a non-smoking teetotaller who, together with his wife, ran a newsagency and a home newspaper delivery round. His wife had read a double-page spread about depression in the Sunday Times. She said, 'Harry, this article is about you.' I was one of the GPs interviewed by the reporter and my name was mentioned in the article. 'Mrs Harry' insisted that he came and saw me the very next day.

Harry was never the life of the party, but five years after they married he became even more gloomy and pessimistic than his 'normal' irritable self. His wife put his changed mood down to taking up a newspaper round and having to rise at 4 a.m. and to worry about his two children. (One had congenital deafness, the other epilepsy.) She was also very much aware that Harry's father had a similar disposition, always picky, irritable and irritating. Neither father nor son spread much joy to those around them. When one of his customers won Lotto, Harry did not join in the spirit of the celebrations. Many of his customers described him as a 'miserable bastard'. But he was honest and reliable so they stuck with him. And his wife was always pleasant and they felt sorry for her.

Harry was thin and wiry and said that food didn't interest him. Apart from his work, he lacked the inclination or energy to go out or socialise. His wife did the business books and made all the decisions. Unexpectedly, she reported that they had an active—or more accurately described, regular—sex life, since he didn't seem to enjoy it all that much.

At first, Harry was unwilling to accept antidepressant pills. He said he would be labelled as a 'psycho' or a 'nutter'. But, with the insistence of his wife, he eventually agreed to a two-month trial of therapy. Three weeks later he said he felt as if a weight was being taken off his shoulders. He asked if the imipramine could affect his sex life. So, with due care, I changed him to fluoxetine.

Lessons learnt

When I was a young 'doc', fifty years ago, we were taught to classify depression as either 'reactive' or 'endogenous'/'melancholic'. The former was regarded as due to an understandable cause such as bereavement or adverse childhood experiences. The latter was usually more severe and seemed to lack an obvious triggering event. We were also aware that some of these patients with endogenous depression had a family history of depression and a 'constitutional predisposition' to be moody, gloomy, pessimistic and focused on the sad side of life.

There was much debate about the validity of the concept of 'chronic depression'. However, I encounter one such person a week in the course of my academic and social interactions. And I come across many more similar patients during my clinical GP sessions. These gloomy souls are missing out on life and close relationships. But they are difficult to get into therapy. They invariably suffer from low self-esteem and this translates into viewing a psychiatric diagnosis and treatment as a stigma.

I try to explain to them that they are similar to people with diabetes who suffer from a lack of insulin. Their depressive symptoms are due to a lack of serotonin and other neurotransmitters. I coax them into trying a two-month trial of antidepressants. About 70 per cent keep up the antidepressants. The results are often mildly dramatic. The rude, gloomy, picky patients become happier in themselves and much easier to live with.

I am a low-prescribing doctor and am conscious of Aldous Huxley's classic book Brave New World, where the populace are kept controlled and content with a dream-inducing pill called 'soma'. But there are many depressed, unhappy, dysthymic people whose lives—and the lives of those with whom they interact— would be much improved with a standard dose of an SSRI.

Professor Max Kamien

WHEN LOW MOOD IS MISTAKENLY ATTRIBUTED TO STRESSORS

Often depressive illness is 'missed' altogether. There are stressors that fuel depressive illness and at the same time distract from it. An older person's inability to cope can be attributed to difficult circumstances, with the implication that a low mood is a 'logical', not a 'pathological', response.

In the following account from 'Helen' of her husband's illness, we once again observe a mood disorder presenting via somatic symptoms which initially mask the depression. Her husband had shown notable resilience in the face of recent setbacks and tough childhood experiences. The latter likely conferred an extra vulnerability that put him more at risk of developing a non-melancholic depression.

Journey to knowledge

 How I wish we had known about depression as an illness sooner.

We decided to take early retirement in 1990. My husband's workplace was closing and offering redundancies. We had been putting as much as we could afford into a super fund and our son agreed to buy our family home. So Bob and I were free to go travelling as self-funded retirees. We were 'on the road' for twelve months, and on our way back to visit family we saw a delightful cottage in a very friendly town and decided to make this our new home.

It was like a honeymoon period, renovating the house and planning and working on a garden together. However, the high interest rate that we had relied on had fallen dramatically and we realised our financial nest egg was not going to last as long as we had hoped. So we looked around for jobs available in our country town. It was the time of the mature-age allowance and to qualify one had to have been looking for work for a period of time. I found a part-time job but Bob, being older, was not having any luck.

It was then that his niggling health issues started: neck ache, hernia problems, headaches, stomach upsets and disturbed sleep patterns. Next, seemingly unimportant things like the noise of a neighbour's cockatoo became an insurmountable problem. Once, when bushwalking with friends in hilly country, he became unable to move up or down the slope. Gradually he was less inclined to socialise and was becoming angry at strangers. There was the feeling that things were getting out of control for him. 'Am I going mad?' he wondered. It was becoming difficult for him just to get out of bed and face each day. And all the time he was focusing on the physical ailments, as his feelings of despair—when everything in life should be so good—could not be explained.

Finally, he decided he must have got Ross River fever while on our travels. We had heard of people who had been infected and how you feel so weak and have aching joints. So we went to the doctor. He listened to both of us and said, 'You have depression, Bob.' 'But what about the hernia?' asked my husband. 'That can wait,' said the doctor.

We were very fortunate to have a GP who understood that just taking antidepressants was not enough. He recommended that we read the book Beating the Blues and suggested that six months' treatment should see an improvement. He arranged for counselling and we learnt about the damage negative thoughts could cause and how to challenge them with positive affirmations.

But then we found out what panic attacks were all about! One day we went for a picnic to a local beauty spot and had to leave when panic set in for Bob. Thunderstorms, which had previously never bothered him, now became terrifying.

One day when he was at the surgery for a review, he developed all the symptoms of a heart attack. The surgery was the best place to be and he was wired up to an ECG—but no heart irregularities were present. Six months later things seemed to be improving and the doctor said, 'Latest research shows that it is best to continue taking the medication for twelve months.'

Well, if you have one wish, all I can say is make it to not have depression. With any other illness we would have had the sympathy of friends and family but, apart from our sons, we had difficulty talking about all this to people. However, when we finally decided that it was not something to be ashamed of and started talking, it was amazing how many people had experienced depression personally or through a loved one. Bob frequently thought he should be able to beat this thing and tried to wean himself off the medication. But after a few weeks all the previous problems would return, so at the end of twelve months the doctor said he thought it would be best if the medication was continued for life.

So that is our story of the medical facts. But there is so much more to this story. We talked as never before and became closer for it. We read everything we could find on how the mind works. We understood how some depression is from a life event and some from a chemical imbalance. We saw the need for medication to be like taking insulin for diabetes, to make it more acceptable. We accepted that depression is an illness, not a weakness. We enjoyed every good day. We used our knowledge to help me cope with menopause. We were more compassionate to a daughter-in-law who had previously had postnatal depression with our first grandchild. At the time we could not understand why she was acting so oddly with all the family in regards to the baby. Her depression was not diagnosed by the medical staff for many months and she was so distressed. It brought a closeness between her and my husband as they both knew what the other one had been through, and both had tried to manage without the pills.

They call it late-onset depression, but is it just the result of a lifetime of events, culminating in one that we just cannot accept? In Bob's case, early retirement seemed to him to be 'cheating'. He had been indoctrinated to believe he had to work till he was 65. Taking ten years off to enjoy yourself seemed wrong to him. When we were self-funded it was acceptable, but for a man who had never been out of work for his entire life, signing on for unemployment support was the last straw.

We realise that the same life event can lead to a different reaction depending on circumstances and personality. My husband lived through the Blitz in London as a child and he now dislikes caves and mines; we can guess a link from all the nights in an air-raid shelter. His father was seriously ill in a sanatorium at the time, too. Bob and his family—mother and three siblings—were evacuated to northern England and billeted with another family who obviously saw it as an intrusion. So they returned to London in time for the doodlebugs and rockets. Being the eldest, Bob had to take responsibility for his siblings though still a child himself, which contributed to a sense of guilt whenever things went wrong, even when it was beyond his control. We all have regrets in life of things done or not done, but some people constantly berate themselves for their inadequacies. Not good for mental health!

I am pleased to say that we are in a pleasant phase of life now. You might call it maturity. We are more tolerant and enjoy the company of family and friends. And we can enjoy the simple pleasures of life because we know we have survived depression and put the black dog back in his kennel. Helen

A feature of Helen's story is how readily the couple educated themselves about depression. Their astute doctor helped them to formulate ways of thinking about risk factors to illness (sometimes conceptualised as the 'predisposing', 'protective', 'precipitating' and 'perpetuating' factors associated with an illness and response to treatment). The GP also understood the vital role of medication in keeping Bob well and was a steady influence in Bob's continuing compliance.

GENERAL RISK AND PROTECTIVE FACTORS IN OLDER AGE

There are known risk factors and protective factors that affect both physical and mental health and also influence how well we manage the process of ageing. In general, mental stimulation, social activities and participation, control of chronic pain and, possibly, grief counselling can reduce the risk of developing depression.

Protective factors include:

- an individual's positive attitudes and adaptability
- a belief system (e.g. religious, spiritual, humanist)
- participation in community
- purposeful engagement
- good nutrition and levels of activity
- financial security (not just income level)
- connection with and support from family and friends.

Risk factors include:

- poor housing standards
- high costs—particularly for accommodation
- low income and financial stress
- being female (females are more often financially insecure, single, and focused on their feelings)

- stigma, discrimination and unhelpful attitudes associated with age
- poor nutrition and lack of exercise
- isolation from community and pleasurable activities (particularly in rural areas)
- lack of access to medical care
- lack of support and contact with relatives and friends.[1]

NOTEWORTHY

Is it sadness or depression?

It is argued that psychiatry is increasingly 'pathologising' normal moods and re-badging them as psychiatric disorder. This allegation has some truth to it. Researchers Horwitz and Wakefield provide a detailed case for this concern in their book The Loss of Sadness. The fact is that the classification of 'depression' has become muddied over recent years, and it remains difficult to discern where the boundaries lie between a normal state such as sadness, and an abnormal state such as depression.

The rejection of the 'binary' model of depression, which divided depression into two types—'endogenous'(from within, biological) or 'exogenous' (from outside, or following on from stressful events)—has meant that depression has become homogenised into one condition, merely varying by severity: 'major depression' or 'minor depression'.

This agglutinated entity has clouded the psychiatric profession's capacity to identify valid treatment matrices for separate depressive conditions, with their differing causes.

Up until the mid-twentieth century, 'depression' meant the severe expressions of biological depression (psychotic or melancholic depression) with no effective treatment and uncertain recovery—sometimes resulting in confinement in an asylum. Such characteristics meant that depression joined with other severe mental illnesses in being stigmatised, discouraging the many people with less severe expressions from attending health practitioners, so diagnosis and detection were limited.

However, with the advent of successful treatment, there has been increased uptake of therapy, both medications and psychotherapies. And with such success comes a move to test any therapy's efficacy beyond its initial boundaries. This extension of therapy (as having universal application—be it a medication or psychotherapy) then became wedded to the new 'muddy' major/minor or severe/moderate/mild definitions of clinical depression, with the boundary between the minor/mild expressions and normal sadness being poorly drawn.

Since the 1980s, 'clinical' depression has been redefined, with the bar for meeting a diagnosis probably being set too low, resulting in many more people with varying levels of depression being diagnosed as clinical cases. Once essentially restricted to the disease of melancholic depression, the new definition encompasses a range of conditions: diseases, disorders, syndromes, even into the sub-syndromal states and extensions of normal mood states, such as grief and sadness.

Alongside this, successful destigmatisation messages have encouraged more individuals to seek recourse to diagnosis and treatment. Additionally, the introduction of SSRI antidepressants which—with very few side effects—lift depression, mute worrying and distress and restore functioning may encourage prescribing to the 'worried well', and those with more transient or 'normal' states of distress. The low cost of antidepressants when compared with psychotherapies is another factor that further skews a leaning to pathologising normal mood states.

Horwitz and Wakefield conceptualise sadness as a natural reaction to a range of negative events in one's life, while clinical depression (principally melancholia) is a mood state that appears without any apparent cause, or is grossly disproportional to any preceding stressor. They argue that psychiatry has confused normal sadness with clinical depression by ignoring the relationship of symptoms to their context: sadness appears in response to triggers (principally losses); the response is proportional in intensity to the loss; and sadness lifts when the loss ends or the individual adapts to it.[2]

So, the boundaries between normal and abnormal mood states have become more diffuse and ambiguous, some individuals are now less ready to experience normal extremes of emotion, and there is encouragement that they should not have to tolerate distress.

A clinician undertaking an assessment of an older person might contemplate whether his or her depression is a normal adjustment process to life's vicissitudes, and thus might benefit from counselling and support, or a distinctive clinical expression that would respond more effectively to pharmacological intervention.

Professor Gordon Parker

5

A structured assessment for depression

Don't let ageing get you down. It's too hard to get back up.

John Wagner

It is important to emphasise that an older person in good physical health has a relatively low risk of depression. So, how many older people do develop depression? Estimates of the prevalence of clinical depression in older age are rubbery, ranging from 3 to 8 per cent. Even the higher percentage is likely to be an underestimate because clinicians, carers and older people themselves don't recognise depression's signs and symptoms.

In aged care facilities, residents are at higher risk of depression, with 10 per cent experiencing major depression and another 20 per cent exhibiting significant depressive symptoms. One study found that almost half of nursing home residents had depressive symptoms.[1] Depression in this setting is often undetected and, even if recognised, untreated. Other psychiatric disorders are also highly prevalent in nursing homes.[2]

THE BLACK DOG INSTITUTE'S APPROACH

In the following paragraphs, we overview the sub-typing model that underpins the Black Dog Institute's clinical approach. The Institute's template does not necessarily correspond to the interview structure and style used by other health professionals.

Depression in older age generally involves many causes, some of which are likely to be physical, so a systematic assessment is central. The logic of a management plan is to work out why this particular individual is depressed at this particular time and for what individual reason/s.

The types of depression

The approach at the Black Dog Institute is to look for evidence of one of three principal types of clinical depression:

- psychotic depression
- melancholic depression
- non-melancholic depression.

Each 'type' of depression has different internal and external causes, thus determining a rationale for differing treatment approaches and for matching the therapy to the disorder.

For more 'biological' mood disorders, the priority will be prescribing and monitoring medication. For a different combination of factors leading to depression—especially to non-melancholic depression—medication may aid improvement, but not be the mainstay of treatment. Yet again, for other non-melancholic states, non-medication options—counselling, problem-solving, psychotherapy and/or anxiety management strategies—will be the appropriate tools.

By the end of the interview/s a clinician will aim to provide:

- a provisional diagnosis
- a differential diagnosis
- a management plan—for discussion with the older person and, if appropriate, with accompanying support persons
- educational information and answers to any questions.

PRIOR CONSIDERATIONS

- Diagnostic guidelines—difficulties arise when identification of depression relies on standard diagnostic systems. These do not adequately capture the different pictures presented by older people with depression.
- Self-report can be an unreliable starting point—older people often under-report or don't recognise feelings of depression.
- A corroborative witness is helpful—the views and observations of a caring relative can be fundamental to

reaching an accurate diagnosis, especially for supplying details otherwise forgotten, and for better 'hearing' and remembering the discussion and advice. Generally, the older person is interviewed individually first, and then the relative or friend is invited to join in the interview.

- Confidentiality and duty of care—though clinical notes are essential, the assessing professional and the older person discuss from the outset what is to be 'on the record' and 'off the record'. It is outlined to the person that information that impacts on the clinician's professional duty to the individual (for example, if the older person has had recurrent thoughts of suicide, and a plan) is unable to be kept private; there is an obligation to inform appropriate family members and supporters.

- Notes of past history—prior to the interview, it can be helpful if the older person and their relative/friend/carer sketches a timeline that lays out the onset of the illness and some details about the main symptoms and signs.

- Prior medications—the older person is requested to bring in all current prescription medications, including complementary medicines, health supplements and vitamins. A list of medications that have been useful or ineffective previously is also of use.

- Referral information—with the permission of the older person, records from previous treating professionals and any investigations and reports are obtained.

THE SEQUENCE OF THE ASSESSMENT

Summary points of the Black Dog Institute's clinical assessment process follow.

The initial clinical judgement is whether the person is depressed. If so, is the disorder severe enough to warrant intervention—is it 'clinical' depression? Is it impacting on the person's capacity to function? The context is also considered: an older person presenting with a host of physical complaints may be very sensitive about being given a psychiatric diagnosis. A practical approach to managing this is suggested in Professor Brian Draper's case notes about Bill in Chapter 4, 'But I am not depressed'.

A common confusion when investigating clinical features is that feelings of depression are an essential marker; this is not always true. As mentioned previously, the individual may instead feel 'numb' and frozen, or highly anxious. In another presentation, an older person may admit to feeling 'down in the dumps' but, as with Bill, this may seem perfectly rational because he or she is experiencing persistent aches, pains and tiredness, loss of appetite, weight loss and insomnia that the doctor can't find a cause for.

Diagnostic options may be less clear or less readily made if an older person has some level of age-related brain changes. These are suggested by chronic unexplained physical symptoms, memory impairment and behavioural changes. (However, as noted, these symptoms can also be manifestations of depression.)

Domains covered in an assessment

- History-taking—this proceeds from open-ended questions at an early stage of the interview to more focused questions after the person has settled. It is usually necessary to allow more time for taking a history from an older person, and to attend to practicalities such as comfortable seating that facilitates communication (at eye level, on the side of the better ear if relevant), checking the person's hearing capacity (ensuring hearing aids are switched on and have functioning batteries) and considering whether cognitive impairment might be obscuring a detailed history. Attendance at the interview of a relative or friend who knows the older person is generally helpful.

- Differential diagnosis—the most common presentations of psychiatric disorder to consider in the elderly are delirium, dementia, depression and anxiety. As a person ages there may be a number of symptoms that overlap with those of other states or conditions (for instance, apathy, delirium and dementia). Additionally, cognitive impairment or mental slowing secondary to depression—known as 'pseudo-dementia'—may be an indication of a primary depressive illness. Classically these cognitive impairments resolve when the depression lifts.

- Medical evaluation—depression can develop in an older person despite the lack of a psychological or social trigger. Any person who becomes depressed for the first time in older age should be suspected of developing a depression secondary to a medical illness until proven otherwise, and so requires a thorough medical evaluation. Additionally, it is noted that depression can be secondary to a physical illness, and/or a side effect of some medications used to treat medical conditions.

- Somatic symptoms—as shown throughout this book, depression in older individuals can manifest as physical symptoms. Though distressing physical symptoms should be investigated at any age, older people with depression are more likely to complain of a host of vague somatic symptoms that have no obvious physical cause.

- Memory impairment—though depression in those who are ageing is often accompanied by memory changes, sometimes the memory impairment is seen as the main problem, and this symptom is misconstrued as dementia (from the person's 'pseudo-dementia' presentation). When depression and memory problems occur simultaneously, diagnosis becomes more difficult. Treatment of the person's depression usually improves his or her memory, though memory may not fully recover. A diagnostic challenge for clinicians is when depression occurs in a person with dementia, so that he or she has, in fact, two conditions.

- Behavioural changes—depression may bring with it quite varied behaviour changes including agoraphobia (where an individual may become housebound with fear), refusal to eat, shoplifting, alcohol abuse, 'accidentally' overdosing and hoarding behaviours that lead to squalor.
- Suicidality—this is a feature of severe depressive states at any age, with a heightened risk of self-harm, particularly in older men. Some clinicians find a direct question appropriate to assess suicide risk: 'Are you having any suicidal thoughts?' Others use a graded approach, asking by degrees: 'Have you thought that life was not worth living?', then moving through some variant of 'Have you had thoughts of death / thoughts of harming yourself / thoughts of suicide / any plans of how you would do this / made any attempts?' If there are answers in the affirmative, then the interviewer will explore any plans or attempts and self-injurious behaviours and then make a judgement about level of risk. (More detail about assessing the risk of self-harm is provided in Appendix I.)
- Past treatments—if there have been previous episodes of depression, past treatments are considered and evaluated for their effectiveness, and any side effects that limited their value.
- The current mood disorder—further into the interview, bipolar disorder and previous depressive and/or manic states are explored—as they are currently, and when they have been at their worst. Depending on how 'psychologically minded' the older person is, it may be easier to obtain such facts from the accompanying relative—and essential if the older person has cognitive impairment.
- Melancholic or non-melancholic?—after assessing the main features of the current episode, the interviewer asks further questions to assess whether the pattern of depressive

episodes seems 'melancholic' (quintessentially 'biological') or 'non-melancholic' (more related to external stressors).

MELANCHOLIC DEPRESSION

Estimates vary about the prevalence of melancholic depression, but the lifetime risk of melancholia is about 2 to 5 per cent. Adding in those individuals with bipolar disorder who suffer melancholic mood swings, this figure increases to around 6 per cent.

Melancholic depression

There are certain features that are more often present in the melancholic sub-type of depression, rather than specific to it, making diagnosis more difficult. The symptoms of melancholic depression may be difficult to separate from the more physical 'somatic' presentation in an older person, but a corroborative witness may have noticed such distinct behaviour changes.

Features include:

- distinctive 'anergia' (lack of energy, not merely fatigue)
- impaired concentration
- slowed ('retarded') and/or agitated movements (psychomotor disturbance)
- in some cases, constipation (though this can be a side effect of medications)
- insufficient food and fluid intake
- anxious and importuning behaviour, with an inability to be reassured
- an 'anhedonic' mood state (the individual gets no pleasure from activities that would normally give pleasure)
- a 'non-reactive' mood (the individual is either not cheered

> up at all by pleasant events, or is only superficially or
> fleetingly cheered up)
> • 'diurnal variation' (mood and the lack of energy are
>   usually worse in the morning and improve later in the
>   day).

Melancholic depression, or melancholia, is a physical or biological state reflecting disrupted circuits in the brain, a sort of chemical imbalance where there is a decrease in neurotransmitter function in neurocircuits responsible for mood and movement. This leads to symptoms (features reported by the individual) and signs (features observed by others) of 'psychomotor disturbance'.

The 'psycho' (of 'psychomotor') refers to the impaired concentration associated with melancholia, where the older person may describe slowed thinking, having a foggy brain, and an inability to concentrate, even for short periods of time.

The 'motor' (of 'psychomotor') refers to the individual's symptoms of 'retardation' and/or of 'agitation'. 'Retardation' is visible: the individual loses the 'light in the eyes', is slowed down physically and mentally, and lacks energy. Many individuals describe the feeling of sinking into a 'black hole' or 'fog'. 'Motor agitation' is another feature present in some, with perhaps a furrowed forehead, slow writhing movements of hands and restless pacing to and fro. The individual may wake early with a churning stomach, preoccupied by worries about trivial issues and unable to be reassured. 'Agitation' tends to alternate with periods of 'retardation'.

Individuals with melancholic depression will often withdraw and lack motivation to mix with family or friends, feeling hopeless and despairing, that there is no future and that they are worthless and a burden. Others feel blank, numb and frozen and unable to experience anything but a 'grey drizzle of horror'.[3]

Psychotic depression

If melancholic depression is diagnosed, the interviewer will probe to see if it is a psychotic sub-type of melancholia. If psychosis is present, usually there has also been very severe psychomotor disturbance. There must be, also, categorical 'psychotic features'—delusions and/or hallucinations. For example, individuals may be delusionally convinced that they are penniless, that their insides are rotting or empty, or that they have done something terrible, or they may hear voices accusing them of being evil or worthless.

If the individual shows indications of a severe melancholic depression with significant guilt (often concerning a relatively trivial event in earlier years), the guilt should be assessed to see whether it is held at a delusional level, as this can be a marker of psychosis.

Bipolar or unipolar course

Another area to assess if the older person is thought to have a melancholic depression is whether the illness course has been 'bipolar' or 'unipolar'. In unipolar depression there are mood swings down into depression, but without any swings up into 'highs'.

A bipolar disorder is indicated by oscillations in mood and energy: during a bipolar 'high' an individual will describe feeling carefree, extremely happy, very confident and energised. He/she may need little sleep, spend money excessively and make impulsive ill-considered judgements. Anxiety disappears and the individual feels euphoric, although there may be some concurrent feelings of agitation, irritability and anger. Bipolar 'lows' are almost always melancholic depression.

Bipolar sub-type: bipolar I, II and III

The sub-types of bipolar disorder include bipolar I, II and III disorders. Those with bipolar I disorder experience extreme mood swings and psychotic features—becoming out of touch with reality in their 'highs'. In bipolar II disorder, psychotic features are not experienced during the 'hypomanic highs', and rarely, if at all, during any melancholic depressive episode.

If a bipolar picture is suggested, it is then important to determine whether 'highs' have occurred spontaneously. If there has been a high only after the person has taken antidepressant medication or after an increase in its dose or following its cessation, then this condition is known as bipolar III disorder. It is a medication-induced state, not a true bipolar condition.

NON-MELANCHOLIC DEPRESSION

Non-melancholic conditions and states are less obviously 'biological' in origin. They are usually the consequence of stressors diminishing the individual's self-esteem—sometimes compounded by the individual's personality 'style' that can increase such vulnerability.

Non-melancholic depression
Non-melancholic depression has no characteristic features. It is diagnosed by the absence of the features of melancholia. Thus, the individual can be cheered up, does not show distinctive psychomotor disturbance, and mood and energy are generally not distinctively worse in the morning.

Melancholic or non-melancholic depression?

The assessment now seeks information that more accurately identifies the sub-type of depression.

- Age of onset of episodes—melancholic depression and bipolar disorder are very rare in childhood and generally emerge in adolescence or early adulthood.

- Developmental history—this gives a 'snapshot' of how the older person has progressed through life until now. It is designed to see if there is any support for a biological melancholic depression and, if not, to determine what factors might have contributed to a non-melancholic depression. Areas covered include family and parenting; early temperament; any birth complications or significant illnesses; evidence of early personality problems; and any issues of abuse (bullying, verbal, physical or sexual abuse) in earlier life. Education, training and work history are also examined, as are current relationships. The interviewer will also look into any relevant medical or allergy conditions and whether there were earlier psychiatric disorders.
- Changes in life circumstances—changes such as retirement, financial status and loss of loved ones are covered.
- A drug and alcohol history is also compiled.
- Stressful events—the interview seeks any stressful events that may have preceded the older person's depression, both to get a general picture and also to help determine if the depression is effectively 'explained' by such stressors. While melancholic depression is less likely to be associated with stressors, stressors may still be associated with its onset. If the individual's depressive episodes happen without any obvious stressor, then this weights judgement to the melancholic sub-type.

PERSONALITY STYLE

The interviewer considers whether there is any impact from the older person's personality style. For instance, is the person an anxious worrier (or does he or she 'externalise' any anxiety via irritability); overly sensitive to interpersonal interactions; socially introverted; reserved in interpersonal relationships; impulsive, with a hair-trigger emotional response to provocation; and/or perfectionistic?

Certain personality styles may predispose individuals to develop mood disorders (particularly non-melancholic depression) following stressful events that have special significance for them because of previous exposure to similar stressors (such as abuse, criticism). This is known as the 'lock and key' pattern, where there is an exaggerated response to a particular stressor because of previous sensitisation that has shaped a unique vulnerability. As an example, an individual may become suicidally depressed when someone criticises him or her unfairly—the 'key' operating on a 'lock' established by having a very judgemental and critical father in the early years.

The more definite personality styles and obvious personality disorders tend to mute with age, as outlined further in Chapter 6.

ARE SYMPTOMS OF DEPRESSION DIFFERENT IN LATER LIFE?

Based on research undertaken since 1985 by the Mood Disorders Unit (the predecessor of the Black Dog Institute), older people were more likely to have melancholic or psychotic depression than were younger people referred for depression. For example, an older person with a psychotic melancholic depression could present with 'retarded' movement and thinking, mimic the picture of dementia or apathy, or have delusions of poverty, illness or persecution.

Older people were also more likely to feel disproportionate guilt, to show agitation (restless, anxious movements) or psychomotor retardation (the slowing of movements and thinking) and/or to be psychotic. These differences were more pronounced in women. A common presentation where the depression is masked by somatic symptoms (the 'depressive equivalent') has been discussed in Chapter 4.

The generation of older people now in their 70s and older tends to under-report their depressive symptoms: an important finding was the discrepancy between self-reported symptoms and objective clinician-rated symptoms. This difference between patients' ratings of their own depression severity and the clinicians' ratings increased linearly with age—that is, the very old were more likely to markedly underestimate the severity of their depression. This underlined that older people tend to be more stoically accepting, and this—and other factors, such as shame and incomprehension about the disorder—may help explain why epidemiological studies underestimate the prevalence of depression in those who are older.[4]

ARE RATES OF DEPRESSION HIGHER IN LATER LIFE?

While symptoms of depression occur in 25 to 50 per cent of older people, rates of clinical depressive syndromes are found to be no higher—and in formal epidemiological studies are lower—than those in the younger adult population.

Older people more prone to depression include those with neurological disorders, including the dementias; those in nursing homes or other residential care settings; those with physical illness or pain; and those who are isolated. When clinical syndromes of depression occur in older people, they are more likely to be severe.[5]

THE MOOD ASSESSMENT PROGRAM (THE MAP)

The Black Dog Institute has developed a Mood Assessment Program (the MAP), where the patient can enter into a computer (or via the website) data about a range of factors that may be relevant to his or her depression (for example, anxiety, mood swings and stressful events). These are weighed up in algorithms which compute the individual's likely mood disorder diagnosis. A MAP report providing this information and treatment guidelines is then sent to the referring doctor.

NOTEWORTHY

The range of depression: a summary

'Depression' has become a diffuse term. At its core is a cluster of feelings and behaviours that can manifest as: a 'normal' mood state, a disorder, or a physical illness.

'Normal' depression versus 'clinical' depression
Most people experience depression from time to time. A setback can make an individual feel sad, helpless or despairing, often with a lowering of self-esteem. But there is a context and the 'down' mood is in proportion to the distressing event. This type of depression soon lifts and the person returns to their baseline mood setting.

With 'clinical' depression, however, the symptoms persist and the condition impairs functioning. The individual can't seem to bounce back to his or her usual temperament setting, having seemingly lost all usual ways of coping. Symptoms persist without let-up for more than two weeks.

Symptoms of clinical depression
These include:

- a severely depressed mood
- lowered self-esteem
- feelings of worthlessness
- thoughts that life is not worth living
- irritability and anger
- some people feel 'frozen', blank or incapable of experiencing emotion.

Other symptoms include:

- multiple, diffuse somatic (physical) symptoms, with no obvious biological cause

- memory and concentration problems
- loss of interest in day-to-day activities
- inability to look forward to or enjoy activities
- disturbed sleep
- withdrawal from friends and family
- behavioural changes, such as agoraphobia
- anxiety
- weight change—either increased from eating comfort foods, or decreased, as appetite is lost
- feeling hopeless and helpless—or numb and distant.

Some causes of clinical (and less severe) depression

Several factors may lower the threshold for developing depression. Some of these factors are also relevant to the development of bipolar disorder—particularly genetic loading, disrupted sleep, and environmental pressures that disrupt 'circadian' rhythms.

- Mood disorders have a genetic loading. A study of family background may identify relatives with depression or bipolar disorder.
- Traits such as high anxiety and certain personality 'styles' can increase risk.
- Medical problems and illness may impair mobility and independence, and/or have a biological impact which could 'cause' depression.
- Disturbing events during childhood and/or lack of parental affection and care (or overprotection) create susceptibility to subsequent stressors.
- Events during the developmental years, such as sexual abuse, disability, birth trauma and injury, can lead to vulnerability to depression.

- Grief (e.g. due to death, injury or illness of someone close, or unresolved family feuds and toxic relationships) can become chronic and unresolved and so precipitate depression.
- Lack of social stimulation, loneliness, isolation, poverty and disadvantage can predispose to depression.
- The stress of differences in cultural background and subsequent isolation can impact on mood, particularly when such individuals have diminishing demands to establish themselves and their families.
- Medications and alcohol may have depressive side effects.
- Guilt issues and undisclosed family secrets may re-emerge or fester and preoccupy a person as they age.
- Physical problems, such as lack of sleep, and varying circadian rhythms, such as at the change of seasons, may impact on the 'biological clock' to cause disruption of emotions.
- Significant financial pressures and threats to security and independence can become a chronic stressor.

Is the mood disorder 'primary' or 'secondary'?
A primary mood disorder means that it is the main or only condition. For instance, if depression is the main disorder, healing it means that other, 'secondary' problems (e.g. sleep disruption) will be alleviated by its correction; it can also be 'primary' in the sense that, of all the other problems faced by the individual, it is having the greatest damaging impact; or it was the first destabilising factor, which then led to a series of secondary problems.

A secondary mood disorder indicates that the mood disorder—for instance, depression—follows as the consequence of a primary psychiatric disorder, such as an anxiety disorder, a primary medical condition (e.g. epilepsy, head injury), or of another primary factor (e.g. alcohol or drug abuse).

Bipolar disorder

People with bipolar disorder (previously known as 'manic depressive disorder') experience mood swings—usually both 'highs' (mania, or hypomania) and 'lows', although some individuals only experience 'highs'. The 'lows' are almost always 'melancholic' depression. Bipolar disorder is thought to be primarily caused by biological factors. It is a disorder that is strongly inherited.

Symptoms of bipolar 'highs' include:

- elation, although sometimes with underlying agitation
- grandly increased self-esteem
- talking more and talking faster than usual
- a 'racing' mind
- abundance of energy and decreased need for sleep
- impaired judgement
- overspending and indiscreet behaviours, including hypersexuality
- marked irritability and aggression (in some individuals).

In older people, manic episodes may be less florid and manifest as irritability or as mixed manic and depressive episodes.

6

Melancholic and non-melancholic depression

Old age comes at a bad time.

Sam Banducci

It is important to reiterate that depression is not the invariable companion of ageing. Of those aged 65 and older, more than 90 per cent can anticipate an older age that is, in the main, fruitful and satisfying. Creating a space to dwell in as we age, however, may take some conscious refocusing and self-management. Some individuals carry an idealised notion that it will just happen, and they are ambushed by the inevitable changes inherent in growing older. To paraphrase psychotherapist Peter O'Connor, our sense of who we are may have deteriorated and be in need of renovation preparatory for this new age. While it may be foreign to the way we have operated previously, assessing and accepting the need for renewal and then beginning the task can make the difference between being 'centred' or 'off-balance' as we age.[1] Some, however, will still be prone to develop or experience a recurrence of an affective or mood disorder. Several illustrations follow of individuals experiencing different kinds of depression, and their treatment and outcomes.

TWO ACCOUNTS OF MELANCHOLIC DEPRESSION

The two accounts following illustrate some characteristic signs and symptoms of melancholic depression—particularly evident in older age. Biological changes impact on brain chemistry, shaping melancholic depression's very 'physical' symptoms. Melancholic depression can start without any external stressors.

Recovery can be assisted by psychotherapy and counselling after the mood state has been lifted by antidepressants or other physical treatment, so that the individual is then well enough to 'hear' and benefit from counselling.

The first story is of 'Brigid's' untreated depression, as told by her daughter 'Bernadette'. This narrative is followed by Professor Osvaldo Almeida's account of Mrs A's 'agitated' melancholic depression and the very positive outcome of its treatment.

My mother's little life

My mother suffered and perhaps died because of endogenous depression [melancholic depression] and I spent most of my younger years looking after her, or better expressed, 'watching' over her.

Her depression started earlier than most, in her 40s. She would sit at the window staring into the distance for hours on end and crying for no apparent reason. My father said she was only homesick for her family far away and would dismiss that it was any kind of illness. My mother's only role was that of housewife and she had no other interests. She never left the house on her own and never mixed with the outside world. She was shy and very deaf and self-conscious about her hearing handicap. She never expressed an opinion or gave an argument. It was as though she didn't care what went on around her.

During the morning hours while she was busy with the housework and taking care of three children, the sadness would leave her eyes and she would methodically arrange the house. But in the afternoons and the evenings she'd sit in the corner and get a helpless sad look, and only after much cajoling—and then only sometimes—would we be able to get her out of her sad mood.

Even as a child I realised that something was terribly wrong with her. I would come home from school and find her sitting by the front window staring out into the street at the hills. She was always crying. Even though she'd stop when she saw me, her eyes were always red and swollen. If I asked if she was alright she'd shrug her shoulders and walk away and find something to do to keep her hands, always shaking, busy. I'd try hard to rush home from school so I'd be there to talk to her, and even though she wasn't much for conversation with me she'd listen, and while she was listening her eyes were focused on me.

Physically, Mum was healthy. The doctor would check her pulse whenever he came for a home visit. He'd look into her eyes, listen to her heart and never found anything wrong. He was a kindly man and I recall how he'd say, 'Why don't you smile, Brigid?', at which she'd look at the floor. He'd talk to my father and I remember him saying that 'Poor Brigid suffers from melancholia and she should get out of the house more', but nothing else was done about it. There was no medication prescribed for her, and knowing how she avoided medicine of any kind, she would probably not have taken it.

When my father returned from work, punctually at 5.30, all our attention would turn to him. Silently Mum would set the table, we'd eat while my father engaged us in conversation, and afterwards my mother would put the boys to bed and my father would retire to his sitting room where he'd work till midnight and listen to records. I'd have to go to bed, therefore my mother would find herself alone again and she'd sit in a corner staring out into the darkness until she'd fall asleep. She never showed any interest to go and sit with my father. Our life was a strict routine and I believe my mother went through the motions of living and was afraid to venture outside her thoughts.

By the time we were teenagers we had accepted that our mother was just 'sad' and we tried to please her and make her as happy as we could. We took her every Saturday without fail to the movies and watched her staring at the screen, lost in the lives of the characters she saw, and for an hour or so afterwards she was excited at what she had seen and chatted with us about the movie. But by the time we'd returned home the magic of the cinema had gone and she'd come back to her reality.

As we got older my brothers and I took it in turns not to leave her alone, to keep her busy, and thus the years passed slowly. There were times when she'd be almost normal, but she would never leave the safety of the house and garden. In all the years I lived with her, she never went for even a simple walk on her own. She had made a prison for herself and couldn't break out of it. Bernadette

There are indications in Bernadette's story of the cost that she and others in her family paid because of her mother's untreated depression. Bernadette exemplifies the 'parentified' child, where roles are reversed and circumstances require the child to mature early and take care of the parent.

In some cases, depressive illness can distort the personality of the sufferer so that their diagnosis—and thus their treatment—is incorrect. For example, depression may be mistaken for dementia, or apathy associated with cognitive decline may be misdiagnosed as depression. The following case study, contributed by Professor Osvaldo Almeida, outlines how, on recovery, Mrs A returned to her competent pre-illness self with no trace of the uncharacteristic behaviours that had been a feature of her disorder but not an enduring part of her 'self'.

CASE NOTES

A case of mistaken personality
Mrs A, 65 years of age, lived with her husband in an affluent suburb of a large city. They had migrated from a small village in southern

Italy in the late 1950s. They were in close contact with their three daughters and eight grandchildren, and had a prominent role in the local Italian community. Mr A had been a successful businessman and property developer, and Mrs A a dedicated wife and mother.

Mrs A's problems began at the age of 63, a few months after her youngest daughter married and left home. She became agitated and insecure, constantly seeking reassurance from her husband that there was 'nothing wrong' with her. She progressively withdrew from her daily routines, including cooking and basic house maintenance, and spent increasing hours in bed in a darkened room. Her daughters organised a roster to look after her and the house but her behaviour did not improve—to the contrary, she became more agitated and disruptive, constantly seeking reassurance from others that she was not 'going mad'. She lost twenty kilograms over a period of twelve months, and although she would accept her meals after persistent encouragement from her daughters, she showed no interest in food.

Her GP suggested that she was grieving the fact that her daughters had left home and prescribed a benzodiazepine to decrease her agitation. After several months of trying different anxiolytics [anti-anxiety medications], her doctor introduced an SSRI [antidepressant medication]—but she became even more agitated, constantly wringing her hands and shadowing her daughters and husband when they were at home. Her sleep deteriorated further and her restlessness during the night led her husband to move rooms.

At that time a psychiatrist reviewed her and suggested that she had 'agitated depression' and a 'dependent personality disorder'. Combined treatment with two antidepressants was introduced but after four months there was no obvious improvement in her clinical presentation—in fact, the shadowing and relentless demand for reassurance from her daughters and husband increased. The psychiatrist suggested that the family was reinforcing her dysfunctional personality traits and that these were, in turn, perpetuating her symptoms. At this point, she was referred for treatment as an inpatient at a public psychiatric hospital.

During her stay in the ward Mrs A spent most of her days hovering around the nursing station, repeatedly reporting to staff that she was unwell, asking them to confirm that there was nothing wrong with her and telling them that she trusted them to make her feel better. She slept fitfully, waking up several times a night and visiting the nursing station to repeat her complaints and requests for reassurance.

Despite constant reassurance from staff, she remained agitated, perplexed and insecure about what was happening. It took only a few days for staff to form the view that she did indeed have a dependent personality disorder that was contributing to perpetuate her symptoms of mixed depression and anxiety. This view was despite advice from her family that she had always been an outgoing, active and confident mother and spouse.

Attempts to optimise her pharmacological and psychological treatment were not associated with any obvious benefits during the first three months of her stay in hospital, and she consistently declined offers to go home for the weekend because she felt she would not be able to cope. Indeed, two attempts to have her spend some days at home with the family failed because of increasing agitation and anxiety.

At this point it was decided to discontinue all her medications, and after a washout period of two weeks, a new treatment regimen was introduced. We noticed a gradual change in her behaviour during the subsequent eight weeks: she woke up less frequently during the night and became less reliant on others' reassurance during the day. Her appetite improved and she even asked staff if she could spend some time at home.

On return from one successful weekend leave, she reported that she could not explain what had happened to her and that the past year 'felt unreal, like a bad dream'. Over the subsequent weeks, she became actively engaged in all ward activities and provided valuable assistance and support to other patients. In fact, after a while she was even telling staff what to do to improve the care of patients!

After six months as an inpatient, she was discharged back home to a delighted and welcoming family. She has remained well for the past four years.

Lessons learnt

The first lesson Mrs A taught me is that one should be very careful not to make assumptions about people's underlying personality traits when they are severely depressed or anxious—what we see may be the product of their underlying disorder, rather than a reflection of their character. (It is very tempting to blame patients' personalities when things do not work the way we expect.)

A related point is that the family usually knows the patient better than we do.

Finally, if one's treatment plan does not work, review the diagnosis and management plan and try again!

Professor Osvaldo Almeida

In summary, with melancholic depression the treatment priority is to address the biological balance and rectify the disruption to the brain chemistry. Melancholic depression is minimally responsive to placebo and to talking therapies (psychotherapy and counselling), but highly responsive to physical treatments, including antidepressant medications.

Below, Professor Peter Rabins discusses the use of the term 'depression' and how it fails to capture the actual quality of the experience. He says that it is a common complaint of patients that existing descriptions don't capture the emotional pain that is uniquely associated with melancholia. His thoughts follow.

CASE NOTES

Does it matter what term we use to label melancholia?

William Styron, in his autobiographical essay Darkness Visible, said it well. 'When I was first aware that I had been laid low by the disease, I felt a need, among other things, to register a strong protest against the word "depression".'[2] Styron attributed the label 'depression' to Adolph Meyer, although Emil Kraepelin, the German psychiatrist who introduced the currently used structure of psychiatry in the late nineteenth century, had used the term 'Manic-Depressive Insanity' long before and believed that the Greek term 'Melancholia' might be preferable. Whether one agrees with Styron or not, any clinician will tell you that his complaint is a common one.

In the past, statements such as this have been attributed to denial, to an inability to describe feelings ('alexithymia'), to the desire to avoid the stigma of mental illness or to cultural factors. Each of these may be true in some cases but I believe the majority of patients I have diagnosed with major depression who have vehemently claimed that the word does not describe how they feel are likely referring to the fact that what they are experiencing is not like the sadness they have experienced at other times in their life but rather a condition that is superimposed upon them; it has changed how they experience their place in the world, turned their usual degree of self-confidence in a negative direction, and changed many vital daily experiences and actions such as appetite, sleep, sex drive and energy/initiative.

Thus the word 'depression' often does not accurately describe what people are experiencing. This leads me to conclude that we need to start all over in defining what we mean by the phrases 'major depression', 'clinical depression', 'endogenous depression', 'depressive illness' and the like.

I believe we need to identify several thousand people from around the world who expert clinicians agree have 'the condition once known as melancholia' and to have them describe their state in detail. From them we can find what is similar across most people with melancholia (I recognise I am making an assumption that this is correct), whether there are variations by culture, age, sex, ethnic background, et cetera (the existing research is very unconvincing in my opinion), and whether there is even a single word that can capture the range of experiences people report.

We now recognise that the words people use to describe pain vary greatly and that it is a subjective experience that defies a universal standard. Whether this will be true of melancholia remains to be seen. However, I think it is time to listen to our patients and recognise that the words we use now and the symptom criteria we use to diagnose and study people with this condition or group of disorders are inadequate.

Professor Peter V. Rabins

SORTING THROUGH THE MAZE OF NON-MELANCHOLIC DEPRESSION

Uppermost in the clinician's mind when sorting through a mood disorder with an older person is:

- What is the principal diagnosis? That is, why is this individual depressed at this point in time? Have I missed an underlying medical condition causing the depression?
- What is the most appropriate treatment—physical treatment, counselling or a combination? With older people, a simple pristine diagnosis and targeted treatment is not always easy, and therapy needs to be pluralistic and tailored to the factors underpinning the patient's depression.
- How best can this treatment be 'delivered', respecting the needs (for example, poorer hearing and eyesight) of the older person,

and the fact that he/she may need more sessions, examples and exercises that are relevant to their age and experiences, and explanations that allow for the fact that he/she might not be 'psychologically minded' and thus need some psychological concepts more carefully illustrated.

- What is the background? Events or interpersonal interactions may cause distress. Such stressors may be chronic, acute or a mix of both. A person who is exposed to a continuing stressor—one the individual cannot control, and from which there is no psychological escape—may develop psychological and physical problems.

- Issues that act as precipitating and perpetuating factors that attenuate the disorder or impede treatment may be proximal (recent) or distal (past) stresses. There may also be other causes—for instance, medication effects or alcohol abuse— impacting on the individual's vulnerability.

As considered previously, non-melancholic depression, also known as 'exogenous', 'neurotic' or 'reactive' depression, is more likely to be brought on by a stressful life event impacting on an individual with or without certain predisposing susceptibilities—such as an at-risk personality style and/or childhood adversity. It is therefore often well addressed using psychotherapeutic strategies.

SOME INFLUENCES ON NON-MELANCHOLIC DEPRESSION

Acute stress may encompass an immediate financial problem, recent retirement, death of a valued friend (or pet) and/or onset of injury or disease. Recovery comes about when the stress (the trigger) is removed or stopped, or the individual learns to adapt to and process the stress more effectively (known as 'neutralising' or 'negating' the stressor). Improvement can happen without the need for professional assistance but counselling or problem-solving strategies are useful if the older person is willing to consider such intervention. Mostly, antidepressant medication isn't necessary.

Chronic stress can include the strain of poverty, an ongoing unhappy marriage, illness in the individual or a significant other and/or troubling continuous health problems. Chronic stress may leave a lasting imprint and a sense of 'learned helplessness'—where the individual feels that he or she can neither escape nor improve the situation. Depression may result from a chronic stressor if the older person is living in a situation, for instance, where he/she is constantly belittled, criticised or isolated. Management of a chronic stress-induced non-melancholic depression mainly involves suggesting and supporting changes to the individual's social and community life and maintaining this new positive view through the difficult period. Even though the cause of such depressions is social, the SSRI class of antidepressant medication can provide some relief, as they reduce the constant worrying many such depressed people experience as a consequence of these stressful and inescapable situations.

Personality style—the individual's characteristic way of reacting to events—can exacerbate risk to the onset, maintenance and resolution of non-melancholic depression. Personality style is usually a combination of personality dimensions. Black Dog Institute research has investigated eight such 'styles', namely: anxious worrying, irritability, self-criticism, sensitivity to rejection, self-focused, perfectionistic, socially avoidant, and a style of personal reserve.

As previously touched upon, the more marked personality styles and frank personality disorders tend to mellow with age: there is a general decline in 'borderline' personality symptoms, as well as other immature and destructive personality styles (such as antisocial, narcissistic, histrionic and sadistic).[3] It is thought that adaptive coping strategies occur in the face of the significant environmental stressors as people age. Older people still do, however, display some of these personality dimensions—in particular, anxious worrying, low self-esteem, and self-critical and perfectionistic styles. Studies also indicate that older people are significantly more obsessive-compulsive and schizoid than younger adults.[4] Such personality styles are relevant to the health care professional, as they will influence ways of framing diagnosis, treatment and long-term management of a depressive disorder.

SOME ACCOUNTS OF NON-MELANCHOLIC DEPRESSION

Next there are some narratives that illustrate facets of non-melancholic depression, and the impact of some of the stressors that cause and prolong it and which, if undiagnosed, can make non-melancholic depression unresponsive because of inappropriate treatments.

The five accounts that follow illustrate some of the factors discussed above: acute and chronic stressors, the impact of personality factors, particular vulnerabilities (the 'lock and key' effect), and 'decompensation' in later life, where exposure to earlier trauma and the effects of ageing lower the threshold for developing non-melancholic depression.

This next report illustrates the contribution of an acute stressor to the development and exacerbation of an episode of non-melancholic depression.

From break-in to breakdown

 Upon meeting my true love, I finally caught up with my life and got it together.

Money flowed to us 'new lovers' and we were able to buy ourselves an old corrugated-iron cottage. We had carefully planned our new life together, but just before our daughter was born—my partner nine months pregnant—we suffered a home invasion in the dead of night. I naturally went into attack mode to protect my partner and tore straight into the burglar.

Unfortunately, I was the one who lost consciousness and shattered some bone in my shoulder joint, which completely put a stop to my job as an architectural draftsman. After minor hospital surgery to free up my shoulder, it was noted in the x-rays that I had also sustained injury to my spinal column. This meant that I could no longer work bent over a drawing board—which brought the Bank onto us, pursuing their mortgage repayments. Our happy home life together took a complete 'arse about face'.

It was three years later that I realised that I may have become depressed and I reluctantly agreed with my partner that another journey to the doctor was in order; I told myself, 'I must tell the doctor the truth.' I had no idea where to turn for help and was worrying myself sick for days on end. I had hit rock bottom. Going against all my fears that the doctor might think I was loony and put me away, I explained my home life situation to her, while trying to appear cool and collected. In fact I was fighting to conceal my emotions, which were beginning to seep through. I announced, 'I don't know where to turn for financial assistance' and that 'I can't join a church group because I'm not religious'—and then quickly I let it out, 'How can I rid my mind of suicidal thoughts?'

The doctor listened attentively to my story and then quietly told me that I was suffering from 'clinical depression' and prescribed antidepressants. She also took the time to explain to me how they worked and that there might be side effects.

I had already moved out of the house and into the converted outdoor laundry so that I could weep alone and not disturb my children or my partner. My partner never complained about our unfortunate situation and gave me the space I needed as I tried to work out what it was that was keeping me downcast.

She took on the running of the home single-handed, two kids in tow, making money from entering recipe competitions (she won many) and house cleaning for others.

Depression was like death to me. Some days I wouldn't come out of my sleep-out at all, and seldom would I allow myself to go out and enjoy family occasions or our old friends' parties of a Friday or Saturday night like we used to do. Finally I came to the conscious decision that I had to help myself; the pills were not enough and for all I knew they could be the cause. Any rate, I was becoming worse by the week and I thought, 'Why wait for death to put things straight?'

I made the effort to take the bull by the horns and went along to a local men's group and also sought out a meditation group. Meditation was something which had dramatically helped me at the time my first marriage broke up, years earlier. The practice of meditation gave me a quiet platform to look within and try and see what it was that this illness was trying to tell me. Having these two outlets was in fact my saving and I eased off the medication I had been prescribed, which was giving me bad side effects.

I finally asked my doctor for a referral to the hospital psychiatrist to gain some understanding of what these chemicals were doing to me. He listened with meticulous interest as I shared my health predicament and then gave me a small questionnaire to fill out. The outcome of this white-paper test was that I was in fact suffering clinical depression, and he added another chemical to my prescription in an effort to help with what he saw as the influence of moods and sent me off saying, 'Look into your relationship with your wife!'

This journey to the psychiatrist allowed me to see my life from a different perspective. I saw that I was beginning to 'role' my partner into my own illness. This disturbed me, so I returned to my GP and shared what I had found. She then referred me to a clinical psychologist, as I felt confident that

I was onto something I could tangibly work with. I took to sharing with my partner exactly what was going on inside my mind the moment these oddities would arise, and found this had the effect of discharging the all-engaging emotional energies of my past. It began a process in me of being able to cry with my partner and speak with true emotion.

Referral to the psychologist was the major breakthrough I needed with my illness. His many techniques helped alter my state of mind whenever I became lost in myself and had the effect of dissolving fear, no matter how deeply I was entangled in depression. His practical suggestions were highly useful as I could bring them into play at any time I was at home feeling stuck with depression's symptoms. Having a practical and understanding psychologist is a must.

Thus, I began to administer to myself 'the turning of the wheel', and I was soon reconsidering getting off the anti-depressants. The side effects, for me, were too substantial and I felt that they were less and less help. I'm off them now, I'm over the effects of the invasion of our home, and I'm well over my breakdown—but though I feel blessed with my family and stable in myself, I'm still very watchful of my moods. Stanley

Chronic stressors are in evidence throughout the next narrative. A lifetime of looking after others, an onerous series of long-term demands that were unappreciated . . . and then 'Violet's' own deteriorating health and constant pain tipped the scale.

This poisonous fog

 'I wish I was dead.' The thought struck like an arrow through my brain. Where did it come from?

Unlike other illnesses that you can recognise, depression starts slowly, insidiously and then, like a putrid grey fog, it

envelops you. My life was far from perfect, but I believed I was managing quite well: I'd been coping for over twenty years—ever since I came home from hospital after drastic spinal surgery.

I'm an 'in-between' person. When my mother and aunt became old I became their carer, with all its ongoing obligations. They were in a wonderful elderly citizens' facility, but it was my responsibility to look after all their medical and financial problems, take them shopping and bring them home for Sunday outings. When my spine began deteriorating I didn't say anything because I wanted to spare them from worry. And during this time our daughter-in-law became pregnant again, having miscarried her first pregnancy, and was confined to bed most of the time. I felt obliged to help our son however I could. So I was under a lot of pressure, being pulled in different directions by my family. I was working in a responsible full-time position so I put my own physical problems aside.

Eventually it became difficult to walk or keep my balance. My legs felt like they were being squeezed by rubber bands and my back hurt. I ignored it as much as possible and relieved the pain with analgesics. I believed it was psychosomatic—caused by worry. My family also thought this because initially the problem was intermittent and I'd be okay for a week or so.

After my mother and aunt died, I told my GP about the crazy feelings in my legs. She was amazed I hadn't mentioned it earlier and referred me to a neurologist. The diagnosis was terrifying. Severe pressure on my spine was threatening paralysis and I needed urgent surgery or I would end up in a wheelchair. This was too terrible to contemplate. I consulted other specialists and they confirmed the diagnosis. Then I was in and out of hospital for six weeks, during which I had two complicated spinal operations—each lasting several hours, followed by weeks in a rehabilitation facility to learn to walk again. When I returned home, I wore a back brace for several months.

On arrival at home I was confused, miserable and depressed. A deep chasm yawned before me. I knew I had to avoid it and try to resume life as best I could or fall into even deeper misery. A chilling dread lurked deep within me at the realisation of how my life had irreversibly changed. Keeping as much independence as possible was important so I pretended to be okay. I went to physio, acupuncture, hypnosis, reiki, naturopathy and chiropractic. I clutched at any straw which I thought might improve my condition. I also tried to resume my previous activities of swimming, gardening and my book club and my usual household tasks. Nobody knew how scared I was or what I felt. It didn't help to hear whisperings among those around me that there had never really been anything wrong and the surgery probably made me worse—despite all the medical opinions I had received.

It's not long, now, before I turn 78. Naturally, deterioration has taken place in both body and mind. Our home is a quieter place. The phone doesn't ring as often and many of our good friends are no longer with us. The children are grown with their own families. Advertisements for the latest household goods hold no interest. I know my furniture will outlive me and end up in the nearest op shop on my passing. I wonder now whether even to buy new clothes—I'll probably never wear out the stuff I have. In short, misery swamps me. It's hard to concentrate. Sometimes I feel I should be doing something more impor-tant but don't know what. I hate myself because I'm unable to keep pace with family and friends. They rush ahead while I trail behind like a sad old dog, pushing my walking frame.

I've been told I manage well, that I'm always cheerful and I don't complain. That's partly true. What's the alternative? If I expressed some of my deepest feelings to those around me they'd feel uncomfortable; tell me things aren't so bad and probably avoid me completely. But an icy hand grips my heart at thoughts of the future. Physically I'm deteriorating and wonder where I'll end up. I'm unsure about my situation and unable to come to terms with it.

This feeling of depression which sometimes swamps me completely is kept hidden. But like a poisonous fog it threatens to engulf and destroy me. I know I must keep on fighting, but for how much longer? Violet

As discussed earlier, certain personality styles can be a risk factor to developing and maintaining depressive disorder, even in older age. In this next report, recounted by Professor Sid Williams, neither Mrs R nor her family could understand why she had become depressed in the face of well-intentioned kindness.

It is the power and solace inherent in skilful therapy that can uncover the significance of events as experienced and processed by individuals—often by comprehending symbols and metaphors and revealing their meaning to the distressed person.

CASE NOTES

Mrs R and the brass plate

Mrs R's first words to me were: 'I'm sorry, doctor, to be bothering you with such a silly thing. I shouldn't be upset.' Her daughter, Maeve, had arranged for Mrs R to see me because of the apparent depression which had suddenly overwhelmed her five months before, following the renovations to the home they shared.

Concentrating as I was on looking for features of depression or other recognisable condition, I missed at first the significance of the home renovations. Mrs R certainly was experiencing symptoms of depression, including sleep disturbance, lack of energy and lack of interest in events which usually would have given her pleasure. Sitting with me in my office she looked very unhappy and a little restless. She continued to apologise for taking up my time.

Her GP had provided a very brief letter suggesting that the referral was at the insistence of Mrs R's daughter. I had the impression that he wasn't too happy about the referral because he didn't consider there was a 'psychiatric problem'. He had carried out general tests to check that nothing else—thyroid under- or over-activity, anaemia, infections, neoplasm, et cetera—was causing her difficulties. Largely because of her age and hints of memory problems he had ordered a cerebral CT scan, which was reported as showing some 'involutional change and minor white matter attenuation consistent with age'. He had started Mrs R on an SSRI antidepressant two months before, but there had been no positive effect. Indeed, perhaps she had been more agitated on the antidepressant. Mrs R certainly had the impression that the antidepressant was causing her problems and she was hopeful that I might advise her to stop it. She didn't like the idea of taking tablets and was worried that she might come to 'depend on them'. She was an active 82-year-old and taking tablets for high blood pressure and arthritis. Both she and her daughter had noticed that she didn't walk as freely as she used to or find it as easy to get out of a chair.

Mrs R was a comfortable perfectionist. That is, she liked to do things well and she liked to keep her house clean and tidy but 'lived in'—she had never been troubled if the children, and later the grandchildren, made a bit of a mess. Her husband had died many years before after a prolonged illness. They had two children—a son and a daughter. Their daughter had never married, had stayed with her parents throughout their lives and had been a 'pillar of strength' to both of them, throughout her father's long illness and in the years following. She had a creative flair and now ran her own successful business.

Mr R had owned and run a local business which had been established by his father. He had also been very active in the local community, coached junior rugby league and served on the local council. Many years before, he had successfully campaigned and helped raise money for the council to build a municipal swimming pool which was, as a result, named after him. Sadly, with waning use of the facility and the fact that it was built close to an expanding shopping centre, the pool was closed and the site sold for further development. Mr R was given the brass plate from the site which recorded, among other things, his name and the opening date of the pool. He had framed the plate in timber and it held pride of place in the family home. By the time he made the frame, however, he was experiencing deterioration in both eyesight and cognitive ability, so the frame was a little crude, out of square and clumsily painted.

Two years before this visit to me, Mrs R's daughter, after careful and respectful discussion with her mother and her brother, came to an arrangement that Mrs R would gift the family home to her son and daughter, with her daughter then buying out her brother's half-share. This arrangement was to everyone's satisfaction. Her daughter, in lieu of rent and to assist her mother, had been in any case and for many years paying rates and costs associated with the property.

Once the property had been transferred, and again following discussion with her mother, her daughter had arranged for extensive repainting of the house and renovation of the kitchen. During the several months that this was occurring, Mrs R visited her sister in Queensland; her daughter accompanied her on the forward and return plane journeys. Everyone was looking forward to Mrs R's response to the repainted home and renovated kitchen.

Mr O, the painting contractor, was present on the day Mrs R returned. He was an old family friend who had taken great pride in returning the house to its pristine state. He had removed all the pictures and photographs, storing them carefully. He had filled and 'made good' all the fixing points for the pictures, with the plan for them to have new hanging points provided as required. He was also proud of the fact that he had reframed the swimming pool brass plate with a Pacific maple frame. He had not charged for this, seeing it as a gift out of respect for his old friend, Mr R.

When Mrs R came home, instead of being pleased about the painting renovation and plate framing, she was immediately shocked and distressed, crying uncontrollably and, as she was later able to tell me, actually angry. She was as surprised and frightened by her response as were her family and Mr O. At the time she could not explain or understand her feelings.

By the time Mrs R came to see me, the significance of the renovations and the loss of her husband's frame for the brass plate was apparent to her and her daughter. Her daughter was mortified, puzzled and defensive about her actions. She had no need to be. Neither she nor her mother had expected this response.

Partly in deference to Mrs R's wishes I stopped the antidepressant and didn't immediately replace it with another, even though there was a strong indication for doing so. Mrs R was convinced the antidepressant was the main cause of her problems. I wanted to return control of the medication to her. As is my custom at that first visit, I saw her alone and spoke to her daughter separately. I explained my understanding of what had happened: that, although she and her daughter had been caught off-guard by her response, the response was not surprising. I then saw Mrs R every two weeks for three months, speaking to her daughter in Mrs R's presence about every three visits, or if a particular issue came up which required a joint consultation.

Mrs R reminisced a lot about her husband, their early life together, their families and the children. We talked about the family's history in the home and the memories associated with it. Mr and Mrs R began living there three years into their marriage. They lived initially in a garage before they had sufficient resources to build their home. Mr R, assisted by friends, family and Mrs R, actually built much of the house, only calling in paid tradesmen (e.g. electricians) when the work was beyond his ability. They were assisted financially in the early stages by Mr R's parents.

Maeve and her brother returned all the pictures and photographs as close to their original places as Mrs R could remember—she supervised this process. The reframed brass plate resumed its prominent position, but Mrs R described a 'tug on her heart' each time she looked at it and thought of her husband's poorly constructed frame.

After six weeks and following discussion with Mrs R, we started another antidepressant—this time a more sedative one given at night, which I thought might help with sleep as well as the depression.

Mrs R more or less recovered and I saw her at intervals for two more years, during which time she continued to take the antidepressant. A year after she presented I tried a reduced dose but she experienced a recurrence of symptoms and returned to the earlier dose. Although relatively well she was a little vague, and after some mishaps and uncertainty with her medications she agreed that it would be a good idea for her to use a medication 'blister pack' dispensed by her pharmacist.

Lessons learnt

The world around holds meanings to us humans, and these meanings are beyond the world's immediate material characteristics. These meanings are tightly linked to memories, and the memories are of emotions as well as of facts and experiences. As Darryl Kerrigan says in the much-loved Australian film The Castle: 'It's not just a house . . . it's our home!'

We all like to feel a sense of control over ourselves and our world. Some like this more than others but all of us need to feel this sense of control to some extent—it translates into a sense of 'agency': feeling that what we think, feel and do matters. We like to feel that we act effectively on the world and people around us. Many older people can be at risk of losing that essential sense of agency.

Being responsible and perfectionistic—both valuable and not at all abnormal characteristics—can make it harder to adjust to change and the loss of a sense of agency and control.

Small changes deep in the brain due to microscopic blood vessel abnormalities (causing the 'minor white matter attenuation' in Mrs R's CT scan) can make it more difficult for an older person to adapt to change, to work through and recover from grief and to employ adaptive mechanisms. At least, that is my explanation for the association of these brain changes with depression in old age. This association has been shown in a number of studies. It is nevertheless possible to have depression in old age without these changes, and to have the brain changes without depression.

Professor Sid Williams

Vulnerability to developing non-melancholic depression can be laid down early in life by certain experiences. As mentioned earlier, there may be a 'lock and key' connection, where particular stressful events have special significance (often unrecognised) for an individual because of earlier exposure to similar stressors. While developing a depressive disorder may seem like an exaggerated response to a precise stressor, information about the individual's background can make sense of their unique vulnerability in a specific context. Editor Parker identifies the triggers for 'Joan' in the following narrative.

CASE NOTES

A new key to an old lock

When Jim Barrett refers me a patient I know that I am in for a difficult time as, while a GP, he also handles most of the psychiatric problems in his practice with great competence.

His referral note was terse, indicating that Joan (a 73-year-old widow) was overreacting to a recent incident at her golf club and that, while he didn't think she had a significant depression, she was miserable, and he hadn't got anywhere in his discussion with her.

Joan made contact by ringing my secretary on three occasions before the appointment date. For the first, she complained about being referred to see a psychiatrist, stating that it was extremely embarrassing and that she felt quite stigmatised. Then, just in case my secretary hadn't passed that message on to me, she rang a second time. On the third occasion, she repeated her complaints and asked what procedures we had in place to protect her identity when she arrived at the psychiatric facility. One tetchy patient and one tetchy secretary—the scene was set.

At the initial consultation with me, Joan was stiff and proud and again emphasised that there had been no need for her GP to have referred her to a psychiatrist. I sat out my itch to become tetchy, and asked her about symptoms. Her defensiveness quickly settled and she acknowledged a significant number of depressive features. Her mood was very low, she had been contemplating suicide and she had even made some plans. She had lost appetite, could only sleep a couple of hours at night and had become quite asocial and isolative.

When asked about precipitants, she described how her depression had started. Her friends had not invited her on a reciprocal visit to another golf club and had not provided any explanation. She had initially felt rejected and then she felt demeaned, unworthy and unwanted.

As I started to take a history of developmental details, she bridled and repeated her concerns about seeing a psychiatrist. I stated that, while it was necessary to get a history, I didn't anticipate that any assistance would require many visits. Her body language intimated that one would be quite enough and that she had 'never' been depressed previously.

Her life history was one marked by poignant and unfortunate events. The seminal experience had occurred in primary school, when the headmistress announced at assembly that a bracelet had been stolen and that a search of all bags and lockers was underway while they remained standing on parade. The bracelet was found in her locker. She assured me—and I entirely believed her—that she hadn't stolen it and that some other girl had clearly wanted to hurt and shame her. She was expelled and her parents found a boarding school in another state so that she could 'start again'.

She started at that school in the new year and, as luck would have it, she found that she was not the only one who had transferred schools. An ex-classmate was quick to inform others that Joan was a well-known 'thief'. Although Joan applied herself academically and received high marks, the stain ensured that she remained ostracised across all her secondary school years. She felt—from the way that people interacted with her—that the word 'THIEF' was branded on her forehead.

On leaving school, she trained as a nurse. In her final year, she developed acute appendicitis that required surgery. Post-surgical complications required three further operations and finally the surgeon had to remove her uterus. She faced the fact that she would never have a child.

Though she had avoided relationships, in her late 30s she married an older man, judging that he would be kind and safe. He died six months later. His estate enabled her to live in a large house with pleasant gardens, and she had enough money to travel and to play bridge and golf regularly. She progressively developed a small set of friends at both, but was distinctly circumspect with them, never giving any details of her personal life but closely observing the niceties of superficial interaction.

As noted, her depression commenced following her golf friends' failing to include her in a reciprocal club visit—almost certainly an innocent error, but one that she had unconsciously interpreted as an echo of the past.

The term 'lock and key' is useful to describe situations where an individual is exposed to deprivational or abusive experiences in childhood that lay down a vulnerability for similar events in adulthood to induce a painful psychological reaction. The latter precipitates the 'key' that opens the predispositional 'lock' to a set of accreted negative feelings. Thus, Joan's precipitant was not only hurtful in and of itself but had been compounded by activating the earlier hurts, humiliations and stigma. To be referred to see a psychiatrist had then further activated her sense of stigma.

I elected not to prescribe any antidepressant medication and suggested that we would spend six to nine sessions going through her life story and coming up with some suggestions as to how to rework relationships with her golf club group. At the end of the third session, she fully understood the reasons why the presenting scenario had been so perturbing, and she observed that talking about her earlier humiliations and losses had, for the first time, given her a perspective and distance. Further, she had received an apology from one of her golf friends (who had also made it clear that the lack of invitation was an innocent error). Her symptoms settled.

Recognising that she had been so reluctant to attend a psychiatrist, I suggested at the end of the third session that she had improved so much that there was no clear need for us to meet again. I anticipated that she would express relief. Instead, her face fell. I quickly suggested that we should review things in three months.

Lessons learnt

This vignette provides three messages. Firstly, in relation to diagnosis and formulation in psychiatry, what might look like a simple—and often not particularly stressful—life event precipitant can often be of far greater psychological magnitude, unearthing resonating echoes of past events (the 'lock and key' model).

The second message was more a lesson on for me. I had interpreted her reluctance and sense of stigma in attending a psychiatrist to be ongoing and had sought to limit our consultations to respect this concern. This turned out to be a major error. For the first time she had been able to openly tell her life story and, in so doing, she had 'unpacked' many of the hurts and losses that had been encrusted onto events and had found that unburdening process very helpful. She had established some trust in me but, by my bringing the sessions to an end, I had effectively betrayed her trust once more and sharply reactivated her sense of loss and rejection. Predictably, I never heard from her again.

A further message was that, while most people appreciate being able to tell their story and—subject to the professional being attentive, empathic and offering commonsense advice—will find the experience positive, I have learnt that older people are even more appreciative. I suspect this reflects the way in which they see themselves as perceived in society: as becoming 'invisible' with age and progressively devalued over time. A therapist who spends time with them effectively provides a contrasting meta-communication—that if they are worth spending time with, they are of worth.

How can such observations be put into practice? Often, by spending more time with older patients, and certainly in allowing them to start the process of terminating sessions. Also, as far as possible, by having a parity-based tone to the sessions so that the individual feels more comfortable and that the professional's status is of little impact.

The Lennon and McCartney song 'When I'm Sixty-Four' affectingly questions whether our 'need' and 'feed' wishes will be met as we age, while Jean Cocteau once observed that 'the awful thing about getting old is that you stay young inside'.

Issues of emotional nurturance are brought to any therapeutic endeavour by older patients as strongly as by younger ones—they just present them less directly, and with well-honed, if not world-weary, defences.

Professor Gordon Parker

The process of ageing, in itself, can render us more vulnerable to non-melancholic depression. As previously mentioned, the biological wear and tear of ageing results in organic brain changes that can function to lower the 'threshold' for depression, leading to increased susceptibility.

A study by Professor Henry Brodaty and others examining vulnerability factors found that older age, experience of severe trauma during the World War II Holocaust, use of immature defence mechanisms and higher levels of neuroticism were significantly associated with post-traumatic stress disorder (PTSD) and psychological ill-health. From this, a profile of at-risk survivors can be identified that may have applications to survivors of more recent genocides and traumas.[5]

Tragic and stressful events from many years before—such as sustained abuse in childhood or the enormity of surviving genocide—can lay a flawed foundation that collapses under stressors that naturally accumulate as an individual ages and accrues the physical impairments of growing older, loss of friends to death, and encroachments on independence and control. This may result in personal decompensation, where a person has reduced resilience to such stressors and a lower threshold for onset of depression.

My husband's invisible scars

 Many books have been written about Holocaust survivors and others who were in prisoner-of-war camps. I have never read about how carers of these (mostly) men managed living with these people after World War II, as many suffered depression, anxiety and nightmares.

I am the wife of a Holocaust survivor. We married in the 1950s. I was born here. He was born in Czechoslovakia and spent four and a half years in Dachau concentration camp in Germany as a political prisoner. His number is tattooed on his forearm.

However, it was not until I married that I knew about depression and anxiety and nightmares. I soon learnt.

The first years were good, apart from the odd anxiety attack, usually during the night. I found it was best to sit up and talk to him until he became calm and went to sleep. After a few more years, health problems started, but nothing serious could be found; depression was the main problem.

The doctor prescribed Serepax and every 28 days my husband went and got a repeat prescription—until he became addicted to them. His doctor did not want to stop them and said he needed them. He became worse, at times taking more Serepax than he should, and if we were going anywhere he had to have one tablet in his pocket—'just in case'.

I heard about a doctor with experience with drugs of addiction, and with his help my husband was able to stop the Serepax; easily done because he wanted to—and I feel 'wanted to' is the key. The depression was still there.

By this time age had caught up with both of us and we were assessed for aged care. When the assessment nurse came to interview my husband, she first spoke with me—he would not leave his bed, so she went to him, took one look and said, 'Depression.' I took him to see his doctor and he was put on one depression tablet each day. It helped.

Christmas is his worst time—cards always remind him of Dachau, when the German guards placed the bodies of the dead around a Christmas tree and made prisoners stand around the tree and sing carols.

I find it is better for me to leave him alone at this time. He knows where I am and I let him seek me if he wishes. However, I am never able to enjoy the time as I would like. My husband was in Dachau for four and a half years, but his experiences are with him until he dies. It is like a life sentence.

I have no regrets about marrying him. I have learnt to cope with his problems. I am sure there are others out there with similar circumstances. Hannah

WHEN NORMAL GRIEF TURNS INTO NON-MELANCHOLIC DEPRESSION

Jenny's following story of her nan shows how grief can morph into depression. The impact of the chronic stressor, grief, has been eased by family support, but Nan has been distressed and ill, losing her hair, isolating herself and experiencing 'erratic' moods. For this age band of elderly people, psychological intervention may be an intrusion: personal reserve, privacy and coping in their own way and time are strongly held values.

Life after 'Pop'

Nan has kept all Pop's possessions—from his favourite coffee cup that still sits in the cupboard, to his collection of brown suits that hang in his wardrobe. At times she sits there and strokes his coat sleeves and inhales the musty smell like a drug. The house they called a home for over 25 years is littered with tributes to Pop. Nan is reluctant to leave even though she is unable to maintain such a large house and gardens. She said it would feel wrong to leave the house with all the precious memories it holds.

For several months after Pop passed away, Nan avoided going out of the house, busying herself with menial chores. My father and I made sure one of us visited her every day. She started losing her hair not long after. The doctor said it could be her age, stress or grief. Her moods became erratic. I never knew what frame of mind she was going to be in when I entered the house so I was always mindful of my approach.

Sometimes just sitting there with her in silence was calming for her, knowing that nothing needed to be said.

There were days when she felt that there was no point getting out of bed. We knew that it was important to help her get back to a sustainable quality of life but never putting Pop aside. We still refer to him in present tense, which helps us all feel like he's here somewhere.

We are a small family unit, with Nan only having two sons, one of whom lives away, and with the other son—my father— only having two daughters, one of whom also lives away. So a lot falls on my father and me; we feel her anger, her pain and her helplessness.

Time passes, and after a while we got Nan back into her routine. This seemed to help steady her moods; knowing that her week was structured and that she had places to be seemed to help reduce her sorrow. It didn't get rid of it and she still does cry, but at least the sadness doesn't last for days on end.

We have had no counselling and little support outside our family. But together we have developed coping strategies that help us in our own way. We don't talk if nothing needs to be said. We know family is our main priority, so if Nan has a sad day and takes it out on those closest to her, she doesn't mean it and everything is fine afterwards. Just little things that we have learnt about each other during this difficult time have also helped strengthen our relationship. She is not cured from her depression, nor do I expect her to ever be. But at least it's at a manageable level and we are all coping. Jenny

NOTEWORTHY

Persuading someone to seek an assessment

You've observed that the older person for whom you care is struggling—perhapswithdrawnoranxious,irritable,notthemself.

Now, how do you get a grasp of the problem? Does it warrant help from a professional? And how do you advance without the risk of making things worse in discussion with them?

Here are some ways that have been found useful in opening up what can be a threatening and painful subject.

First ask yourself if an assessment is needed

Hopefully, your intuition and knowledge of your spouse, relative or friend will determine whether any mental health assessment is warranted. For someone affected, having the family doubt their mental health is likely to be quite painful in itself, let alone the processes faced by an older person adjusting to age-related changes—some of them quite searing.

Seek advice for yourself first

It may be useful to consult with a counsellor or the GP yourself prior to any assessment of your spouse/relative/friend. Before you broach the subject with the person, it is helpful to have a grasp of what you think might be happening and a sense of your objectives: what do you want to find out, what would you like to see happen? How you come across in such a discussion is crucial; you need to be a strong and reassuring presence.

How do you bring up the subject?

Many high-profile people have talked openly about their bouts of depression and how they managed them. A web search will reveal the names of actors, sportspeople and politicians who have spoken about overcoming their mood disorder. That such public figures are open about their mental illness may make the subject a little easier to raise. Another possible entry point may be a medical check-up necessitated by the presence of troubling physical symptoms. Or there may be an influential family member or friend who they will listen to.

When might be a good time to talk?
You probably know the situations when you feel most comfortable together and when there is a time that you can talk with the person without pressure or interruption. Decide how far you want to press the subject. There is likely to be natural resistance or denial initially—the person may be frightened and defensive. If it is too difficult at first, now that you have opened up the discussion you could mention a particular time when you will broach it again. If the older person is still very much 'in command' of the family, you may wish to include all the relevant family members in the discussion. It can be wise to brief them anyway so that all are clear about what is happening.

What might you say to your relative or friend?
You can let him or her know what symptoms and signs you've noticed and why you are concerned. Though you are probably a familiar contact, it may still be awkward to raise a sensitive subject that is so close to a person's sense of themselves, particularly as he or she may feel very lost. Try to press on gently. You know his/her psychological 'style' and this can help shape your approach. They may trust you and be relieved that you are presenting an escape from the tide of dark feelings that is threatening to engulf them.

Guides to successful communication suggest that the important struts in any discussion include:

- support and acceptance—not rushing in to swamp the individual with advice
- taking things at his/her pace
- genuine respect for the individual and his/her point of view
- validation of what he/she is saying, and empathy with their problems and distress. Listening comes first and is crucial.

What will an assessment achieve?

An assessment will help to decide whether the person's symptoms are mainly due to depression, another psychological condition or a physical problem. Assessment may result in a diagnosis and a plan of management. Alternatively, there may not be a clinical problem at all.

Why not just 'wait it out'?

'Waiting it out' is not usually the best option. If it is a depressive illness and it is left untreated there can be unfortunate consequences.

If the need for assessment is accepted

Do your 'homework' and seek a professional who is well versed in assessing older people. Then offer practical support to your spouse, relative or friend: make the appointment, take him or her to the interview. Ask if he/she will allow you to be included. Often a supporter can 'hear' the advice and management options much better than someone who is tackling a mood disorder, and who is elderly and perhaps not very psychologically minded. If he/she is then prescribed medication, you can encourage compliance, anticipate any side effects and discuss these with the health care professional who is monitoring them.

Your value here is also to ensure that there is a schedule for follow-ups, and that you understand which professional is responsible for what part of the treatment and who is coordinating it. Discontinuity of care—where the elderly person gets 'lost' between specialists and nobody has a clear idea of the 'game plan'—can be a reality that leads to loss of faith in the effectiveness of treatment, and breeds non-compliance and more chronic disability.

Finally, when supporting an older person in distress, it is of use to ensure that he/she is receiving adequate nutrition and fluids, to monitor medications for adherence to correct dose and frequency, and to watch for any risk of self-harm.

7

Late onset: depression specific to ageing

... age is the awkward period when Father Time starts catching up with Mother Nature.

Harold Coffin

At a recent gathering of older people, Ruth was greeted by the hostess as she arrived. 'It's so lovely to see you, Ruth. I'll catch up with all your news in a minute. Wait here with me while people arrive: first we've got to have the "organ recital".'

Ruth, surprised, had not expected a musical event, but she soon understood. As each guest came in they gave the hostess an update of their health—yes, the coronary bypass op was very successful; no, the doc had decided to leave the prostate in place; thanks, the lungs had settled down, the cough was nearly gone; yes, the blurry vision had improved since they'd last spoken ...

LATE-ONSET DEPRESSION (LOD) OVERVIEW

Late-onset depression (depression occurring for the first time in later life) differs from early-onset (recurrent) depression. There are differences in causation, neurology, clinical features and outcome. Late-onset depression is more closely associated with somatic symptoms, cognitive deficits, cerebral structural abnormalities, vascular disease and poorer treatment outcomes.[1] Genetic factors more related to cerebrovascular disease (disease of the blood vessels, especially the arteries that supply the brain) rather than to depression itself also play a role.

Other influences that increase vulnerability to a first-onset depression in older age include the losses and impairments that accumulate at this age, such as death of spouse, social isolation and loneliness, the side effects of medications, alcohol misuse, prodromal (possible initial signs of) dementia, personality factors and adverse life experiences.

However, a cognitively intact older person in good physical health without a past history of mental illness has a relatively low risk of depression.[2]

VASCULAR DEPRESSION AND OTHER MANIFESTATIONS IN OLDER AGE

'Vascular depression' is first-episode depression arising in older age and caused by cerebrovascular disease. This is a non-dysphoric depression (depression without the 'blues'), characterised by apathy, psychomotor retardation, reduced insight and mild frontal executive cognitive deficits. The nature and degree of the underlying biological processes and the extent of the damage to parts of the brain is associated with treatment success. Risk factors for vascular pathology include hypertension, type 2 diabetes, peripheral arterial disease and smoking.

Other types of depression that become more prevalent with age include the more severe manifestations—particularly with psychotic features; and, in up to 15 per cent of older people, a more minor sub-syndromal depression. As mentioned previously, although a sub-syndromal mood disorder has fewer depressive symptoms, it still causes considerable distress and incapacity, and increases the individual's risk of developing clinical depression.[3]

PHYSICAL ILLNESS ASSOCIATED WITH OR CAUSING DEPRESSION

Don't worry about your health. It'll go away.

Anon

Depression in older age may arise via biological mechanisms, including structural damage in the brain; it is associated with most neurological conditions such as Alzheimer's disease and

Parkinson's disease, and with neuroendocrine disturbances such as hypothyroidism.

Other physical illnesses that can cause depression in older people include occult (unrevealed) cancer, vitamin deficiencies, anaemia and infections. Depression may be present long before any other symptoms or signs of underlying physical illness can be established, though an absence of any psychosocial reason for depression may provide an indication. A thorough medical examination is always paramount.

When an individual is diagnosed with a serious illness such as cancer or dementia, this in itself may precipitate a reactive depression. Suicide risk is increased in the three months after such a diagnosis. [4]

DEPRESSION DUE TO OTHER FACTORS ASSOCIATED WITH AGEING

Other facets of ageing associated with depression onset include disability, restriction of activity, chronic pain and the dependency associated with age, and loss of accustomed social role.

The medications that are often required in older age can also cause or exacerbate depression, particularly antihypertensive drugs, steroids, analgesics, benzodiazepines and antipsychotics.

Social isolation—and its relief by alcohol—exacerbates depression, as do traumatic early life experiences (such as childhood abuse, parental alcohol abuse or war-related trauma) reactivated by the frequent and cumulative losses that accompany advancing age. [5]

LATE-ONSET DEPRESSION AND CONFUSION WITH DEMENTIA

Depression may resemble dementia, confusing diagnosis and management. An older person can become unwell quite rapidly, with signs such as confusion and agitation dominating. He/she may 'disappear' behind the illness—presenting with symptoms and behaviour that is very distressing to the family and quite unlike his/her 'normal' self.

In contrast to the potential for under-detection of depression in an older person, there may be over-detection of dementia, with a latent expectation in relatives and health care workers that dementia is to be expected, and with any change in behaviour thus attributed to this. If this mistaken diagnosis is not tested further, treatment that could resolve a masked depression will not be pursued. Dr Lana Kossoff in her account following illustrates how she picked up the cues that led to a very different outcome for Mr H.

EFFICACY AND ACCEPTABILITY OF ELECTROCONVULSIVE THERAPY (ECT)

Dr Kossoff's account, together with the one that follows by Professor Brodaty, also demonstrates the benefits of ECT (electroconvulsive or 'shock' therapy). Depression in the older age group can be quite treatment-resistant due to the biological changes of ageing, yet ECT is often very effective. This treatment arouses prejudice—partly because people immediately think of the film One Flew Over the Cuckoo's Nest, and partly because it is used in very ill individuals who may have trouble giving informed consent (though a relative is permitted to do so in cases of life-threatening depressive illness). However, despite the stigma surrounding it, ECT is well tolerated and frequently restores individuals to their previous good functioning, especially in cases of intractable depression and where medication is ineffective or not tolerated.

An understanding of ECT's mechanism of action still eludes research: it is not yet known which of the myriad post-ECT biochemical alterations in the brain and periphery—individually or in combination—mark its therapeutic effectiveness. The clinicians' reports throughout this book, however, resoundingly speak for its efficacy, safety and tolerability, particularly in frail elderly people. Dr Lana Kossoff describes a successful outcome in the case of Mr H.

CASE NOTES

Cancel the funeral director

When I was working as a consultation-liaison psychiatrist in a general hospital, I was asked to assess Mr H, an 87-year-old man. Mr H was unable to give me any history so I spoke to his delightful wife, who said her husband had been in good health throughout his life. She said he was living actively in retirement by spending time with his family, enjoying exercising, going on holidays and working as a treasurer for the local club. Mr H and his wife enjoyed raising money for charity and were well-respected members of their local community.

However, about twelve months before, Mr H had a fall, and although he didn't need to go to hospital, the fall did slow him down—to the extent that he couldn't participate in his favoured activities for over a month—and he became depressed. His local doctor started him on antidepressant medication and after a few months of treatment, coincident with Mr H's physical symptoms improving, his depression resolved and the antidepressant was ceased.

This time Mr H had been admitted to hospital. About two weeks before I was asked to assess him, he had been brought to the Emergency Department in a severely deteriorated state by his wife. He was refusing to eat and drink and kept throwing himself on the floor. Attempts were made to communicate with him, but he wouldn't speak. He appeared very confused and was subsequently admitted to the geriatric ward. After the standard investigations came back as normal, the treating geriatrician concluded that Mr H was probably suffering from a rapid-onset and terminal dementia; he sought a second opinion from the neurologist, who concurred.

By this stage Mr H was being nursed on a mattress on the floor, as he would throw himself off any bed or chair. He was sedated and the palliative care team was asked to provide an assessment about what could be done to make this man's last days more comfortable. Almost as an afterthought, the geriatrician remembered that Mr H had had an episode of depression twelve months earlier, so decided he should make a referral to a psychiatrist for a further opinion.

On the day I went to assess Mr H, Mrs H was present and was able to give me a longitudinal history. This revealed in particular the very short time span of the decline in Mr H's intellectual capacities (he had had no cognitive deficits three months earlier). Mr H was lying on a mattress on the floor. He was pale, thin and dehydrated, had his hands held tightly around his neck, as if he was trying to strangle himself, and on a couple of occasions grabbed the plastic beads from around his wife's neck, again to try to strangle himself. While he could convey no history, he said, 'I have done bad things with Suzie,' but could not elaborate. He appeared to be consumed by guilt over things that had occurred in his past. Over the one-and-a-half-hour interview he spoke only a few words. I told him my first name and asked him, an hour into the interview, if he could remember it. To my surprise, he stated my name was Lana.

The longitudinal history that I had obtained from Mrs H, Mr H's suicidal behaviour and guilty feelings, coupled with his ability to remember my name over an hour into the interview, led me to conclude that a more plausible explanation for his presentation was a severe melancholic depression. After the clinical assessment, I met with Mrs H in the interview room, where she told me that she had a funeral director booked to come to her home that evening to talk about arrangements for her husband. I said to her, 'Cancel the funeral director; I think we can help your husband.'

We obtained approval from the Mental Health Review Tribunal for urgent, involuntary electroconvulsive therapy (ECT). Mr H was only able to have five ECT treatments (due to heart rhythm problems); however, within two treatments he was sitting up in a chair, and after five treatments was eating, mobile and relating warmly with other staff and patients on the ward. Within two weeks he was discharged home and was prescribed antidepressant medication. Mr H was closely followed up as we were concerned he could have a relapse, but this did not occur. Indeed, he spent the next five years of his life participating in his previously enjoyed charity activities, working as the treasurer of the club and spending quality time with his wife and children. He subsequently died from an unrelated cause at the age of 92.

As an old-age psychiatrist I had previously seen these 'miraculous' recoveries from depression, but my physician colleagues had not witnessed such an extraordinary response to treatment and invited me to present at the physicians' Grand Rounds. The physicians were very interested in the case and, in particular, how ECT can be of such great value. They also noted how important it is to take a longitudinal history of the symptoms of dementia, as it is unlikely that someone within the space of three months can develop severe cognitive deficits to the point that they can't function.

Lessons learnt

I believe my physician colleagues learnt a valuable lesson from this case. Melancholic depression, particularly in the elderly, can mimic a number of cognitive disorders, including dementia and delirium. Unless one spends the time to take a careful history, usually from carers or relatives, the diagnosis can be missed. Yet the treatment for this type of depression can be very effective, and the quality of life for sufferers and their families can be greatly improved.

It was also pleasing, from that time on, to receive more regular and frequent referrals from the hospital's physicians so that I could assess puzzling cases lest a depressive illness was being missed.

Dr Lana Kossoff

SUDDEN AND ACUTE PSYCHOTIC DEPRESSION

In editor Brodaty's account of late-onset depression, we see a man with strong previous resilience develop a sudden and acute onset of psychotic depression. Mr D responded well to a course of ECT. Such an acute onset of depression may presage later, as yet undetectable, serious physical illness—a conjecture always at the back of the treating clinician's mind.

CASE NOTES

Mr D's first and only episode of depression

Mr D had survived the Holocaust, during which he had lost a wife, two children, several siblings and both parents, and migrated as a penniless but skilled cobbler from war-torn Europe in 1951. He built up a successful shoe-repair business, diversifying into leather goods, and retired when aged 78.

A robust, healthy, sociable and well-liked man with a large circle of friends and loving children, Mr D had a reasonably harmonious relationship with his wife. They lived independently in their own home and enjoyed seeing their three children and seven grandchildren. Apart from high blood pressure, now treated and under control, and a recently developed irregular heart rhythm, Mr D had remained healthy and—up until this episode of depression—happy and enjoying life.

Mr D's depression came out of the blue just after his 90th birthday. There was no warning. Over a few weeks, he lost his spark, appetite, and twelve kilograms weight. He no longer wanted to socialise and became obsessed with money, claiming he was penurious. He would exhort his wife to buy only half a loaf of bread because they could not afford more. His children showed him bank books, reassured him that all was well financially, and hid bills so that he would not be alarmed. All to no avail.

Clinicians knew that the most likely cause for his psychotic depression was an underlying physical condition. Extensive investigations failed to find any evidence of cancer, a blood clot to the brain or abnormalities in his blood. The exact cause of Mr D's depression remained a mystery. The best cause that his treating doctors could come up with was that maybe the culprit was a clot to his brain, as a result of his atrial fibrillation, that had been too small to be detected by brain scan.

Whatever the cause, treatment was urgently needed, as Mr D was wasting away and tormented by his psychotic melancholic depression. Several antidepressant medications over four months, supplemented by psychological therapies, failed to alleviate his misery and continuing weight loss. A course of electroconvulsive therapy (ECT) was recommended and Mr D and his family consented with trepidation.

This treatment was dramatically successful and convinced the previously sceptical staff in the operating theatre in which the ECT was administered of its value. By the third treatment Mr D was eating again and putting on weight. By the sixth treatment he was cured and he remained well. That is, until about a year later.

This time his GP noted that Mr D's abdomen was swollen, and he organised a CT scan which demonstrated an enlarged liver with likely metastases (secondary tumours) from an underlying primary cancer. Five weeks later Mr D was dead.

Lessons learnt
What did I learn from this case?

Firstly, I knew but this confirmed that an underlying physical cause should always be suspected when depression comes on for the first time, especially in late life. Here was a man who had robustly dealt with the worst psychological disasters a person could endure. Additionally, 'old age' is not a diagnosis, and turning 90 was not the cause of his psychotic depression. Hidden cancer manifesting as depression months or a year before the cancer becomes apparent is well described and really does occur. Yet knowing this, and despite modern investigations, the cause remained elusive.

Secondly, even when depression results from an underlying physical condition, traditional treatments for depression can still be effective.

Thirdly, age is neither a barrier to successful treatment— and certainly not to ECT, which has a good track record in older people—nor to recovery. Indeed, Mr D's last year was very happy and contented.

Professor Henry Brodaty

THE POTENTIAL FOR CONFUSION BETWEEN APATHY AND DEPRESSION

The symptoms of depression in an older person can be confounded with another syndrome: apathy. Apathy is a state, not a distinct disorder—and, predictably, does not respond to antidepressant drugs.

Though we can all be 'apathetic' at times, apathy in an older person often reflects cognitive dysfunction—here, of the 'executive' area of the frontal lobe. Apathy is manifested by inaction and lack of interest, together with reduced initiative, motivation, spontaneity, emotion and affection. There is also a lack of persistence when something requires effort, and a blunting of affect or feeling. Anxiety is usually absent, as is suicidality.

Apathy is a frequent companion of neurological disease, and is common in dementia and schizophrenia. It can be associated with medical, drug-induced and socio-environmental conditions as well. To make matters even more complex, apathy can also be a symptom of a clinical depression; in other words, apathy and depression can overlap. The problem lies with misdiagnosing pure apathy as depression.

Because of a lack of standardised diagnostic criteria, the 'organic' apathy that sometimes accompanies old age is difficult to identify. For example, it is hard to tease out the difference between lack of motivation and cognitive impairment. The person's history and clinical impression can, however, add to evidence from rating tools.

Apathy is important to identify as it has a different treatment course to the interventions used to treat depression. If there is misdiagnosis then the stage is set for non-compliance with treatment and poor outcomes in rehabilitation, together with carer frustration at what may be misperceived as 'not trying' and 'giving up'.

The following report, a case from editor Brodaty, describes an individual with apathy. This is followed by a summary of apathy and its markers in the 'Noteworthy' section at the end of this chapter.

CASE NOTES

Apathy versus depression

In 1985, James Blackett, a 67-year-old man, was hit by a car while crossing a road in the centre of the city. He sustained a closed head injury but recovered fairly quickly, with only an hour of anterograde amnesia [inability to remember the very immediate past]. However, he was a changed person. He appeared to have no interest in activities and did not perform his work as before. A CT scan of the brain was normal and his Mini Mental State Examination was 30/30.

Eventually he was diagnosed with depression. Over the next five years he received a number of courses of treatment with different antidepressants, individual psychotherapy and group therapy, and eventually ECT. All to no avail.

When he came to see me in 1990, his opening statement was: 'I've lost the need to talk.' This intrigued me. Depressed people usually say, 'I don't feel like talking.' His wife confirmed this symptom. She said at dinner time if she asked a question he would respond. If she remained silent, he remained silent. He appeared to have lost initiative. His Mini Mental State score remained high at 29/30.

The clinical picture seemed more like a frontal lobe syndrome characterised by apathy and lack of initiative. I organised an MRI scan and neuropsychological assessment. The MRI scan did demonstrate some damage to the frontal lobes which had not been visible on the CT scan. The neuropsychological assessment showed clear indications of frontal lobe damage, with impairment in executive function such as planning, organisation and generating a list of words.

What this case demonstrates is the difference between apathy and depression. Apathy is commonly mistaken for depression, particularly in people with cognitive impairment. I am often asked to treat an older person's 'depression'. On enquiry I am told that the older person just sits in a chair doing nothing. On closer questioning, the older person denies feelings of sadness, tearfulness or wishing to die.

Apathy can occur during a depressive episode. The distinction between apathy and depression can be difficult. However, it is an important distinction because antidepressants are of no benefit to a person with apathy (unless it is secondary to depression). Treatment for apathy requires a structured program of activities and clear suggestions and recommendations to the person with apathy; in essence providing surrogate frontal lobe functions. There is scant evidence to demonstrate that any medication helps, though there is some evidence that the cholinesterase inhibitors which are used as treatments for Alzheimer's disease (for example, donepezil, galantamine, rivastigmine) may have some benefit for apathy in people with Alzheimer's disease.

Professor Henry Brodaty

OLDER AGE PRESENTS MORE TREATMENT CHALLENGES

I'm so old they've cancelled my blood type.

Bob Hope

Treatment in older age is associated with multiple difficulties. Comorbid (coexisting) disease and physical problems such as high blood pressure and physical frailty, plus a greater propensity to side effects, make the management of depression challenging. In the following case notes, Professor Sergio Starkstein presents the progress of 'Mr Blais', who was fortunately given the appropriate treatment for his mood disorder and was consequently then able to access treatment for his disabling Parkinson's disease.

CASE NOTES

Never give up!

I frequently see patients with Parkinson's disease (PD), who also suffer from non-motor problems such as depression, anxiety and apathy. Most patients respond well to appropriate psychotherapy or pharmacological treatment. Sometimes psychiatric problems are quite severe and treatment becomes challenging.

A year ago, Mr Blais was referred to me for assessment and management of his mood disorder. He was a 69-year-old retired man who had been suffering from PD for nine years. His motor problems had gradually increased and he was admitted to hospital to improve his motor disability and lack of response to anti-Parkinsonian medication. The neurology team suggested that he might benefit from a neurosurgical technique called deep brain stimulation, which has proven useful to treat patients with moderate to severe PD.

Six months before hospital admission, however, Mr Blais developed paranoid delusions, with the fixed belief that his food was being poisoned. He refused to eat and had progressively lost 20 per cent of his usual weight. The use of a number of antipsychotic drugs had no effect on his delusions and, additionally, made his motor symptoms worse. He also had psychotherapy, which proved ineffective. Additionally, he had a severe major depression, with no response to usual antidepressant treatment. Given his complex psychiatric status, the neurology team decided to defer neurosurgery and he was admitted to hospital, given his deteriorating medical condition.

At admission Mr Blais was so frail that he had to be fed by a tube inserted into his stomach. A family meeting was held and a decision was made to continue with palliative care, given the lack of response to treatment for his psychological and motor symptoms. The medical team made a referral to our psychiatry consultation-liaison team to explore therapeutic options.

When I met Mr Blais he presented as a cachectic [abnormally low weight, with muscle weakness and general bodily decline], dishevelled man slowly mobilising in a wheelchair. He answered my questions with single words, and his speech was difficult to understand. He stated that his refusal to eat was due to his conviction that his food was poisoned and that he was unable to swallow. A test to check his swallowing capacity was normal, although he remained unconvinced of the result. While his cognitive status was within the normal range for his age, Mr Blais was certain he was becoming demented. A decision was made to transfer him to the inpatient psychiatric unit and we discussed with the family the possible use of electroconvulsive therapy (ECT). We explained to the family that this treatment had proved to be effective in many patients with PD, and he accepted to undergo twelve sessions of ECT, with his wife's consent.

Mr Blais started two sessions per week of ECT, and by the end of the fourth session there was a clear clinical improvement. By the end of the twelve sessions his appetite had returned to normal and he was steadily gaining weight (at the time of discharge his weight was 60 kilograms, as compared to 44 kilograms at admission). He expressed no further paranoid ideation [thoughts], he was no longer depressed, and the feeding tube was removed. His mobility also improved and he was able to walk with the help of a walking frame. He became fully independent with his activities of daily living and his speech was easy to understand. He and his wife stated that ECT was instrumental in managing his paranoia and depression, and expressed their desire to continue with fortnightly ECT sessions. Four months after leaving hospital, Mr Blais continued to do very well. He had a good appetite, was walking with the frame and even danced at his wife's 50th birthday.

While Mr Blais's psychological status showed a dramatic improvement, he continued to suffer severe motor fluctuations due to his PD. Given his psychological improvement, the neurology team accepted a request to reconsider neurosurgery for his severe motor problems.

In conclusion, Mr Blais was a patient with a severe neurological problem and comorbid psychiatric disorders. It is not unusual that, in elderly patients with psychological problems that are refractory [resistant] to usual medical and psychological treatment in the context of a chronic and progressive neurological disorder, that treatment may become palliative only. This case demonstrates that a more aggressive therapeutic approach to problems that are potentially reversible may render excellent results in both the psychiatric and neurological domains.

Professor Sergio Starkstein

INVESTIGATING 'EXECUTIVE' FUNCTION IN OLDER AGE

Late-onset depression is often characterised by a decline in the brain's 'executive' or organising capacities: such individuals are less able to control their thoughts and actions and show disinhibition, rigid thinking, inattention and a decline in memory. Accompanying this, such individuals are more likely to be troubled by rumination—repetitive and circular negative thought patterns. 'Clinical' rumination is likened to problem-solving gone awry. Studies are now examining which executive function links decline in late-onset depression, to enable the development of therapies to circumvent the spiral into psychiatric illness.

PROGRESS IN THE TREATMENT OF OLDER-AGE DEPRESSION

In summary, sound progress is being made in preventing, diagnosing and treating late-onset depression. Ongoing management using a range of therapies has restored many older people to their former quality of life, and there is promising research that indicates new modes of intervention.

NOTEWORTHY

Some markers of apathy versus depression[6]

The symptoms that follow are used to differentiate the conditions of 'apathy' and 'depression'.

Symptoms of apathy
In this condition the individual:

- shows reduced initiative and motivation (rather than cognitive impairment)
- lacks spontaneity and energy
- lacks persistence
- lacks emotion and doesn't care
- is not suicidal

- is not usually anxious
- has a 'flat' affect
- usually does not have 'vegetative' symptoms (such as fatigue, weight change and insomnia), though there may be loss of interest in food and sex.

Symptoms of depression
In this condition the individual:

- is 'down' and may be tearful
- sees no point to life
- shows lowered self-esteem
- may be suicidal
- would 'rather be dead'
- may be anxious
- shows vegetative symptoms—such as impaired sleep, appetite, weight and libido.

Symptoms in common
- lack of interest/initiative/motivation
- decreased libido/concentration.

Also see:

K. Berman, H. Brodaty, K. Seeher and A. Withall, 'Pharmacological treatment of apathy in dementia: a systematic review', American Journal of Geriatric Psychiatry (accepted 25 February 2011—Ref: AJGP–10–145R2).

H. Brodaty and K. Burns, 'Non-pharmacological management of apathy in dementia: a systematic review', American Journal of Geriatric Psychiatry (accepted 25 February 2011—Ref: AJGP–10–146R2).

8

Therapies and the role of the therapist

If I knew I was going to live this long, I'd have taken better care of myself.

Mickey Mantle

It is often assumed that older people are unable to benefit from psychotherapy or counselling—that they are too 'concrete', not psychologically minded, or that they will be resistant because of the attitudes held by their generation. Thus, they are less likely to be referred for 'talking therapies' or other forms of psychological therapy. Data confirm that those who are older in Australia, for instance, are two-thirds less likely to be referred by a GP to a psychiatrist, and even when they do see a psychiatrist their consultations are often shorter.[1] Of people who are referred on, those who are older are less liable to receive psychological therapies and more likely to receive biological treatments such as pharmacotherapy and electroconvulsive therapy, even when allowing for diagnosis.[2]

THE BENEFITS OF PSYCHOTHERAPY FOR OLDER PEOPLE

Environmental variables that bolster a good response to psychotherapy include a satisfying social network, the presence of a confidant or supporter, and a quality place of residence. Other variables that predict better response to psychotherapeutic intervention are younger patient age, female gender, stable pre-morbid personality, problem-solving-based coping styles and absence of concurrent physical illness.[3] However, there are numerous examples throughout this book that underline the benefits of psychotherapy in older age.

Therapists, during assessment of an older person, may follow a loose logic of sorting through which factors can be broadly assigned to one of four quadrants: social/environmental, interpersonal, biological and/or psychological, with the treatment then following aetiology (the suspected cause).

Mr B's story below, related by Professor Nicola Lautenschlager, illustrates how medication was ineffective for treating his non-melancholic depression, but how psychotherapy helped to uncover and resolve the real reason for his 'dis-ease'.

CASE NOTES

There was no time to say goodbye

I remember well how excited I was as a young trainee in psychiatry when we were introduced to psychotherapy and over the years had the opportunity to learn specific types. All of us as trainees had to complete several psychotherapies with patients with mental health problems, and an experienced supervisor would listen and/or watch the taped sessions and give us often harsh but always helpful feedback with advice about how to improve our skills.

At that stage I already had a keen interest in the psychiatry of old age and was surprised and disappointed when I became aware of the commonly held belief that older adults, most of the time, would not be able to benefit from psychotherapy. The thinking was that they would have become too inflexible with age to be able to change. Often Sigmund Freud himself is quoted in this context, having deemed psychoanalysis as not suitable for adults older than 50 years of age. But older adults often surprise us with their resilience and enthusiasm for life when we least expect it and this applies also to psychotherapy in old age.

In this situation, a GP had referred an 85-year-old gentleman to me, questioning whether he might be developing dementia since he seemed to have memory problems.

When I met Mr B he was friendly and polite and happy to talk about his life and his symptoms. I quickly became aware that he was educated and thoughtful and further testing luckily ruled out any dementia at this point in time. However, my heart sank when I heard his story, and I remember the feeling of sadness taking possession of me when I listened to him.

He lived alone in a large house and his wife had died more than ten years ago. They had had a loving relationship over many decades when she suddenly died one night, next to him in bed, from a heart attack. He described in detail how he had been unable to help her or to say goodbye, and how since then his life was empty. They did not have children, and only a few friends, and so for more than ten years he had lived isolated and alone in his home. Additional physical illnesses also kept him from leaving home most of the time. Despite counselling by his GP and being prescribed tranquillisers and antidepressant medication, he did not improve and began to want to die. He also complained to his doctor that his memory was going.

After having ruled out the presence of a dementia syndrome, I referred Mr B to a colleague who specialises in psychotherapy for older adults.

Just recently I met Mr B again for his twelve-month follow-up appointment. I was delighted to see him smiling and to witness his new positive outlook on life. His psychotherapist, who has seen Mr B weekly, had focused on his loss and had conducted many sessions aimed at helping Mr B make progress with his grieving and giving him a sense of being able to say goodbye to his wife properly. Since these sessions, the depression and death wishes have vanished and have been replaced by healthy grief for the loss of his wife. Mr B now leaves his home more often and has made new friends. He was extremely grateful for the psychotherapy sessions.

This experience was another reminder for me that we should not withhold psychotherapy as a treatment for depression just because a person is old, but rather work hard to be able to offer more of it.

Professor Nicola Lautenschlager

Skilful diagnosis and flexible therapy is evident in 'Rita's' story, from Professor Joel Sadavoy, and this account again resoundingly confirms the success of psychotherapy in a person of advanced years.

CASE NOTES

The shifting realities of therapy

The elderly depressed person who comes for help often describes an array of immediate problems that at first sight are the 'cause' of their depressed feelings. However, experienced therapists have learnt to look beyond the obvious and to try to understand the deeper story. In the right therapeutic environment, a person's real life story may emerge for the first time. I hope that the case that follows illustrates the layers of complexity that underlay this 75-year-old patient's initial complaint of depression and the therapeutic approaches that emerged from a full understanding of her story.

Rita, a pseudonym of course, was the youngest of three girls born in Europe to a Western European middle-class Jewish family. She was the favourite of her caring, intelligent, strong and loving parents. She did very well in school, but did not have it easy, even before the war. She was often lonely because her sisters never played with her, and as a child her self-esteem was low because she felt inferior to them.

Life as she knew it came to a sudden end when she was twelve and the Germans invaded. Her parents dispersed her sisters and Rita to different places in the country, having paid families to keep them safe. Rita spent the war as a hidden child, from the ages of twelve to seventeen living with four different families. She recalls that her only thoughts were for the reunion with her parents. Rita never saw her parents again. She subsequently learnt to hide her feelings and developed an artificial stoicism that she maintained for the rest of her life. She was content with being numb, which allowed her to defend against the terror of being alone.

After the liberation she reunited with her sisters, but eventually confirmed that her parents had been murdered in a concentration camp. Thereafter she began to reconstruct an external life that belied her inner emptiness. She went to school, married and had two daughters, before migrating to Canada, where the family lived an intellectually and socially fulfilling life. She did not work, but lectured about her experiences of the war, and people marvelled at her strength and capacity to carry on despite all that had happened to her. She thought of herself as always partially on automatic emotional pilot, apparently engaged on the surface but always holding her true emotions in reserve. Through her adult years as a mother and wife, life was relatively smooth, and when there were problems she went to great pains to maintain emotional calm.

Then, in old age, her life once again transformed. Her family as she knew it disintegrated in a short period of calamity heralded by the professional disgrace of her prized older daughter, a successful professional who encountered ethical problems, leading to her public disgrace. Emotions which she no longer could deny or numb flooded into Rita. For the first time in her life she became overtly depressed, and at the age of 75 she came for help.

Rita said she was depressed because of her worries about her daughter. She presented with symptoms of moderate depression, with daily crying, impaired sleep, loss of appetite, withdrawal of interest and reduced motivation and experience of pleasure. She said she would be happy to die, but would not actively attempt suicide. At first blush, this was a common form of depression associated with a specific problem that should have responded well to a combination of medication and focal psychotherapy to help her work through the disillusionment about her daughter.

Indeed, in the first several weeks of treatment her depression stabilised on the combination of psychotherapy and medication—but then the full complexity of this problem began to unfold. Her second daughter revealed that she had been abused by her father as a young child, unbeknown to Rita. A short time later, Rita herself had a very mild stroke. While it was not sufficient to impair her functioning, it made her own vulnerability evident to her. As a last straw, her husband began to show signs of early dementia. And because of their feelings about their father, both daughters cut off contact with Rita.

This story, while somewhat more dramatic than most, is not different in form from many presentations of depression in late life. What initially looks like one issue in therapy evolves in a short time into something quite different, often because the lead problem is but the vanguard of other problems.

For Rita, now 76, the sudden transformation in her life evoked severe emotional conflicts, not only because of the pain of the recent events, but because the losses precipitated by those events mobilised old grief and feelings about herself that she had never put to rest. Her belief in the strength and support of her family had given her an external coating of security and safety and normalcy. This was now irreparably breached.

Needless to say, she now had therapeutic needs far beyond those first presented. Because of the loss of her other sources of comfort and intimate relationships, therapy became the only place, she said, where she could safely talk about all aspects of her life and about her pain. She revealed that it was the first time in her life that she had talked of the two worlds in which she had always lived—her adult 'present' world of friends and family, which she said often felt empty and false, and the world she had lost in the war . . . which secretly had always been the one more real to her, despite being unbearably associated with unresolved mourning.

From the point of view of treatment, Rita's story illustrates the complexity of psychogeriatric therapy. A complex situation requires a model of therapy that has room for flexibility to change with shifting realities in the patient's life, and that is simple enough to be practical. Rita needed four main things: education, adaptation to current realities, correction of many distortions of her thinking, and help dealing with the past as it now invaded the present.

From a therapist's viewpoint, Rita's needs were reframed as follows:

- she had to deal with the destruction of her idealised view of her older daughter, and shortly thereafter with the illnesses that she did not understand in her husband and herself
- she had to reframe her view of her family and her adult life in light of the new information about abuse in the family
- she had to develop new strategies for relating to her daughters
- she had to address her repressed loss and abandonment— remnants of the war re-evoked by current separations (the war continued to intrude into most of the issues: she frequently talked about how the calamity of her present family life felt like the effect the Holocaust had on her before)
- she needed to manage hopelessness associated with older age—'What have I to hope for now?'

How did therapy progress?

First, as therapist, I had to recognise that brief focal interventions were not going to solve this situation and a longer-term perspective was necessary. As we began she confronted many things, for instance, encountering and dealing with the loss of the husband she once had. This intensified lifelong feelings of emptiness, only now she said that because of her age there was no hope of repair. When younger she could fight, but now she did not want to. She said if it were not for her caring for her family she would end her life.

Working with ageing survivors of massive trauma like the Holocaust inevitably means working with unresolved and, for some, unresolvable massive grief. It means addressing the severe identity disturbances and sometimes impaired capacity for intimacy associated with the numbing effects of trauma. Rita herself wondered at one point if her need to contain her feelings may have damaged her relationship with her children. This kind of therapy was also concerned with re-establishing Rita's sense of the continuity of her life. For example, she had always kept separate her inner world of loss, a life that had frozen her at the moment she was sent away by her parents. Living in two worlds prevented her from experiencing herself as a fully integrated person. To some extent she has felt like a stranger in her own life.

Themes of understanding who she 'really' was emerged repeatedly in the therapy, including approaching very intimate issues about her identity as a woman. Only in the therapeutic relationship has she allowed her full inner self to emerge. Hence this relationship has taken on a depth of meaning which she had never experienced elsewhere. The story of the final outcome remains to be seen, but Rita to this point has adapted to her painful struggles and has maintained the courage to carry on with her life. Therapy continues—likely an essential part of her continued survival.

Lessons learnt

Of course I cannot convey everything here, but I hope Rita's story demonstrates the rich complexity of depression in late life and helps to show how a therapist can make sense of a life like Rita's, to offer hope and healing. I learnt from her how a person can tolerate the intolerable and continue to bounce back from repeated assaults. She also reinforced for me how crucial the therapeutic relationship can be. The nature of the problems in her family meant that there was no emotionally safe place for her anymore. At this stage of her life, it was only in the process of therapy that she has been able to fully reveal her pain and isolation without fear.

Perhaps most important: Rita reinforced for me that the mere passage of time in someone's life does nothing to dampen the sharpness of memory, nor does it diminish the need to explore and express these memories to reconstruct the wholeness of one's identity and self.

Professor Joel Sadavoy

COGNITIVE BEHAVIOUR THERAPY (CBT)

Cognitive behaviour therapy is a standardised therapy that teaches the individual how to challenge and change dysfunctional thoughts, rather than trying to alter painful feelings directly. CBT focuses on altering maladaptive values, attitudes and thinking patterns. The model is based on Aaron Beck's (1976) theories of depression, and proposes that it is not the event itself, but rather how the depressed person interprets it that determines his or her feelings.

There are four main strategies, combined with 'homework' tasks, that are used to help the individual gain a greater sense of self-efficacy:

- identifying negative thoughts
- evaluating the validity of those thoughts
- substituting more realistic, positive responses
- modifying dysfunctional attitudes ('schemata').

Research indicates the efficacy of CBT for depression in older people.[4] Modifications for age ensure its greater success—see the 'Noteworthy' section at the end of this chapter. In the context of ageing, CBT needs to be more eclectic and to reference 'dynamic' issues in the person's life and relationships and relevant past events, as well as engaging with themes more common in older age, such as loss, low self-esteem and anxiety about the future.

It is a common scenario, as Victor observes in the next narrative, that 'sufferers of depression seldom seek help until they reach crisis point'. When he finally sought help, Victor successfully combined a variety of supports: medication, counselling, group therapy and CBT.

Challenge the thought, change the mood

> . . . there is nothing either bad or good but thinking makes it so.
>
> Shakespeare, Hamlet

Sydney was celebrating. The Olympics were in town and our brash metropolis, so often indifferent to strangers, was as full of bonhomie as a big country town. And where was I? Alone in my apartment nursing a crippled knee; isolated and immobile and prey to all manner of negative thoughts. The early retirement I had elected to take at the relatively youthful age of 64 and which had cut me off from an extensive social network no longer seemed such a bright idea.

Where were the fruits of sweet retirement Voltaire had written about, and where was the old enthusiasm that had seen me take that great leap into the unknown just twelve months previously? Why was I being engulfed by a flood of negative thoughts and nagged at by a tape recorder in my head that I couldn't turn off?

I tried watching the wall-to-wall TV coverage of the Games but concentration had deserted me. My once-inquisitive mind took no interest in the outside world, intent only on turning in on itself. This hadn't happened overnight. Some months earlier my arthritic knee finally gave up the ghost and I was pencilled in for knee surgery at a yet to be determined date. Even with crutches and painkillers, getting about was extremely painful, so I unwittingly stopped doing the things that gave me pleasure: mixing with friends, going to a movie, seeing a play, eating out. I know now that activity is the enemy of depression but back then I had innocently cast it aside and without it I had no defences against the advances of the black dog. I was an easy, almost willing victim.

I have been told that sufferers of depression seldom seek help until they reach crisis point. This was certainly the case with me, but once I reached out, help was fortunately on hand and treatment began almost immediately. There was the medication, in my case one of the older-style antidepressants usually more effective for people of my age. And there was counselling, group therapy sessions and a technique, new to me, called cognitive behaviour therapy (CBT). Essentially, the idea behind CBT seemed to be 'challenge the thought and change the mood'. Of course, it wasn't quite as simple as that; it had other strings to its bow, such as refocusing on the positive, managing problems and restoring balance to one's life. But its mood-changing properties were what worked best for me. I became an instant convert.

The Olympics have long gone; the dogs have barked and the caravan has moved on. And so it has been with my life since CBT but it is now the dog that has moved on. It's still there in the background but I have been given strategies for keeping it in its box. I consider myself one of the lucky ones, for there must be hundreds, possibly thousands, of people isolated by age and infirmity who are being visited by the kind of negative thoughts which made my life such a misery. Will they need to reach crisis point before they seek help? And when they do, will help always be available? With an ever-growing ageing population, these are questions which need to be urgently addressed. Victor

INTERPERSONAL THERAPY

Interpersonal therapy has also been found to be an effective treatment for depression in older people. This therapy helps people find new ways to relate to others, and to forge strategies to resolve losses, changes and conflicts in relationships. It assists people to build or better use their social support network, thus facilitating crisis management.

Interpersonal therapy proposes that the onset of any depression occurs in a social or interpersonal context, and that understanding this context can help the depressed person to identify the triggers and reasons for their depression, deal with them, and prevent them recurring. This therapy usually focuses on current rather than past relationships, looking at the immediate social context, and attempts to intervene in symptom formation and in the social dysfunction associated with depression, rather than aiming to change more enduring aspects of personality.[5]

OTHER PSYCHOTHERAPIES

There are many variations on psychotherapy—in addition to one-on-one talking therapies there are, for instance, music, art and writing therapies—and many 'brands', each with different emphases and approaches. Lists and descriptions are available on the internet. These more specialised therapies are usually offered in an inpatient setting.

THE ROLE OF THE THERAPIST

Good therapists have skills in common, regardless of the therapy they espouse: they are empathic (good listeners), non-judgemental (trained to listen without being critical), and they do not dictate what an individual 'should' do. The therapist provides a setting of unconditional positive regard for the client, and may encourage a person with depression to 'ventilate' (talk about things that are concerning and preoccupying them). Therapy may be structured to a particular pattern or follow the priorities of either party.

Sometimes the therapist needs to be mindful that he/she can unconsciously (or consciously) experience negative counter-transference towards an older patient, which may result in, for instance, ageist attitudes and therapeutic pessimism.

The trusting and accepting relationship that grows between the individual and the therapist (the 'therapeutic relationship') provides a microcosm—a smaller, safer version of the outside world—so that interactions with the therapist and resulting insights can be used as a means of understanding the way the individual re/acts in real life. The dynamic that grows within the therapist–patient relationship is a large part of the efficacy of therapy. 'Positive transference'—the individual's regard for and trust of the therapist—helps generate the energy and confidence to enable him or her to take up the tools for recovery; 'positive counter-transference' is the similar experience for the therapist.

Skilful psychotherapy can be protective at other levels, too. Feelings of relevance and purpose may be bruised as age forces older people from their accustomed roles. Being respected and attended to, despite initial reluctance at the 'pathologised' setting, can provide great solace.

In the next account, from Professor Dan Blazer, what began as mild psychotherapy has evolved into a comforting and supportive relationship that is valued and enjoyed by both doctor and client.

CASE NOTES

The old VIP

My experience with very important patients (VIPs) has mostly been inconvenient, unpleasant and unproductive. And somehow they often manage not to pay (for reasons I cannot fathom), so the experience is unprofitable as well.

A couple of years ago, I received a call from the son of a very prominent older man. The man's name would be recognised by almost everyone in our region. He was depressed, according to his son, and might be losing his memory as well. I could have claimed a schedule entirely booked for weeks in advance. Yet, in the spirit of full disclosure, I received the call while I was waiting to hit off the tenth tee at a local golf course. I could not assert that I was too busy. Therefore I agreed to see his father and set a time, hoping that he would not show up, as I was certain he had bounced from one doctor to another.

To my surprise, the 85-year-old VIP arrived at the scheduled time and had never seen a psychiatrist before our visit. Prior to entering my waiting room he checked in with our accounting department, arriving 45 minutes early so that he could make certain that he finished the paperwork before our appointment. He was alone, and upon introducing himself joined me in my office.

As he was a businessman with a widespread reputation of being able to charm one's socks off, I was on my guard. Yet I found myself instantly warming to him. He seemed honest and sincere and though he was not quite certain why his son had asked for the appointment, he was polite, appreciative and willing to talk. Yes, he had been feeling down recently but he thought it was because he could not walk down the street of his small town and just greet people as he had in the past. He felt like a stranger in his home town! Small towns had changed. In the past there were usually three or four restaurants where good friends dropped in for a cup of coffee in the morning or a leisurely lunch. Now there was no place other than McDonald's, and the fast-food site was so noisy and rushed that one could not sit and talk. He daily spent time at his office but other than a constant stream of people who wanted some favour, such as a letter of recommendation, few came to visit him. His wife had 'a life of her own' visiting family and friends so he was often at home by himself during the evenings.

The old VIP met criteria for major depression, but not severe. He experienced trouble sleeping, had lost about two and a half kilograms, was mildly agitated and definitely less interested in his activities than in the past. He experienced very mild memory impairment that in no way interfered with his usual activities. He did, however, have trouble hearing, as do many older adults, especially in crowds. In the confines of my office, we communicated without difficulty. I began him on an antidepressant. Six weeks later he told me he was sleeping better and was less irritable. After our third visit, his son accompanied him and I spoke with the son privately.

I explained that I did not think his father needed formal psycho-therapy, yet the son believed he did. So I agreed to continue to see the old VIP. I did not expect him to be willing to meet so regularly (he lived in another town and was often called on for meetings or special engagements), yet he agreed. Over the subsequent two years he has rarely missed an appointment. Every time he is forced to reschedule he informs me days in advance and always apologises.

How has the psychotherapy progressed? I encouraged him to exercise more and he agreed to regular visits to a local gym where he swims and works with light weights. Overall, he has been most willing to listen to suggestions I make, noting that I am certainly correct that he must change his behaviour. Frequently, however, he does not follow up on my suggestions and is later apologetic. I began to write 'prescriptions', usually two copies—one he keeps for himself and one he gives to his staff assistant. This plan has led to a number of changes, such as a willingness to give his staff assistant more authority to screen the multiple requests made of him. He admitted that he has felt overwhelmed with many of the requests and was not certain how to manage them. Despite the obvious demands upon his time and his person, which we discuss frequently during our sessions, he has never expressed any sense of self-importance deriving from these requests and responsibilities, but rather a deep sense that he should help his friends and society when he can. Many of the requests do not come from anyone he knows personally.

Yet this is only part of the story. We continue to meet about every three weeks. And the old VIP and I just talk. Following a few such 'sessions' I realised that he is truly lonely and isolated, much more so than his overt lifestyle reflects. He has no-one with whom to talk. His family, though very supportive, are also extremely busy. During monthly family gatherings, which include over twenty people when grandchildren are counted, the old VIP usually sits in his easy chair observing the cacophony of noise and the flurry of activity around him. Yet his children have on more than one occasion not only arranged a vacation for him but have accompanied him and his wife to negotiate the difficulties of travel. Rarely, however, do his children sit with him at his beach cottage and talk on the deck.

His fantasy is to build an old-time 'filling station', such as peppered the southern United States years ago at nearly every rural crossroads. These petrol stations served more purposes than simply providing fuel for a pick-up truck. One could buy various sundries or simply drop by, pull up a chair into a circle and talk. No Twitter, no Facebook, no texting. Simple, slow, relaxed conversation about sport, politics, the weather, families and getting on in the world. Of course, the old VIP had 'gotten on' very well, so well that he could have purchased half the county in which he lived. Yet he could not purchase or build back the community which he feels he has lost over the years. 'I have outlived them all. No-one left with whom I can talk.' And so we talk. He tells stories, interesting stories, and I listen. At times he is frustrated and we do some problem-solving together. I wonder, however, if our conversations may be no more complex than if we were just chatting in a restaurant or sitting around the pot-bellied stove in a filling station.

During my training to become a psychiatrist I was taught the dangers of counter-transference, namely how our preconceived perceptions of our patients shape our interactions before we even meet them, and potentially throughout our contact with them. My feelings about older people with views of themselves as deserving special treatment due to past accomplishments has been an issue for me since I can remember, for reasons not important to review here. Despite the fact that I gravitated to geriatrics for my specialty practice because I truly enjoy most elders, I am innately suspicious of those who ask for special privilege. The old VIP taught me most important lessons.

VIPs, given their position in society, often receive increased deference and unique favours. That I knew. Yet the old VIP pays a price that most of us do not recognise. First, he is called upon for special favours—favours that often overwhelm him. Second, regardless of one's position in society, loneliness is a very real problem that transcends psychiatric diagnoses and 'doctor–patient relationships'. Third, the old VIP can experience depression like anyone else and deserves my best care, the same care I try to provide to all of my patients. Yet his care must be contextualised, just as the care of each of my patients. Have I been derelict to my responsibilities as a psychiatrist by trying to be a friend to and conversational companion with him? Perhaps, yet it feels right and in this case I am going with my feelings, maybe against cost-effective practice.

The old VIP is happier than when I first saw him, he is functioning quite well and he often tells me how much our visits mean to him. We care for and about our patients. I do wonder at times whether I am not the doctor I should be because the old VIP in some ways takes the 'work' of therapy out of our relationship. I enjoy his company and I appreciate that he seems to enjoy mine. I believe we must recognise that if we truly wish to help our patients, often it is important that they care about us and our friendships with them as well as our professional competence.

Professor Dan Blazer

SENSITIVITIES OF THE 'THERAPEUTIC ALLIANCE'

No matter how sincere, open and skilled a clinician is when offering therapy and solace, interactions both inside and outside of the world of therapy are delicate, and sometimes reactions are also outside rational control. The patient undergoing therapy is unwell, often vulnerable, and sometimes feeling very invaded. The therapist, despite compassion and sensitivity, can evoke a reaction in the patient that is beyond the control of each, as can be seen in the next report, contributed by Professor Robin Jacoby.

CASE NOTES

What's in a name?

Clinical failure teaches more than success. Not only do you learn about the patient but also about yourself.

When I first met him, 'Patrick' was in his early 70s, a gardener-cum-handyman to aristocrats, and lived with his wife in a cottage on their estate. He was manic and was hospitalised. As I recall, there was nothing particularly remarkable about his manic mental state on that first occasion. He was somewhat disinhibited and irritable, not really challenging in his behaviour, but his wife was getting no sleep which was why he needed to come in to hospital. When he recovered from his manic state he soon fell into the Slough of Despond.

Patrick's father, a businessman, had been a strict, domineering, highly critical person who had shown his son no affection. Patrick had not lived up to expectations and was told by his father that he was a failure. As was often the case in those days with the unsuccessful in well-off English families, Patrick was 'sent to the Colonies'—Australia to be precise. There, still in his twenties, he worked on a farm, suffered a depressive breakdown, was admitted to a mental hospital and subjected to ECT [electro-convulsive therapy] without anaesthetic. He returned to England and did manual jobs, married a delightful and capable woman and had a son. He was a quiet, very deferential man who may not have been very bright but was loyal and hardworking. A good marriage is a favourable prognostic factor in psychiatry and this appears to have worked for Patrick. He had no relapse of his affective illness until old age.

Sadly, however, when his affective illness returned, it was one of those malignant bipolar disorders that never really gets better. The periods of remission between his manic and depressive episodes never lasted more than a few months and got shorter over the years. His depressions were so severe that we had to offer him ECT, and eventually his manic episodes would also respond only to ECT. Happily, the treatment with anaesthetic and kindness from everyone was accepted quite readily by him. Eventually, we reached a more or less (usually less) satisfactory steady state with maintenance ECT once a month. However, Patrick's depressions were painful to witness and his manic state was not much better because he was clearly pretty miserable then, too.

I have always objected to the promiscuous use of first names with older patients. It is now almost universal for staff to address patients in this way but I never did it unless invited by a patient. I always use 'Mr' or 'Mrs' plus the surname and expect to be addressed as 'Doctor' in return. When I spoke to Patrick I would call him Mr K . . . I believe that most older patients prefer it, but that probably tells you something about me.

One day, several years down the line, Patrick came into our clinical meeting to tell us how he was getting on. He was in a mixed affective state, certainly very depressed but manic enough to mention things he would never normally utter. He began to say how difficult he found it to relate to me. He was grateful for what I was trying to do for him but he found it hard to feel at ease in my presence, which made it difficult to tell me how he was feeling. Everyone else, he said, called him Patrick but I called him Mr K . . . I explained that it was my way of showing him respect but if he wanted me to call him Patrick, I would. There was a long pause . . . someone coughed. Then he said quietly, 'You remind me of my father.'

I do not recall how I extricated myself from that conversation. All I can remember is how distressed I felt. On the whole I think that I have related well to my patients, although no doctor invariably succeeds. My formality, intended as a mark of respect, was symbolically authoritarian for Patrick. It represented power, in the face of which he had been deferential all his life, his first paternal experience of it having been entirely adverse. But I do not believe that this was the essence of his difficulty relating to me. By this time we all knew that he was never going to be completely well again; he himself knew it. His father had imprinted on him a permanent sense of failure and here was one of his greatest failures of all: he was not going to recover. When he was depressed he abjectly blamed himself. When he was manic he felt that his father would have blamed him. In his mixed affective state that day both versions applied and merely increased his dejection. It distressed me then and, long after Patrick has died, it still distresses me now.

Professor Robin Jacoby

As the more educated and affluent post-war generation ages (the so-called 'baby boomers'), there may be a dramatically increased demand for psychotherapy because of awareness of its availability and effectiveness.[6] Despite initial unfamiliarity with psychological concepts, those grown older are often the most appreciative and receptive of therapy of any age group, whether therapy is brief or extended. They have sharp antennae for the subliminal medical attitude, 'There's nothing more that I can do for you'—and, reciprocally, appreciate the chance to review their life's course, and perhaps set off on a new direction rather than remaining stranded. American research found that management of depression in older people using combined antidepressant medication and psychotherapy helped around 80 per cent of the group to recover and remain well.[7]

OVERVIEW OF TREATMENTS

A recent review of research literature listed the treatments with the best evidence of effectiveness, in this order: antidepressants, electroconvulsive therapy, cognitive behaviour therapy, psychody-namicpsychotherapy,reminiscencetherapy,problem-solvingtherapy, bibliotherapy (for mild to moderate depression) and exercise. There was limited evidence to support the effectiveness of transcranial magnetic stimulation, dialectical behaviour therapy, interpersonal therapy, St John's wort and folate in reducing depressive symptoms.[8]

A recent study from Holland concluded that bright light therapy may hold promise for alleviating mild to moderate depression in those who are older. Patients exposed to three weeks of one-hour early-morning bright light therapy (pale blue and of approximately 7500 lux) experienced a lifting of their mood and a lowering of the stress hormone cortisol.

Improvement in mood via bright light therapy is attributed to a resetting of the body clock that normalises the body's natural circa-dian rhythms by influencing the hormone melatonin.[9] Disturbance of circadian rhythms is also implicated in seasonal affective disorder (SAD)—a mood disorder that arises at the change of seasons—and bright light therapy has been found to be helpful for treating SAD also. Disruptions to circadian rhythms are also implicated in post-natal depression.

Advances in neurobiology and brain imaging technology are helping to link research findings from different fields of emotion and mood, and enable the 'mapping' of depression. Charting the physiological changes involved in emotion during ageing will better pinpoint the biology of mood disorders in the elderly, and the phys-iological effects of bereavement. Biological markers that may be present in the blood are also under investigation. There are already ways of testing for individual differences in rates and effectiveness of metabolism of medications (how the body processes the drugs).

MODIFYING NEURAL PATTERNING

Recent laboratory and functional findings have led to reassessment of brain 'plasticity'—that is, the capacity for the brain's further development and reorganisation after we have become older. Until recently it was thought that the brain upon maturation had little potential for regeneration, though improvement and compensation—over a limited period—had been observed in individuals with brain injuries such as stroke or trauma. However, it has only been recently noted, from training sessions with individuals, and from autopsy, that new neurons are produced in the mature brain and that existing neurons can revitalise. Optimistically, lost functions can be reacquired and new skills mastered by even the oldest old. The 'Noteworthy' section at the end of Chapter 1 has already outlined some facets of neurogenesis.

It's known that neural patterning can be modified by medication—for instance, see the case notes about Harry in Chapter 4. There are also other tools that can assist our brains to forge fresh neural pathways. Techniques such as meditation, relaxation, yoga and mindfulness therapy are effective—with repeated and committed practice—and can inhibit the brain's amygdala from driving disturbing emotions to the left pre-frontal cortex of the brain and into our awareness. Such practical mental and physical exercises can assist us to adopt new habits and ways of thinking and unlearn those that are less suitable.

ACQUIRING NEW HABITS AND SKILLS

> The trick is growing up without growing old.
>
> Casey Stengel

Unlearning 'bad' habits and substituting new and better habitual ways of functioning is a skill all in itself. New habit formation— or old habit 'extinction'—takes varying amounts of time, commitment and effort. There is much advice available from therapists, libraries and the internet about tricks to help effectiveness and motivation, and about how to substitute better routines that are incompatible with the unwanted behaviour. Gathering information about tackling habits will also help identify ways in which individuals 'self-sabotage' . . . it is natural to subvert new behaviour by reverting to past routines. Targeted interventions and follow-up by a therapist is helpful.

It is also an expected feature of our natural resistance to change that we may revert, even after initial success, to previous habits—consider for example the number of times that a smoker has to give up cigarettes before there is complete success. Such slips require an even more concerted effort to re-adopt and more thoroughly establish the new and preferred behaviour.

NOTEWORTHY

Modifying 'talking therapies' for older people

The following techniques help make psychotherapy more accessible to older people. None of these therapies is likely to be of major benefit in cases of melancholic or psychotic depression when used alone, but they can assist if used in conjunction with medication. The following points are adapted from an article by Koder, Brodaty and Anstey.[10]

Making therapy more effective for older people
- Therapy techniques need to be adapted to the normal cognitive changes associated with ageing, such as slower new learning and less rapid ability to shift between abstract concepts.
- Shorter and more follow-up sessions, slower pacing and awareness of an older person's possible difficulties with hearing, vision and mobility make therapy more effective.
- Cognitive, sensory and perceptual impairment may be helped by the use of printed material, frequent reviews of progress, bright lighting, low background noise and sitting closer.

- A more concrete, problem-solving approach is helpful, where practical situations can be discussed and greater weight placed on action and goal-setting.
- Education level, degree of 'psychological mindedness' and any cognitive changes should be factored in.
- 'Homework' and use of role plays is effective in fostering learning.
- 'Attributional' retraining may counteract the loss of the older individual's sense of control. This means training people to reframe their views and attribute 'failures' to external, unstable and specific causes, and 'successes' to internal, stable and global factors.
- Be aware that cognitive 'styles' can be common to a group of a particular age. Older people may be reluctant to ask questions if confused, may show personal reserve, and have different ways of viewing problems.
- Beliefs about the origins of depression need to be challenged—older people may take on the passive role of 'waiting to be cured' by the physician, or may fail to acknowledge or understand that symptoms are manifestations of a depressive illness. They need to become active partners in their own therapy, taking responsibility together with the therapist for finding effective ways of recovery.
- Education about the purpose and uses of therapy should address some of the underlying issues of ageism and shame.
- The sense of being 'too old to change' must be disputed. Cognitive behaviour therapy can be reframed as helping an older person to learn how thoughts can influence mood so that this strategy is seen as a tool to enable better

management of depression—in contrast to advocating that the therapy can 'cure'.

- Therapist respect for the older person and his or her wisdom and experience enhances the power of therapy, as does therapist collaboration with the therapy's direction and goals.
- Possible difficulties can arise for an older person in accepting the credibility of a younger therapist, as well as harbouring feelings of stigma about being 'in therapy'.
- Therapists should be aware of the possibility of their own negative counter-transference feelings towards certain older people, and adverse expectations about success with older patients, mingled with pessimism about growing old themselves.
- Gradual termination of therapy is recommended, as severing relationships is a sensitive area as people age. Also, more gradual 'tailing off' of therapy preserves what has been learnt.
- Group therapies have potential for those who are older: a group can lessen isolation and encourage more open discussion.
- Involvement of significant others (e.g. spouse, relatives or close friends) in the latter stages of therapy can enhance its retention and application.
- The offer of regular review plus support in case of crisis appears to be especially valued by older people. Booster and follow-up sessions also help maintain therapeutic gains.

9

Ageing and coping
with care

I still have a full deck; I just shuffle slower now.

Anon

Gerontology is currently moving from a multidisciplinary to an interdisciplinary science. There is growing integration of health care professionals around awareness of the complexities of age as shaped by birth cohorts (or groups), the social history intersecting their biographies, genetic make-up and the overlay of social class, gender, race and ethnicity. The current 'crop' of people 65 and over, and subsequent generations, will have very different expectations of growing older to those of our predecessors and will drive these processes further.[1]

AGEIST STIGMA AND AMELIORATING IT

Being old is when you know all the answers but nobody asks you the questions.

Anon

To date in Westernised countries, older people have often been accorded low status. Ageing is associated with the three Ds: disease, disability and death (not to mention dementia, delirium and depression!). In the context of free-market-based economies, age is associated with decline, limitations and increasing irrelevance and cost; youthful 'can do' is more pertinent to earning capacity and the ability to secure what is valued materially.

Some sociologists argue that as people age they shape their future choices on the basis of their past patterns (so-called 'continuity theory'). This behaviour is seen as adaptive, consistent with past habit and accords with others' expectations. Continuity theory argues that such habituation explains the circumscribed social experience of older adults: as people age and relinquish physically or mentally demanding spheres, the remaining roles available to them become more rigidly theirs alone, and there is a dearth of new and respected roles that they can transition to.

Stigma can arise from feelings of uselessness and irrelevance in response to such increasing constraints, and shame makes older people less likely to acknowledge distress or seek and accept help. Self-stigma also makes us see ourselves as 'too old to change' and may, as well, reduce our expectations of therapy should we engage in it. Additionally, and as mentioned before, when psychological help is sought, 'reverse ageism' can lead to an older patient questioning a younger therapist's competence. The therapist, too, needs to unpack any covert ageism in his or her own 'baggage'.

ENCOURAGING A SHIFT IN ATTITUDES TO AGEING

> We've put more effort into helping folks reach old age than into helping them enjoy it.
>
> Frank A. Clark

A radical shift in attitudes to getting older would make the single biggest difference in older people's lives. The widespread negative perceptions of older age seriously limit the opportunities, activities and choices open to those who are ageing and also diminish their sense of what is possible. Stereotypes are translated into disrespectful and disempowering behaviours and practices—by friends and families as well as professional caregivers. Older people may then internalise such attitudes, further decreasing their sense of self-worth.

Such ageism could be replaced with a positive view of older age as a time of opportunity, continued contribution and fulfilment of ambitions. Helping the public become aware of the way they regard older people, assumptions in the workplace and the things that older people are excluded from is a start. Positive attitudes are encouraged by policy and legislation that leads to culture change. Age discrimination legislation can also help and laws can set the stage for changing the way people behave. Attitudes align themselves to harmonise with new behaviours.

Greater visibility is effective. It is possible to do more at an organisational level to instil positive attitudes towards older workers and customers, and to seek out, train and employ older people in appropriate jobs. More conspicuous involvement of older people in the community, for instance as aides for disadvantaged younger children, would also help bring ageing out of the shadows.

BETTER INTEGRATION OF CARE FOR OLDER PEOPLE

For the frailer aged, a smaller support base and rising costs of care are already driving new solutions. An Australian university is currently setting up an integrated 'one-stop shop' to improve continuity of health care and community support for those growing older. It aims to prevent the dislocations that arise when different types of care are managed by different tiers of government, and plans to better link sub-acute care (palliative care, rehabilitation and older persons' mental health), residential and community-based aged care.[2]

CARE FOR THE OLDEST OLD

If you live to be one hundred, you've got it made. Very few people die past that age.

George Burns

It has been said that this is 'the age of age'. The steady increase projected in the number of oldest old makes even more relevant the motto adopted by health care workers—that they are aiming to add life to years, not just years to life. Broadly, there are two levels of residential care for those who have become too infirm to manage in their own home: high care is provided by a nursing home and low care by a hostel. Each facility supplies personal care, meals, laundry and cleaning. High-level care also includes 24-hour nursing care.

In the last decades much effort has been put into the design and management of such care options so that the residents (and staff) don't regard such accommodation as 'God's waiting room'. However, there is still a lot of financial pressure on both government-run and on privately owned facilities to return value for the money invested.

Community care is a choice for older people who wish to remain in their own home, but who are having difficulty with home and self-maintenance. Tailored support services are available in this situation, including home-delivered meals, transport and domestic help, home modifications, counselling and intensive 'care packages' that comprise home nursing and day centre activities.

WHEN THERE IS ENOUGH TIME FOR PHYSICAL CARE ONLY

> Small grandchild touching aged skin: 'Gran, why do you always wear gloves?'
>
> Anon

A continuing dilemma remains in high-care institutions: the intention to deliver compassionate care may not be enough to offset the depersonalisation inherent in a large facility. Under-trained and low-paid staff work at heavy nursing jobs under time pressure, which means that each shift is occupied with providing basic physical care, with little time left over for interaction with their charges.

'Maria', in the following narrative, shows the pressure on nursing home staff to complete a never-ending round of physical care which robs them and their charges of time for interaction and mutual nurture. The frail elderly, as do we all, flower in the warm contact of personal relationships, but various pressures mean that it is very difficult to provide nursing home care that is able to meet multiple physical and psychological needs.

Dorothy slips through the cracks

 As a migrant, an unrecognised midwife and a single mother of two, I supported my family by caring for the elderly in local nursing homes. Most of my working life concerned a 50-bed facility, operated by a qualified nurse with four carers. Night duty consisted of only two carers, headed by a professional nurse who most of the time was bogged down by administrative duties. At least a quarter of the population was incontinent, the physical nature of duties was arduous but in order to be with my children during the day I had to do it.

Changing soiled bed linen took half the night, then we had to start all over again. Regardless of youth and fitness, around 3 a.m. my knees would begin shaking uncontrollably, signalling complete exhaustion. The two of us worked like machines, there were no tender words or reassurance during the changing process; we had to be efficient and time conscious with the only goal in sight—preventing the development of decubitus [bed sores] at all costs.

One day, however, I had the pleasure of admitting Dorothy, a 75-year-old lady. Her only reason for seeking supported care was anxiety—left by fear when her elderly neighbour was robbed and beaten a short while before. Dorothy was a delightful person, looking for security, companionship and belonging. Sometimes her juvenile humour brought me to tears of laughter. To combat her boredom, she helped me in the laundry. One night while folding the giant underpants, she asked my opinion about the fashion, women wearing pants. 'I like to wear pants' was my reply. Then she lifted some huge bloomers, commenting: 'Look, with black stockings these would be awesome on you!' I would have loved to take her home, to be my mother and the grandmother of my children.

This dream quickly faded due to her unacceptable death. The downhill road started very early. Since the majority of the population was bedridden or suffering dementia, Dorothy found herself lost in the crowd. While I was able to light her angelic smile, it was a short discourse—I had to carry on with attending to 'real' need. One night, only some weeks after she had arrived, I was standing behind the front desk when she passed by without noticing me. Calling after her seemed not to catch her attention and when I approached and cuddled her she gently pushed me away, asking, 'Do I know you?' I was shaken and to check her thinking I asked, 'Dorothy, how old are you?' Looking through me with sightless eyes she replied, 'I don't really remember, but living on the old age pension has made me feel ancient.' That same night she slipped in the bathroom and broke her hip. After the operation to repair it, she returned to the nursing home and passed away shortly after.

The reader may conclude that, as these events happened in the 1970s—in the 'stone age'—things have surely significantly changed since then! Nothing could be further from the truth. Nursing homes are under more pressure than ever before and the numbers of elderly are increasing with unprecedented speed. In the Western world many of the older generation are left alone as the nuclear family shrinks. Separated, invisible and unrecognised, despite their immeasurable wisdom, they quickly disintegrate mentally and physically. As a measure of their frustration, they support the aim of Dr Death—to legalise voluntary euthanasia.

In ancient Greece, democracy was widely supported by the Council of Elders. This group was committed to maintaining a well-ordered human life—a life lived in the polis for the polis. The desired outcome for individuals, young and old, was 'eudaimonia', the flourishing that comes from the exercise of a virtuous disposition. Another inspiring example: in today's China an astronomical number of elderly gather daily in parks to practise mental and physical exercises to keep them mobile—engendering self-respect and a feeling of belonging.

Happiness is the glue that unites us all into a cohesive whole, and it has only a limited connection with financial profit. Bureaucrats and bean-counters need to recognise (on their way to older age) that the elderly in our society are an ASSET, not a liability, and that we are all better off by their inclusion. Maria

Interviews with nursing home staff conducted by the National Ageing Research Institute (NARI) indicated that staff appreciated the rewards derived from good relationships with residents, and had a strong desire to meet residents' emotional needs. However, staff continuity was a problem, as was lack of time to deliver holistic care.[3]

Some opinions from older people about improving the quality of their residential care are collated in the 'Noteworthy' section at the end of this chapter. Their reactions and comments outline ways in which more 'soul' could be added to combat the impersonality of institutional care.

DEPRESSION IS A PROBLEM IN RESIDENTIAL AGED CARE

Every man desires to live long, but no man would be old.

Jonathan Swift

Depression is under-diagnosed and under-treated in aged care facilities. Depression in this setting may be up to three times the rate of that in older people living in the community. Again, there is the notion that being 'down' is normal when one is older. Complicating this further is difficulty with diagnosis and, as mentioned earlier, the potential for confusion with other disorders, such as dementia or apathy. And dementia itself is associated with depression.

While every decade sees improved conditions for those in institutionalised care, the institutions themselves can be inherently 'depressogenic' (tending to cause depression). When questioned about their experiences, residents disclose feelings of fear, isolation, loss and helplessness, additional to the strain of coping with cognitive and physical impairments. Furthermore, pain management may also be inadequate.[4]

FINDING MEANING IN LATE LIFE

It's sad to grow old, but nice to ripen.

Brigitte Bardot

Much current research focuses on what contributes to meaning and purpose in older age. Aged care residents in one study identified two main values as being important to them: being 'good' and being 'of use'. Being good was linked with achievements—such as being a good worker, a good provider, a good husband, wife, mother, son or friend. Associated themes included having independence, working hard, helping others, making a contribution, not complaining and not being a burden.

Loss of function and independence with increased age posed a major threat to the second value: being of use. Some residents were able to find ways to be of use to others within their care facility and were proud of this contribution. They also drew pride from remembering and talking about their past lives and achievements. Having someone to listen to them and who valued their stories was comforting and affirming.[5]

Don't make them feel older than they are

One might ponder whether depression in older age is the mark of mourning rather than melancholia; mourning for both the self-lost and a self-to-be-lost? Shying away from company, not wanting to participate in activities, fearing intimate contact with friends and families lest it betray one's forgetfulness are only part of the territory of age and these can be utterly debilitating.

In more concrete terms, the most pressing concern for the older generation is not being made to feel older than they actually are. Likewise for family and professional carers of older people, it is essential that they are not the sole 'ears' of those suffering from the slings and arrows of older age.

Part of the solution to depression's onset in later age is not only its management but also finding ways to mitigate its effects. Carers must have supervisors that they, too, can turn to for attention and feedback. Such supervisors must have ready access to research in the fields of dementia and depression which advocates new approaches to caring and being cared for in this age group.

Recently, my eleven-month-old son needed to be seen by a doctor. We entered the waiting room. It was filled with older people—and silence. However, by the time we left, the five elderly gentlemen closest to us were engaged in conversation. My gregarious son had crawled to each of the men, 'introduced' himself and made them laugh. The lift this scrap of young life had brought to the melancholy atmosphere in the surgery was palpable, and both my happiness and my son's wellbeing were enhanced by the visit. This experience made me wonder if 'crèches' that used the skills of the older generation were possible. By that I mean combining children with people over 70, carers with nannies, family members with mothers. As a family living far from our grandparents, we often long for a grandmotherly touch or a grandfatherly joke that is the unique feature of this older generation, who, without the pressures of work and with the hindsight of experience and child-rearing, are able to 'be with' children in ways my partner and I cannot.

After my parents could no longer look after my grand-mother at home, she went into the local nursing home. The home and the staff were perfectly good but I thought her rapid decline was due to two things: restrictions on contact with her grandchildren—for whom she was a significant figure and who did not judge her slight dementia and slowness of body; and the Anglo-Saxon environment of the home—being Croatian, she was culturally in a foreign milieu which made her feel like an outsider.

Her estrangement brings me to my last point: that early cultural ties and histories resurface at the end of one's life and they need to be accommodated and interwoven into every-day life. To neglect such possibilities of comfort is like refusing to give a tired child their favourite doll. It ignores opportuni-ties which can allow the self to foster a psychical reintegration (rather than disintegration). This brings the subject back to the community. If, as the etymology of the word 'community' suggests ('with unity'), we understand our own happiness as interlinked with that of others, then the imperative to connect with older people and their carers becomes not an act of charity but, rather, a contribution to our social, generational and personal wellbeing for each of us.

Combating depression in older people might at a first glance seem like reflecting mirrors: where to start and how to pinpoint the origins? For carers, the task is often daunting, multifaceted and demanding. Perhaps the most frustrating aspect is the paradox of how to make someone happy by arguing that life looks good, even as the person approaches its end. How do you comfort and enliven those who, truthfully, have some challenges to be glum about?

Perhaps the approach needs to be gentler: we can hear, see and even predict the feelings associated with ageing, and as a result we can listen and take action to counteract rather than ignore such feelings. Feelings of dejection through losses, the burden of failing health and irrational fears in the face of these pressures need to be expressed, otherwise denial and stigma thrive.

We can value the hindsight of older people and use it to engender some kind of foresight to smooth both their and our path. We can act in solidarity with them to enhance the experience of these last valuable years. Claire

OPTIMISING THE QUALITY OF AN AGED CARE FACILITY

. . . old age needs so little but needs that little so much.

Margaret Willour

Quality of life at any age is assessed by socioeconomic and physical measures including the income, housing and health status of individuals, then measures of how a person judges his or her life. The greater the individual's feelings of wellbeing and satisfaction with their lot, the more he or she is likely to engage in social activities, cultivate friendships and pursue interests; and these are all associated with increased life expectancy and improved health.

Most residential aged care facilities attempt to add as much quality of life as possible within institutional constraints. Researchers

Knight and Mellor aimed to capture what characterises a satisfying old age, and the most effective ways of providing the resources and programs to achieve it. They put together a framework to measure dimensions of social inclusion, prior to interviewing residents about their satisfaction with their aged care facility.

Their study considered variables such as:

- features of the aged care facility (size, location, age and ownership)
- resident factors (level and type of dependency, age and sex)
- impact of the facility and type of residents
- staff factors (staff satisfaction, professional development, care hours and staffing level, quality of volunteers).

These residence, resident and staff variables contributed to resident satisfaction, defined in terms of:

- accommodation (room size, storage, etc.)
- the facility (design, accessibility, outdoor areas, etc.)
- social interaction (level of activity, social life, contact with outside world, etc.)
- meals (amount and choice of food, temperature of food, etc.)
- staff care (staff attitude, respect for privacy, promptness in responding to requests, etc.) and
- resident involvement (level of input to decision-making in the facility).[6]

General findings from their study are collated, together with other research findings, in 'Noteworthy' immediately following.

NOTEWORTHY

Types of support older people prefer
Older people who required a high level of support, either in their own homes or in an aged care facility, were asked what

helped them to be more genuinely content. Here is a rephrasing of some of their wishes.

They sought:

- to be useful—active providers in the community; part of something bigger; not a burden
- for others to show a recognition of their past; and attention to and respect for what they had to say about the past and the present
- to be given genuine choice and more opportunity to decide, individually, what they would do and when—though they were grateful for the efforts of those who cared for them, and aware of the demands of such physical care
- more sensory richness in institutional settings, though they realised that functional design must be the basic template
- to be assisted to be as independent as they could be within functional limitations; for instance, 'colour highways' that help the forgetful to be more independent, and 'memory boxes' filled with personal photos and mementos outside their rooms
- a softening of the clinical feel of institutional settings, by colours, scents, outlook, furnishings, touch, animals, access to outdoor spaces, appropriate lighting . . .
- better solutions to risk—converting the conservatism arising from risk awareness into more creative ways of risk management
- for staff to have the opportunity to be more person-oriented and not so task-oriented; for tasks to be secondary to the person
- to see staff able to form more of a relationship with them,

thus creating some feeling of teamwork and 'family'—and thereby providing greater job satisfaction for staff too.

Markers of depression in aged care facilities include:

- weight loss
- reluctance to participate in activities
- forgetfulness
- repeated negative comments about staff or other residents
- flat and unresponsive presentation, monosyllabic answers to questions
- difficult or demanding behaviours
- general demoralisation; themes of not having anything useful to contribute
- expressions of hopelessness; questioning the point of going on.

Some remedies that can ameliorate depression in aged care include:

- ongoing support and regular visits from family and friends
- families being encouraged to develop relationships with key staff members; this also ensures useful feedback about how the resident is managing
- allowing prized personal belongings from the resident's earlier life—for instance furniture, framed photographs and favourite music can personalise a residential space
- while cognitive behaviour therapy and medication may be less useful to older residents, talking through the reasons for depression can help
- art and music therapy, exercise programs and pet animals may all help to reduce symptoms of depression
- more opportunities for visitors and staff to spend time talking with residents and forming relationships
- a regular 'talk and walk' program that combines conversation and exercise

- a 'life story book' can provide an absorbing interest, and also helps staff to get to know residents at a deeper level
- a visitors' book, so family and friends can coordinate visits
- appointing a key worker for each resident—a staff member who acts as that resident's advocate
- as much autonomy as can be garnered for each resident; and choice about style and time of activities to enable more personal control, involvement and purpose.

Adapted from research by Dr Dimity Pond and Professor John Snowdon from an article by J. McCredie,[7] and an article by Dr Tess Knight and Professor David Mellor.[8]

10

Managing severe depression

The Living Will
Last night, my wife and I were sitting in the living room and I said to her: 'I never want to live in a vegetative state, dependent on some machine and a fluid diet. If that ever happens to me, just pull the plug.' She got up, unplugged the TV and threw out my beer.

Anon

Depression in those who are older can present challenges due to the biological changes of ageing. All medications have the potential for side effects. It is wise to check what these may be and whether comorbid (coexisting) conditions increase particular risks. Otherwise, treatment for depression that appears later in life is similar to that used for younger people with depression, with some differences in application, as outlined below.

- Medication usually has to be started at a lower dose and increased gradually to minimise side effects; it needs to be prescribed and titrated very carefully.
- Side effects and past response determine the choice of medication.
- There is a risk of interactions with other medications that an older person is likely to be taking, including complementary and alternative drugs, supplements and vitamins.
- Some antidepressant drugs, for example tricyclic antidepressants (TCAs), are more likely to have side effects and so are used less often.
- Selective serotonin reuptake inhibitors (SSRIs) may be less effective than dual-action antidepressants or a TCA in the treatment of melancholic or psychotic depression.
- Atypical antipsychotic medication may be used to augment antidepressants in the treatment of psychotic depression.
- Antidepressant medication may take longer to work in older people—trials of six to eight weeks or longer may be required.

- The use of benzodiazepines for insomnia and anxiety should be minimised. These provide only temporary symptom relief without addressing the actual depression, and possibly increase suicide risk. They may also increase the risk of falls and confusion.
- Treatment resistance is more likely when there is physical and psychological comorbidity.[1]
- When a person loses capacity to give informed consent, it falls to the closest relative or friend to give proxy consent.

Following initial good response to antidepressants:

- antidepressant treatment should be continued for at least six to nine months to prevent relapse or recurrence
- in older people at increased risk of depressive relapse, antidepressant treatment should be continued for at least two years
- in the case of those who have experienced three major episodes of depression or two severe episodes (e.g. have been hospitalised), it is recommended that antidepressant therapy be continued for life.[2]

'CLASSES' OF ANTIDEPRESSANTS AND TYPES OF DEPRESSION

Put simply, antidepressants fall into three classes: narrow-action, dual-action and broad-action medications. Broad-action medications are generally the most effective to combat melancholic depression.

In some cases where an individual has never taken an anti-depressant before, the clinician may start with a narrow-action antidepressant and then, if there is no benefit over a few weeks, move to a broader-action antidepressant or add an 'augmenting' medication to the antidepressant.

Although medication is the mainstay for severe depression, it does not mean that other support isn't needed. It's important to address problems that arise in tandem with the mood disorder via the most appropriate strategies—counselling, psychotherapy or other supports. While antidepressant medication (and sometimes the addition of other psychotropic medication) is a key component for the treatment of melancholic depression, some patients require and benefit from electroconvulsive therapy (ECT).

In studies of those with psychotic depression, antidepressant medications on their own assist about 25 per cent of patients; antipsychotic medications on their own assist some 33 per cent; while the combination of both of these medications assists about 80 per cent of individuals to achieve remission. Following remission, the antipsychotic medications can often be tapered and ceased. ECT may sometimes be required and beneficial.[3]

Individuals vary in their ability to metabolise drugs, with most drugs being cleared by liver enzymes. If the liver enzymes are overactive, those who are 'rapid metabolisers' may excrete most of the medication dose without it gaining 'traction'—thus, they may have little benefit and few or no side effects. Conversely, 'poor metabolisers' have or develop enzymes on exposure to medications that are slow or poor in metabolising drugs, so that such patients only need small doses to obtain benefits, and 'normal' doses may risk side effects.

THE USES OF ECT

As covered earlier, ECT is a useful treatment in melancholic and psychotic depression that has failed to respond to medication, or when depression is very severe. Extra precautions need to be taken with the anaesthetic, but older people tolerate the treatment quite well and may have better therapeutic response than younger patients. Professor John Snowdon describes the outcome for three of his patients.

CASE NOTES

ECT and late-life depression

I don't want to have ECT (electroconvulsive therapy). Not really. Well, not at all! However, over the last twenty years I've told count-less junior doctors and medical students that if ever I am one of their patients and I present with a seriously awful depressive illness, I want them to order ECT for me. I say it again. This is a living will, if you like!

I've told them I'd like them to try other ways of getting me better first—to try to understand why I'm depressed and to deal with obviously reversible causes. If I have what I think of as a biological depression (as opposed to one brought on by environ-mental or psychological influences), I've told them I'd like to try antidepressant medication first, unless I'm suicidal and so distressed by my depression that my doctors think it heartless and potentially risky to delay giving the treatment we know works best and fastest for psychotic and melancholic depression. If that's the case, I want it—even if at the time I'm indecisive and seem unable to give informed consent.

ECT is commonly dramatically effective—so why would I hesitate? I suppose it's partly a fear and dislike of having an electric shock [despite being anaesthetised and unaware]. We don't like the idea of being knocked out by anything. As I see it, ECT causes a shake-up of brainwaves sufficient to cause a brief period of unconsciousness (if one wasn't already anaesthetised). The fact that the shake-up of brainwaves, and changes in the disposition of neurotransmitters and electrolytes in the brain, are responsible for the improvements seen following ECT does help, it's true, to tell me it's worth it. But I suspect I'll be unable to think logically about whether to have ECT if I become severely depressed. That's why I'm writing this down while non-depressed.

I myself am an older person—aged 70. One of the great joys in life is when someone with a depression that's come on in late life gets completely better as a result of our treatment. I'll tell you about three people. One is 'Max', aged about 69, a delightful, outgoing, active man who, out of the blue, for no obvious reason, developed severe depression. He worried that he would not have enough money to go on living, he felt he'd let down his girlfriend, he lost ability to plan or think of anything other than negative perceptions, he thought of himself as worthless and he said that life wasn't worth living. He appeared not to have plans for suicide but nevertheless we kept a close eye on him. He looked glum, worried and slowed-up.

Max did not want ECT. We gave him antidepressant and anti-psychotic medication and he remained in hospital on a Mental Health Act order. He could not decide if he wanted to be in hospital but he had no better alternative. He did not think we'd be able to get him better. He saw himself as doomed.

After days of distress and no improvement we applied to the Mental Health Review Tribunal for authority to give Max ECT. He wasn't strongly objecting but nor was he consenting—and it was apparent that he did not have capacity to make informed decisions.

After having a number of ECTs (using the latest and best technology, and with an ECT expert supervising each treatment), Max made a complete and wonderful recovery. His relationship with his lady-friend again became active and joyful. His recovery made us all feel cheerful. He resumed all his activities and felt fully back to his normal self—so much so that he regarded himself as too strong and stable ever to have another depression. So after a few weeks he stopped taking his antidepressant medication, defying the strong advice we'd given him to stay on it!

Max became very depressed again. He came back into hospital—not quite as severely ill as the first time, but almost so. We recommended ECT. He said No! He commented that he always felt terrible after ECT. He declared that nothing could help him.

We said with confidence that ECT would certainly get him better again. 'Trust us!'

Because Max again was indecisive we felt it necessary to get the mental health tribunal to approve our plan to start ECT soon, to minimise the period of distress. He was given ECT and stayed on some medication.

After twelve ECT treatments he was minimally improved. I'd expected him to be much better by then. He'd become more certain that ECT made him worse and it should be stopped. However, we felt sure that ECT was the only treatment likely to cure him. We added a small dose of nortriptyline (an antidepressant) and obtained approval to continue treatment. And after a one-week gap and then two or three more ECTs, he was much better. After a few more he went home, remaining on a dual-action antidepressant. I can't say that Max accepts that ECT was responsible for his recovery. He will need continued follow-up by our community team to help overcome anxiety and concerns related to diminished self-confidence.

Another case to mention is that of 'Ellen', aged 92, a marvellously feisty woman who's been through heartaches in her time but always came back on top. She developed a severe psychotic depression last year and it failed to respond to medication and non-pharmacological approaches. An MRI showed some vascular changes in her brain, which could partly account for some treatment resistance. Because of heart problems there was a risk in giving her an anaesthetic [when administering ECT], but we and her family could not bear to see her continuing in distress. She was given four ECTs and became much more cheerful. A medical problem caused us to postpone further ECT; when the problem resolved she was still fairly cheerful and positive so we kept her on antidepressants and monitored progress. However, after two months (still on medication), her mood slumped and she again showed signs of psychosis. ECT was recommended and after three

ECTs she appeared well. After detailed discussion with her and the family, we arranged for Ellen to have maintenance ECT once a month. We and they consider it worth the risk in order not to have further prolonged interruptions to her enjoyment of life. She stays content and feisty!

ECT works, and those who seek to have it banned should look at the evidence. There have been studies that show who it's best for. I empathise with those who don't want to have it and for whom other treatments seem sensible, maybe preferable, and feasible. I have to admit that sometimes (never disastrously, thank God!) I've held out rather too long before agreeing to give ECT to a patient. For instance, 'June' was a very care-eliciting lady who seemed to get mental rewards from interfering with staff and other patients. She did not fulfil criteria for major depression or for any disorder that Professor Max Fink and other authorities say will respond to ECT. We called it atypical anxiety–depression. After months in hospital we gave her ECT and she got better. I'd been wrong not to give it earlier. Later she became mentally disturbed as before and we started ECT again. Once more her mood returned to normal and she had no residual memory problems. She has maintenance ECT, recently reduced in frequency to monthly.

I don't want to have ECT—unless a caring therapist is able to show me or my family that ECT really is what's needed!

Professor John Snowdon

THE USE OF LITHIUM THERAPY

Lithium 'prophylaxis' (treatment that prevents or stops a disorder) has been found to be effective in cases of severe and recurrent depression, and in the management of recurrent brief depression. Additionally, lithium therapy has been shown to significantly reduce the risk of suicide in those with recurrent depressive episodes.

In the next case note, from Professor David Ames, the effectiveness of lithium is demonstrated in the treatment of an elderly woman who had received extensive prior interventions for her very disabling and recurrent depression.

CASE NOTES

Recurrent severe depression and lithium

In 1990, while working at a large psychiatric hospital, I was in charge of the inpatient care of a woman in her 70s who required treatment with an extended course of ECT for severe depression characterised by distressing nihilistic delusions. Her history indicated nearly twenty prior similar episodes requiring inpatient treatment, usually on the psychiatric ward of a large general hospital. On this and previous occasions she had responded well to ECT but in the past she had always relapsed with severe depression within one to three years despite antidepressant prophylaxis. She had never experienced a manic episode and had never been treated with lithium.

My attitude to this case was 'nothing ventured, nothing gained'. I had been trained in the use of lithium by Brian Davies in the early 1980s and had been impressed by its efficacy in preventing recurrence of depression in some chronically relapsing cases. I started her on lithium and followed her for over fifteen years until her death from an incidental age-related disease. During this decade and a half, her husband entered a nursing home and later died; she had to leave her family home to live with her daughters; one of her three daughters developed a cancer with secondaries; and her grandchild suffered a retinal artery occlusion. The patient had at least three episodes of severe sciatica over this time, all of which required hospital care, and she was never free of discomfort and mobility limitation secondary to her back problems. Nevertheless, during this whole period she had only one depressive relapse, which remitted rapidly after inpatient treatment with ECT, and she remained cheerful and engaged with life and her family for over 95 per cent of the follow-up period. Lithium was very well tolerated and I reviewed her quarterly, with lithium blood levels performed a few days before each quarterly visit, and thyroid and renal function tests conducted annually.

Lessons learnt

What did I learn from this case? That even the most severe, recurrent, relapsing psychiatric disorders may respond to appropriate therapy, and that it is possible to use lithium safely over long periods in quite elderly patients. It does not help everyone, and not everyone can tolerate it, but when it works it can transform a life previously characterised by intense recurrent distress and suffering.

Professor David Ames

THE VALUE OF SOLACE

Don't let what you cannot do interfere with what you can do.
John Wooden

There are some cases where compassion is the most important contribution from a clinician to those facing intractable illness. The comfort provided by the steady compass and regard of health care professionals, and family and friends who keep vigil with the individual during his or her suffering, is sometimes unrecognised—except by the patient. Professor Kenneth Shulman recounts the experience of three of his patients.

CASE NOTES

When the black dog doesn't retreat—providing solace

Three lives where the therapist's compassion provides comfort

I have been a geriatric psychiatrist for over 30 years. As a clinician, this has been a most gratifying experience highlighted by a sense of satisfaction that the vast majority of people who suffer from depression can be helped. Not infrequently we see dramatic changes, from an importuning, agitated and dysfunctional individual to a delightful, bright, animated and productive human being. What could be more satisfying and rewarding?

It goes without saying that one is never 100 per cent successful. However, what do we do when the black dog doesn't retreat at all? What do we do when we encounter a very small but extremely challenging group of patients whose depression is truly intractable? It is an entirely different challenge for a clinician who is faced with the reality that no matter what they do, they cannot change the course of the illness. Somehow this is more palatable in medical and surgical circles: we accept the fact that metastatic cancer is an intractable, progressive condition ending in death. The sub-specialty of palliative care aims to help people die as painlessly, comfortably and with as much dignity as possible. But what of intractable depression? Do we do the same for this sub-population?

In recent years, I have followed three patients who have posed just such a challenge to my sense of therapeutic zeal and have forced me to come to terms with the fact that I will not be able to make a dent in the clinical course of some people's chronic or recurrent depression.

Mrs A began seeing me in her mid-70s while her husband was alive. She had a history of recurrent and remitting depressions which did not respond to pharmacological or psychological treatments, but responded dramatically to ECT. After her husband's death, she became depressed once again but this time refused ECT or repetitive transcranial magnetic stimulation. I persevered with multiple trials of combination medications, including monoamine oxidase inhibitors, but to no avail. I have continued to see her every six weeks to bimonthly, and each session is virtually identical. She is full of self-deprecation, hopelessness and passive death wishes. She becomes tearful and bemoans the fact that she is still alive. She often resists my home visits, making excuses for why she is not presentable or able to see me. However, inevitably she relents and sometimes even greets me with:'Doctor, I thought you'd given up on me—deservably so,' she adds. Mrs A is now in her mid-90s, still at home living with her sister, and we play out the same scenario every few months.

Mr B is a Holocaust survivor now in his late 90s. He began seeing me while still in his early 70s for a somatisation disorder. He complained of persistent severe headaches for which there was no neurological aetiology [cause], and for which there was no satisfactory treatment. Despite many attempts at pharmacological therapy and even ECT, he continued to complain of intractable headaches with episodic agitation. His family acquiesced to his request and that of his wife to remain in their home and they have around-the-clock help. Mr B is now frail, but his headaches persist in episodic fashion. The importuning and agitation persist and yet I come for visits every few months. They present me with a bottle of wine on each occasion, a gesture of appreciation for my visits, despite the fact that no improvement has been forthcoming.

Mrs C has a very strong family history of recurrent agitated depressions. She herself suffered from post-partum [postnatal] depression, but remained well for most of her adult life, until she again experienced a severe intractable depression in her 60s, for which she was referred to me. Eventually, ECT effected a dramatic remission but over the subsequent years, the states of remission became shorter and shorter—for the last five years she has required maintenance ECT, and has not remained well for a period of more than six weeks. It is heartbreaking to see her transformed repeatedly from a bright, animated and carefree individual to one who is severely agitated, importuning and overwhelmed. Despite maintenance ECT and multiple attempts at every mood stabiliser and antidepressant available, she continues to relapse. Yet, I continue to see her and her devoted husband, who come to me each time despite the fact that I have been unable to prevent the relapses. During the brief remissions, prior to the inevitable and dreaded relapses, they both express their appreciation—'Doctor, you're the best.'

These three patients have severely challenged my capacity to persevere in the face of intractable and persistent psychic pain. The capacity to tolerate one's own helplessness as a physician needs to be learnt. I was not taught this but learnt it by experience and indirectly from one of my mentors, Felix Post, a pioneer in geriatric psychiatry who was often blunt in his communications. As a senior registrar when I was covering his clinical outpatient practice, I vividly remember a patient who revealed: 'Dr Post told me I was a hopeless case but that he would still see me—this was strangely reassuring.'

This is an aspect of clinical medicine and psychiatry that is not highlighted. We do need to acknowledge and not abandon the small number of patients who we cannot help and who continue to suffer—yet who still benefit from the sense that we have not given up on them.

Professor Kenneth I. Shulman

OVERCOMING AND MANAGING RECURRENT DEPRESSION

> People are like stained glass windows. They sparkle and shine when the sun is out, but when the darkness sets in, their true beauty is revealed only if there is a light from within.
>
> Elisabeth Kübler-Ross

'Suzanne' tells in the following account about her increasing ability to recognise her depression as it develops, and to employ tested strategies to see her through it until her black dog is once more reduced to 'a mere shadow on a sunny wall'.

Climbing the slippery slide

 I lie awake in the dark long hours... Low energy levels dull my awareness. Repetitious loops, fixations and swollen worries dominate my negative mindset. I gag on my morning muesli.

'I can beat this!', 'Keep on... it's not so bad!', 'Others cope with a lot worse!' The stuff of my useless self-talk. Tears, trembling and ragged breathing drag me slowly through the endless do-nothing days. Finally I recognise the terrain. Yes, I have been here before—the black dog is definitely at my heels. I need to take action... slow down its blundering momentum. My symptoms are escalating. It's time to unpack my care kit and call in assistance.

My safety rails—to prevent the tumble into depression—are medication, exercise, my supportive health care professionals, my husband, and just giving myself 'time off' for a while.

Medication
Tricyclic medication doesn't sound as groovy as Prozac. However, sometimes the heavier guns have to be aimed at a recurring

depression in an older person. For me, the side effects begin immediately—dry mouth and my ears ringing with tinnitus. I sweat intermittently through a constant woolly feeling. But my doctor reassures: 'It will take at least two or three weeks for your mood to lift and for the side effects to settle.' He tells me that some parts of depression are biological, and its physical momentum is intensified by the collapse of the neurotransmitters serotonin and dopamine, vital chemical messengers that keep the brain happily ticking over and the body healthy; antidepressant medication works to boost their supply.

I begin to sleep better and a healthy interest in food is returning. The side effects diminish. Yet the black dog is still panting and scratching.

So, medication is only part of the solution when my life force is low.

Exercise

There's something about its rhythmic action. Exercise gets energy flowing in my dull, heavy limbs and dissipates some agitation. I take it gently at first . . . not ambitious hikes—but I walk a lot. I'm out when the sun is shining, usually late afternoon, and head for a destination that combines Nature and privacy. I'll sit on a rock to rest and contemplate a simple mantra: 'Trust/Accept/All things must pass.'

Awareness

But fear and despair still carry me to some dark places, isolating me in lonely landscapes, pushing me to irrational suicidal thoughts. Can I convince myself to stay calm? I strain and jolt with my fears but I tell myself: 'fake it until you make it'. I might be able to take charge. I will . . . I have before. Trust/Accept/All things must pass. Yes, even clinical depression.

Roadside assistance

Two helpful professionals wait by the road.

A psychologist enables valuable insights through plain talking. I partly understand that some habitual negative thinking affects the way I perceive myself, others and events. And I find alternatives to substitute for my self-critical thoughts, warped thinking and mental biases. Black dog can be talked down through techniques adopted from cognitive behaviour therapy; however, I have to actively learn this and make it part of my everyday thinking. Sometimes something as simple as being aware of and dispensing with the 'SHOULD' statements can be effective. Or I check whether a 'label' I give myself or another or an event is accurate.

Often I am on automatic pilot—I live my days doing things but not really experiencing them and my mind pulls me every which way. Then, I find calm and endurance coming with concentrating on moment-to-moment experiences but without evaluating them as good or bad. Such 'mindfulness' meditation is a boon.

Also, I see a natural therapist, and I begin to eat six small meals through the day. This is designed to regulate blood sugar—the theory being that it could help with many general symptoms. My small meals contain high-quality whole foods and I add supplements such as vitamin B complex, fish oils and minerals.

My partner

My partner has been hurled into a carer role. I am so fortunate—he listens to my fears and fuzzy logic with great patience. Him just being there is my comfort . . . around the house or garden somewhere doing ordinary things. It is very reassuring. He coaxes me into a warm fragrant bath when I sometimes lose the plot. During the restless nights, he hugs me. He offers companionship as we watch inane TV shows and DVDs and cooks many tasty meals. He carries on his everyday life, laughing and responding on cue in the most ordinary way. When I'm not feeling normal this gives me enormous hope that I can feel that way again too.

My day job

'We teach what we most need to learn' applies to me. For years I enjoyed the calming and grounding effects of regular yoga practice, and this developed into study and qualification as a yoga teacher. Then I became a yoga teacher—while in the depths of despair. There wasn't much choice; I was committed to teach my two weekly classes. I feel vulnerable, somewhat fraudulent, self-conscious, tired and drawn. This shouldn't be happening to me!

However, somehow I manage to get through each week. Despite my shortcomings, I can still offer something to my students and they to me.

It takes willpower to get there but the ground I gain gives a shot of much-needed positivity. 'Laughter yoga' blossoms in the classes. Slowly I reconnect with the two-way street of sociable living.

A pet

Black dog lies heavily on me of a morning. It's no good staying in bed, allowing it to feed off my negative energy. However, a beautiful Siamese cat lives with us. She springs lightly on the bed each morning.

'Hello! It's time to play!'

If I don't stir she will curl happily under my arm and purr awhile. This therapy pet is blithely unaware of black dog. Mercurial and in the moment, she is supremely comfortable in her skin. As I sit by the sunny wall in the back garden, she shows me she has all the time in the world just to 'be'.

Writing

Sometimes a rough recycled notepad helps me rant, ramble and repeat, screw up and toss. My notebook has become a resource. It records some of my toughest days, psychologist visits and outcomes, medication dosages, dietary advice, dispassionate thoughts, doodles, affirmations, literary references and philosophy.

The 'to do' list

I've halved my 'to do' list, watered it down, let it slip, backed off to sit with things . . . that's so necessary for my mental and physical health. Nothing is ever perfect, all is in flux, there will always be leaves on the path. 'Don't take it on!' I now tell myself. 'Manyana, manyana' is my new mantra. Better to be a grandma comfortable in her skin, than a depressed, weepy family elder.

Little things from big things grow

In the acute phase of depression, I can't socialise. In time, visits from close friends and doing small things together or talking over a cup of tea helps to get me back on the road. When I can barely concentrate to read, there is pleasure in flipping through art books. Gazing at paintings takes me to places away from myself. They provide inspiration and ideas for future artwork. Meanwhile I make do with simple knitting—a rag rug. A few basic household chores give shape to my flat days.

Self-acceptance

This is a thought that crops up often with my depression. Sometimes I've had to surrender completely to my helplessness, finally realising that those close to me will support and accept me as I am. I've felt afraid of being seen as unworthy when I'm not coping. I fail my own unrealistic perceptions and expectations. What is beyond these feelings, this vulner-ability? Fear of total exposure? Being stripped bare? My own mortality? Even when black dog has been reduced to a mere shadow on a sunny wall, there is an issue of self-trust and self-love that is demonstrated in my quest to secure self-acceptance—that peaceful state that it seems takes a lifetime to reach. Suzanne

In the final narrative in this chapter, 'Molly' describes her passage to quiet acceptance of her recurrent bouts of depression. While the biggest problem is seeing the way out, she says, 'I know by now that there is a path and that I will find it.'

Going with the flow

I have always lived amongst the trees and I am surrounded by shades of green. The old cherry tree has now finished flower-ing and forms a dense green umbrella. The snowball tree has wept its million pure white tears and they lie on the ground like snow. I sit here when the breeze is blowing and imagine it is snowing all around me. The whiteness on the tree and the ground gives the air an incredible brightness.

The blackbird sings all day, on and off. He perches in the cherry tree and begins his song in the morning when it's still dark, and in the evening it's the last thing I hear. He is marking the days for me just now—beginning and ending them. It's as if he sings only for me and not for his territory or his mate or the young birds in the nest. I need his song now when I am in my struggle time.

The depression and anxiety close around me like darkness. Fear accompanies the physical symptoms and I am even afraid of the fear itself. Time slows down, the days take forever to pass. Mornings are the worst. Waking up and getting out of bed is stepping into the unknown. How will it be today? Will anxiety and panic envelop me or will I cope? I wonder about depression. Sometimes I think there is a purpose in it; it's a kind of burnout. Some say it saves you from madness by shutting down the mind and body until healing can take place. It does force me to take stock and see what I have been doing to cause it. Mostly, negative thinking is the culprit: my mind goes round and round and spirals down, taking me with it. When I look back over the past few weeks I can see the signs—but only retrospectively. The biggest problem is seeing a way out. I know by now that there is a path and that I will find it, but believing that is quite another matter.

Depression first hit when I retired from work. At first I thought it was some terrible illness, and it took many months and several doctors before panic attacks and depression were found to be the problem. Although retirement was the catalyst, looking back I can see the signs. I shut my feelings away. Because I didn't tell anyone my problems, they grew and overwhelmed me. At first I hoped to defeat depression and be the way I was before but now I have come to realise that this is unlikely. I aim to learn to live with it, accept the bad times and enjoy the good times when the shine is back on the world. Sometimes I take tablets but they don't help much, and I still have to face life when I go off them. I have been to a psychologist and this was good but counselling is too expensive to have on a regular basis. I live in the country and when depressed find it very difficult to drive myself an hour and a half each way for appointments. I have also read many books, each claiming to know the cause and the cure. Often I used to think that the author was right and that it was just a matter of doing some little thing differently and I would be cured. But now I know there is no easy answer. The experts have many different suggestions so perhaps they don't really know either. Maybe there are different reasons, different solutions. Maybe there is no solution—for me.

I try to do the things which I know from experience will help me. Each day I do several short relaxations and I walk and eat as well as I can. I keep busy. I go out and connect with others. I talk when the words seem frozen within me. I smile on the outside. Creative activities really help; drawing, music and writing. I keep a journal and record my progress and the day's activities. It's my dialogue with myself. I try to answer my own questions. Writing these words helps me most. Somehow words form a river.

Yes, the river. Once a day I go down the hill, threading through the melaleucas, scuttling the stones and skidding on the steep path. The sound of the rushing water grows louder and stronger. I break out into the open. The restless grey water hurls itself over the top and smashes down to the bottom of the weir. This is what it's like inside me—this greyness, this meaningless force, taking me who knows where.

Yet it's going somewhere, that river. It never gives up. It is forced to keep moving to the sea by the weight of the water still coming from somewhere up in the mountain, by its own self. And it tells me something. It tells me I will keep going, even when I see no reason. Although I think I have stopped, withdrawn from life, I am still moving. I think about going with the flow, keeping my head above water and reaching the peace and expansiveness of the open sea. Out there the greyness is gone. The water is pale green and translucent. The bay is fringed by casuarinas waving their branches in the breeze. The sky above is sunny and tranquil and stretches on forever.

I'll get there. It will happen. I know: I've been there before. Molly

Professor Peter Rabins practises at a university centre and in a department of psychiatry that focuses on caring for people with severe illness. He is referred many individuals who have 'failed' treatment elsewhere, and individuals seeking a second opinion regarding the next steps in treatment for a condition that has not responded to treatment. In 'Noteworthy', below, he addresses the known treatments in a logical sequence.

NOTEWORTHY

Treatment-resistant depression

Depression is mentioned in the Bible and by Hippocrates and those descriptions match exactly the disorder we see today, so we can learn a lot about depression from past descriptions. Two wonderful sources of information are Burton's The Anatomy of Melancholy, written in 1621,[4] and historian Stanley Jackson's Melancholia and Depression.[5] From them it is clear that most cases of what we now call 'major depression' resolved spontaneously within six months to a year. However, there have always been people, perhaps 15 per cent of individuals with major depression, whose illness becomes chronic and often disabling.

While modern studies have identified 'risk factors, predictors or correlates' of chronic symptoms that do not respond to treatment, no factor can predict with any degree of accuracy who will and will not recover. Thus it is only 'after the fact' that we know someone is not responding to treatment or is undergoing a spontaneous response.

Over the years of seeing patients referred for 'treatment-resistant depression', I have become aware of several generalisations. The following paragraphs describe them.

Many patients described as 'treatment resistant' have
not had adequate trials of standard treatment

This may be because the physician prescribing a medication or therapist providing psychotherapy was not well versed in the treatment, and thus 'under-treated' by not prescribing a high enough dose, not waiting long enough to see if there would be a response, or by not adapting the treatment to the needs of that individual. Sometimes the problem is that the patient experiences side effects that limit the amount of time on a treatment or reports side effects that an experienced clinician could support them through; or the patient attributes to the treatment a symptom that is actually from the mood disorder rather than from the therapy. Or there is the 'impatient' patient who gives up on the therapy and does not want to persist, even though more time is needed to determine if the medication is, in fact, working.

Sometimes there are medical issues that are
undiscovered and are causing, perpetuating
or mimicking depression

The list of such potential causes is long, and includes medications that cause depression (steroids and antihypertensive medications such as reserpine and alphamethydopa are two examples); diseases that cause depression, such as occult (hidden) cancer, hypothyroidism or low thyroid, elevated cortisol, vitamin B12 deficiency and Parkinson's disease; or disease that mimics depression, such as early dementia with apathy.

Sometimes the psychiatric diagnosis is not correct

Patients who experience a condition called a 'mixed state', in which symptoms of low mood (depression) and elevated mood (mania or hypomania) occur simultaneously or in rapid succession, might need a different treatment than would be prescribed for a more typical depression.

Sometimes there is a complex mix of psychosocial and/or medical and/or psychological issues that are not dealt with
Treatment here might be best if different approaches are used to treat the different problems, either simultaneously or sequentially. First determine the order in which these problems would be best addressed.

ECT is by far the most effective treatment for severe depression
Sometimes ECT is not offered or the patient does not accept it. Bilateral ECT, in which electrodes are put on both sides of the forehead, can be effective when unilateral ECT has not been. Sometimes ECT is stopped too early, before a full recovery is obtained. If there is any evidence of benefit, I encourage people to continue until it is clear that no further benefit is to be gained. Sometimes a second or even a third course of ECT works when carried out months or even years after an adequate but failed course.

A common issue in treatment-resistant cases is that people lose hope and give up. I admit that I have had patients over the years who seemed to have failed every treatment, yet who either spontaneously improved after years, or who benefited from a medication or medication combination that had not previously been tried.

A final note is that a very well designed and large study, the STAR*D Trial, compared a number of steps that can be taken in changing treatment regimens. My clinical experience disagrees with the primary findings of the study, and I am left with the awkward conclusion that either my clinical experience is mistaken, that the study included subjects who are dissimilar to those I see in my practice, or that there were basic flaws in the design of the study. I am not sure which of these is true or if a combination of them is correct, but I remain convinced that the large majority of patients with treatment-resistant depression can be helped if they and their treatment teams use known treatments in a logical sequence that maximises the assessment of effectiveness of each treatment.

Professor Peter V. Rabins

11
Ageing and self-efficacy

> We are all happier in many ways when we are old than when we are young. The young sow wild oats. The old grow sage.
>
> Winston Churchill

The Centers for Disease Control (CDC) in America has a healthy ageing program that indicates the benefits, well into our 60s and 70s, of taking action to reduce the risk of developing chronic disease and injury. Exercise, stretching and preventive measures such as flu shots and disease screening are valuable; regular checks of vision and hearing are helpful (with updates of spectacles and other aids), as is exercise that improves balance and flexibility to prevent falls.

There is also consistent evidence of the positive effect of a generally optimistic outlook on life: optimists live longer and healthier lives and have a lower risk of heart disease.[1] If you've been given lemons, find a recipe and make lemonade.

Additionally, those growing older are advised to consciously maintain engagement with friends and activities that give pleasure; improve everyday diet; avoid consuming alcohol to excess; and cease cigarette smoking, all of which will facilitate healthy ageing and enhance a sense of purpose and control.

IDENTIFYING THOSE AT HIGHER RISK

A large across-cultures study carried out over four decades by the United Kingdom's Medical Research Council indicated that a person's ability to complete everyday tasks helps predict mortality. Assessment measures found to be linked to current and future health may now enable identification of people who will benefit from intervention to keep them active for longer.

Findings, corrected for age, sex and body size, established that those who performed better at four particular tasks were more likely to live to 'a riper age': gripping (strong hand grip); walking (brisk stride); rising from a chair with vigour; and balancing on one leg.[2]

THE IMPORTANCE OF PERCEIVED CONTROL

How an individual views a situation consciously and unconsciously influences the capacity to cope. The following story about 'Margaret', related by Dr Chanaka Wijeratne, indicates how far an otherwise resilient and competent person can 'decompensate' as a result of both a physical and a psychological assault. It is also instructive how quickly she recovered when she was able to feel in control again.

CASE NOTES

The indiscernible limp

The referral had been taken by one of our aged care psychiatry team's community nurses. The patient was a 73-year-old woman who, during the course of a telephone triage, had described a plan to commit suicide. Now, apart from caring for our patients, the management of the suicidal patient and prevention where possible of suicide is the métier of a psychiatrist. So my mind immediately turned to risk factors for completed suicide—predictors from large populations that are applied to individuals. An inexact science of course but our patient had a much lower risk than a man of the same age and had reported no significant physical illnesses, although she was widowed, lived alone and appeared to have developed depression. An urgent assessment was arranged.

Margaret arrived in the clinic with a book and a shopping bag, a fit and indeed imposing-looking woman who wore an air of defiance. She was easy to engage and with little prompting said she would jump from a cliff top she had selected, at a specific time of her choosing. She did not view it as an act of suicide; rather, a way of regaining control of her life. In any case, she continued dispassionately, she had always believed in euthanasia and the seawater was merely a filter into the next life.

She was adamant that she was not depressed, because she felt numb—in fact no emotion at all—but her self-esteem had plummeted and a sense of futility about living had crept in. She dated these changes to being mugged a couple of years earlier, near a railway station. A man—she knew immediately from the odour—had grabbed her handbag from behind and unsurprisingly she reacted to her assailant and a struggle ensued. She fell and sustained a fractured ankle, which was stabilised with the insertion of a pin and plate. She had planned her suicide for the anniversary of the mugging, six months or so hence.

I enquired about the consequences of the fractured ankle and surgery. No, there was no real pain or disability, and indeed she had walked up the corridor and stairs to my office with no hint of either. And no, she hadn't suffered flashbacks or nightmares and had been able to return to her usual haunts after the surgery, although she felt more security conscious in general and her sleep had become disturbed.

She had never previously thought about taking her life, let alone suffered depression. A story of feeling unloved by her mother, a harsh father and a husband who had gambled away a lot of their money suggested a capacity to weather troubles. Without any children of her own, she had taken pride in her work as a teacher, in particular engaging her more troubled pupils, who would be invited home. She had worked tirelessly for various charities since her retirement.

I prescribed an antidepressant that she ultimately could not tolerate and referred her to Susan, the clinical psychologist who worked with our team, for help with improving her sense of safety. Margaret returned to see me every month and received a time-limited course of cognitive therapy from Susan. She reported feeling better but the anniversary date loomed closer and she still harboured occasional thoughts of jumping.

At this point I received a letter from a solicitor who was assisting Margaret with her application to a victim's compensation tribunal. Now, there is a rather gloomy view in psychiatry about the effects of a compensation claim. These range from the spectre of a medico-legal quagmire perpetuating the symptoms, to the less gracious view that the patient may be embellishing their symptoms for financial gain—so-called 'compensation neurosis'—to the perception that even a good medico-legal outcome does nothing for the patient's wellbeing. Thankfully the matter was resolved quickly, although it was not about the money (which she donated to charity), but rather that she felt her distress had been recognised.

She started to feel very much better, more like a human being she said, and much less likely to jump . . . until a routine appointment at the orthopaedic clinic to check on her foot. She returned indignant at the treatment she had received from a registrar, who had been rude and refused the surgery to remove the pin and plate that had been promised by her surgeon. Her symptoms returned so that she was again tearful and irritable, once more feeling like a non-person, and the thoughts of jumping had returned at a more intense level.

Should I try another antidepressant? No, she hadn't taken to them, no doubt as much because of the physical side effects as for the sense of being controlled by them. Would hospitalisation provide some temporary sanctuary? No, for the same reason. In any case, her problem was more obvious. The metal in the foot was an ongoing symbol of the day her spirit had been assaulted. The surgeon's reply to my letter was swift and far more courteous than the manner of his trainee. Subsequently the pin and plate were removed and Margaret reported a closure of the whole incident. There were no plans to jump at all now and, in any case, there was a dog—an abused dog from the RSPCA a friend had brought her—to care for. That was close to the last I saw of Margaret, after some fifteen months of therapy.

Lessons learnt

The lessons are manifold, some are relearning from previous patients. Like many people from older generations, Margaret did not recognise the word 'depression', yet irritability and the inability to feel any emotion are common mood changes in late-life depression. Margaret's plan to commit suicide some months ahead contrasted with the impulsivity of many suicide attempters. She was preoccupied by the mugger's violation of her humanity so perhaps this was time she intended to use to search for positive engagement with others, who turned out to be various health care and legal professionals. As much as I followed the textbook in managing her distress, it was my advocacy on her behalf to her lawyer and surgeon that led to an initial, and then a sustained, recovery. I also wish I had thought of the dog, because we forget that older people, who no longer work or care for their own brood and suffer multiple bereavements, are often disconnected and isolated.

Finally, I am so accustomed to my older depression patients' demonstrable signs of physical illness—the Parkinsonian shuffle, the long medication list or the brain scan showing strokes—that I underestimated the significance of the metal in the foot. The act of being mugged and humiliated could not be removed, but its stain could.

Dr Chanaka Wijeratne

In the account that follows, 'Martin' summarises what he and his friends have found helpful as they age. This is a 'potpourri' of what they consider to be the best protective approaches to growing older: the 'usual suspects'—regular physical exercise, attention to diet, seeking out mental stimulation, maintaining an optimistic outlook and engaging in activities that add to a sense of purpose in later life.

Prescription for a healthy life

 As passengers on a recent cruise, we sat down nightly for dinner with our fellow travellers and discussed our lives and times. Diverse and often conflicting perspectives were aired from our table of eight—which included couples from Australia, Europe, the Middle East and South America, aged 60 and older. We fell into discussion about how best to mitigate or cope with some of the challenges of later life—including warding off depression.

Our exchanges about our life experiences led us to consider how we were each coping individually. The ethos of the ship was focused on healthy living through regular exercise and stimulating entertainment. We agreed that our active engagement on shipboard was an approach that could be equally applied to everyday living as we aged.

Here is a potpourri of what each of us has found helpful.

Daily physical exercise

Flexibility exercises, aerobic activity involving large muscle groups and resistance training are all easily modified to accommodate the vagaries of age. The many experts, classes and resources available ensure that a program can be crafted that suits tastes, varying levels of disability and timetables. Including friends in a routine is so much the better and shores up lapses in motivation until the exercise habit becomes a valued part of every day.

The importance of regular physical activity is being increasingly recognised with its role in improved productivity, reduced sick time and boosting morale. It's not just another item on our 'to do' list: we agreed that time taken out to exercise refreshes and enables us to do more. And there are benefits that accrue in the years to come.

Attention to diet

We older people can neglect diet and take a 'feast or famine' approach—either big, rich or oversize meals outside the home or a grab-and-nibble tea-and-toast regime at home. It is easy to put together an attractive array of nutritious foods with help from the web or from leaflets at the doctor's or Senior Citizens' Centre or municipal library. Freeze half that casserole for later, ensuring one fewer dish to cook and more variety for next week.

Maintaining mental alertness

We were all spooked by memory decline. We could see it in ourselves and, before that, in our parents. Also of concern was our declining ability to learn and retain new information and process calculations, find our way, and cope with and understand new technology. (Oh well, one can always call on the children!) To combat this we felt that mental and physical stimulation helped with attention and alertness: reading; playing games; TV and radio programs; visits to art galleries and museums; learning another language; free classes and educational tours. An added bonus is the friendships and further activities that grow around these. One of our group said there are mind 'workout' exercises available on the internet. Some of these programs were based on research from reputable universities.

Maintaining mental wellbeing

Perceptions and expectations can play a major role in late-life emotional health and satisfaction. If an older person develops a true depressive illness, this needs help from health care professionals; however, for average ups and downs of mood, cultivating pleasures such as going for a walk or drive, visiting cinemas and theatres, having a massage, a long hot bath, enjoying the garden, eating favourite foods, watching sport events, contacting friends and playing with a grandchild and/or pet can be just the ticket. For longer-lasting happiness, we agreed about the effectiveness of activities that require skill, concentration, feedback, deep absorption and a sense of purpose.

For times of setback, provided you are sure that any problem is within your power to manage, inspirational or self-help books list coping strategies for managing difficult circumstances and teach how to challenge and change automatic negative thoughts. Humour, music and staying connected with others—especially if you are lucky enough to have a cherished partner—are also balms for the soul.

Adding in meaningful, personally gratifying, absorbing activities throughout life (such as community volunteering, church work, writing, dancing, gardening, political activism, a choir) can save us from becoming grumpy old men/women and give a broader horizon to each day. Figure out your signature strengths (e.g. critical thinking, perspective, perseverance, justice, teamwork, appreciation of beauty) and then try to find avenues in life to exercise them.

In short

We agreed that we can create a buffer against the impact of stress, adversity—and ageing itself. Research shows that the outlook for the over-60s is positive. Our health and income levels are better than any previous generation, and behaviours, thinking patterns, and emotional and spiritual aspects are factors we have significant control over, and which have much more impact on health and satisfaction in the seventh and eighth decades of life than was previously realised. So, successful and healthy ageing is a goal that—with some effort—is well within our power. Martin

CONTENTMENT IS NOT LINKED TO POSSESSIONS

> What do the ancient purveyors of physical immortality have in common? They're all dead.
>
> S. Jay Olshansky

To reiterate, the recipe for 'successful' ageing includes a mix of remaining sociable, active and independent, finding substitutes for activities that are no longer possible, and not feeling sorry for oneself. A sense of wellbeing comes from sharing and reciprocity with others and is achieved from having purpose and meaning in life rather than from material gain. And satisfaction comes from within oneself and from relationships rather than from external 'success'.

Contentment is linked to non-materialistic involvements and experiences, such as:

- relationships, experiences and interaction with others
- belonging to a cohesive community
- marriage and family
- efficacy and the sense that life goals are being progressed
- feeling that there is meaning in life
- being involved with something bigger than oneself, be it spirituality, a nurturing life philosophy, religion
- health and vitality; being physically active and maintaining mental capacity
- fulfilment at work or in a pursuit such as volunteering.[3]

THE ROLE OF RELIGIOUS AND SPIRITUAL BELIEFS

Religious and spiritual beliefs contribute strongly to successfully navigating the shoals of ageing. Professor Dan Blazer has studied the role of formal religious belief in a group of older people living in the community: there were substantial correlations between religious attitudes and happiness, and feelings of usefulness and adjustment, and such correlations tended to increase over time.[4]

Harold Koenig, a psychiatrist at Duke University in North Carolina and co-director of its Center for Spirituality, Theology and Health, outlines ways in which religion is beneficial to believers. Religion's emphasis on acceptance and forgiveness of self and others, its hope for healing—yet providing a context and role models for suffering, and its promise of life after death—encourages both a sense of control and self-determination individually and a supportive community collectively.

Religion is supportive in that it reduces deviant behaviour and thus lowers the risk of acute and chronic stressors, and it gives both a cognitive and institutional framework which confers order and meaning and buffers stress. Religious belief also provides social resources and enhances psychological resources such as feelings of worthiness.[5]

Sociologists are able to describe aspects of religion that account for positive effects on morbidity and mortality from an epidemiological perspective. Factors common to religious precepts and good health nostrums include healthy behaviours and lifestyles, health-promoting beliefs and personality styles, belonging and fellowship, the physiological effects of positive emotions, and the benefit of cognitions such as hope, optimism and positive expectations.

TO SUM IT ALL UP

Factors contributing to successful ageing include staying active, maintaining a level of social support, feeling as if we are contributing or reciprocating with others, and, hopefully, developing a foundation for healthy social relationships early in life.[6]

NOTEWORTHY

Strategies for maintaining a positive outlook

Current research indicates the long-term value of cultivating the following habits as best as possible within the individual context. These points have been adapted from Sophie Scott's book Roadtesting Happiness.[7]

Goals are dreams with a deadline

- Practise optimism. It is possible to scan thoughts for pessimistic tendencies and reframe them into more upbeat versions. Repetition can make this habit more habitual. Optimistic people tend to be pro/active, and studies indicate they live longer and healthier lives than do pessimists.
- Switch off rumination. Replaying events and situations that cause distress and anxiety doesn't help—past a point—make sense of them, but such replays can nourish a morose feedback loop. Such thoughts may be extinguished by substituting another activity that is incompatible with them.
- Beware unhelpful comparisons. Many are tempted to compare themselves unfavourably with their peers and feel resentment or envy of the seemingly trouble-free and successful passage of others through life. This diminishes their own accomplishments (and likely overestimates those of others), and lessens grace and self-possession.
- Be grateful. Studies indicate the value of gratitude and being aware of and listing the good things that have happened each day.
- Make a community commitment. Those who help others experience a 'helper's high' and put their own lives into

perspective. Volunteering confers substantial mental and physical health benefits.

- Live in the here and now. Research highlights the value of developing that part of the mind that does not 'think', so that the individual can observe and notice what is around him/her in the 'now' and use all senses to appreciate it.
- Adopt big changes little by little. Large goals or major life changes can be reached in due course by breaking them down into a series of smaller, more easily achievable steps.
- Resilience can be increased through stress-management strategies. Cultivating habits of, for instance, meditation, regular exercise, spending time with friends, and relaxation techniques can provide invaluable everyday tools and a 'credit' balance for when it is necessary to draw on such reserves. Three protective factors in particular have been found to contribute to resilience: positive personality traits, a close bond with an emotionally supportive family member, and receiving support from community or peers.
- The enduring values found to be associated with contentment are gratitude, forgiveness, compassion, generosity of spirit and altruism.

12

Caring for the carers

Husband: 'What do you want for Christmas?'
Wife: 'A divorce!'
Husband: 'I wasn't thinking of spending that much.'

Anon

This chapter looks at the role of family and friends as they support relatives through the course of growing older, and sometimes additionally through depression and/or dementia. A carer's role is difficult and selfless. Those who support carers, such as geriatricians and community care workers, emphasise that if you are a carer you should maintain your own life, health and interests as much as possible. Like the instructions accompanying the oxygen mask that drops from the overhead console in a plane, you need to access your own oxygen first to sustain yourself before you can look after someone else.

CHARACTERISTICS OF CARERS AND CARE RECIPIENTS

A study in 2009 of US caregivers shows that women made up the majority of carers of adults 50 years and older, and most juggled unpaid caregiving with their paid work. Care recipients were proportionately older: in 2004 those aged 75 and older represented 55 per cent; in 2009 they had become 63 per cent, and a higher proportion had dementia. The carers' average age had risen too—from 48 to 50 years of age.

Carers now, however, have less paid help. In the US the use of aides and housekeepers reduced, from 46 to 41 per cent; paid help also declined. Perhaps in response, unpaid caregiving supplied by other family and friends rose, as has the proportion of carers who are male.[1] These figures indicate the risk for chronic stress in carers and subsequent burnout and depression.

THE STRESS OF BEING A CARER

Though much information about carer stress and characteristics is extrapolated from studies of those caring for individuals with dementia, a comparison between carers of those with dementia and those with depression found few differences,[2] and thus we will continue to extrapolate. Carers have high rates of depression: up to 20 per cent of those caring for people affected by dementia are assessed as being depressed. Those who are motivated by a sense of duty, guilt or social pressures are likely to feel more psychological distress than those with more positive motivations.[3] Others may derive positive feelings from caring—being able to reciprocate 'brownie points' built up after a lifetime together, feelings of altruism, enjoyment of doing a job well and satisfaction in seeing a loved one happy. However, the stress of being a carer often overwhelms such emotions.

An illustration of the tremendous stress that carers carry is outlined in the following narrative.

Back from the abyss

My husband doesn't know me anymore. It isn't that he just doesn't want to for some silly reason, or that he is cross with me. He doesn't want a divorce. There's no other woman in his life. He just doesn't seem to know who's who. Even those who were once closest and dearest to him he treats like total strangers. When I visit him at the respite centre where he has been for the past six months, he looks at me quizzically, then bursts into tears. When I leave he sobs his heart out. Who or what he is crying over is anyone's guess. Tragic doesn't even begin to describe the situation.

I haven't been so well myself lately—steadily recovering from surgery for oesophageal cancer and in between fighting depression in the form of anxiety attacks. I always prided myself on being a very upbeat person—nothing fazed me. Grew up in a time when 'depression' was only discussed behind closed doors and sufferers were shunned and often institutionalised. Personally thought depression was a lot of hooey. After all, what did I know?

I am not in any pain—that is, as in ache—but anxiety overwhelms me at times. The emptiness of my day-to-day existence becomes intolerable. A numb, heavy feeling drags me down. I feel I can't cope. All I want is for the evening to come so I can take to my bed, swallow a sleeping pill and sink into oblivion. Will I ever feel normal again? They say it takes time but when you are already in your 80s there isn't that much time left.

Today the word 'depression' is out in the open and bandied about like measles and chicken pox. Talks on the radio and TV, newspapers and magazine articles abound. Everyone is openly worried, even the government and medical profession. Statistics indicate that one in five people already suffer from depression.

Easy to say to the sufferer 'pull yourself together', but when the black dog strikes it's like a tsunami rolling in over you. You gasp for breath, hyperventilate, begin to shake and sweat, the terror is overwhelming. In desperation I call one of my daughters. She comes running. What would I do without them! I see the concern in their eyes and hate myself for being so weak, mastered by something beyond my comprehension.

Currently I seem to live in waiting rooms and at the chemist. Prescriptions fill my bedside table. There was a time when I hated even to swallow an aspirin, never mind how bad the pain. Now here I am—pill-popper deluxe. To crown it all I have a bad reaction to one of my medicines: result, tinnitus. Bells ring constantly in my head. I am reminded of the old nursery rhyme, 'With rings on her fingers and bells on her toes—she shall have music wherever she goes.' Can things get any worse?

I met my husband when I was 23 and he 26. A man of many talents making his way in the world, achieving his goals, taking big decisions, head of an 11,000-person workforce. We have three daughters. As they grew up, my husband, a perfectionist, was always pushing them to excel: his favourite mantra, 'I'm sure you can do better.' Today he doesn't recognise them. They bring him gifts; he looks at them with suspicion. 'Dad, I brought you this teddy to keep you company. When you feel lonely you can take it to bed with you. We miss you.'

My husband had been getting more and more forgetful. Looking back I think I see where and when it all started. He did not really want to leave his beloved home town to move to a new country. On the day the packers arrived he sat in front of the computer typing out the addresses of all our friends in readiness for Christmas. Nothing would budge him. He always designed and made our Christmas cards. I handled the packers and packing alone. Three years later he fell and split the cornea of his left eye. Today he has a glass eye. After emergency surgery, we arranged for him to go straight into care. I joined him at his respite centre for a month. He slept in room 30 and I in number 9. For 57 years we had shared a double bed. Sleeping alone proved a whole new experience; no more just turning over for a cuddle.

Why did I put him in care? There was no way I could go on looking after him once he came out of hospital. He followed me everywhere like a puppy. His continual questions, the same ones repeated a hundred times, were mind-boggling. The fact that I was myself recovering was beyond his grasp.

I visit him regularly but watching him decline is gut-wrenching. He just sits in his chair staring at the TV, taking nothing in. 'I just want to die,' he tells me, his black mantle of depression suffocating him. 'Why don't my mother and father visit?' he asks. 'My brothers promised to take me to Huntley Bay—I know they bought the tickets. The train leaves tomorrow.' Huntley Bay was where he was born and the district where he worked, places he keeps recalling and begging to go back to. I inform him his parents, like his two brothers, died a long time ago. 'Why didn't someone tell me?' he asks.

Tomorrow is Christmas Day—a day I thought my husband and I would never share again. It will be a big day that will include our daughters, grandchildren and friends. Thanks to the wonderful care and love shown my husband by his carers he is more settled today and I can rest, knowing he is in good hands. My hair has grown back, I have put on two kilograms and medically I have been given the all-clear.

Accepting things today as they are has helped me cope with our present circumstances. I'm so thankful to all those concerned with my welfare who have supported me patiently— their thoughts and prayers are much appreciated. And I'm grateful that in many ways, compared to others, we are still very fortunate. Ivy

THE CHALLENGE OF MANAGING CARE FROM A DISTANCE

The following account is from the daughter of a strong and self-sufficient woman, the matriarch of her family, suddenly and shockingly reduced to a shadow of herself. There are themes of distance, role reversal, stoicism, seeking care, stigma and trust, guilt and being torn between responsibilities.

'You'll love it once you're in!'

This was my mother's method of enticing us as young children to plunge into the North Sea in the bitterly cold English mid-winter. It became a family catchphrase, synonymous with the way my mother would take life in both bands and wring the maximum from it. A strong woman both physically and emotionally, she would bounce back from life's adversities in a way that has left my sister and me, even to this day, embarrassed by our tears. Unhappiness and illness were self-indulgences not to be tolerated.

So my father's phone call surprised me. It was unusual for him to initiate contact and when he spoke it took me some time to comprehend. Apparently my mother was sick, but the information was vague. She hadn't hurt herself and as far as I could gather had no infection. Prompted by my husband, I offered to return to England. We had spent Christmas there six weeks earlier and selfishly I hoped my father might say it wasn't necessary but immediate relief was evident in his voice and I knew I would have to go.

I was totally unprepared for what I found when I arrived. The usual effusive greetings were replaced by a quiet stillness. In fact it was several moments before I registered my mother sitting motionless on the sofa. She looked shrunken, older, greyer—and yet only six weeks had passed since I had last seen her. Maybe I had been too caught up in the festivities to notice her decline then but there was no denying it now. My father was obviously looking to me for solutions and his helplessness made me conscious of the fact that to even begin to deal with this there was going to have to be a role reversal. I was no longer the child; I would have to take charge.

'Has she seen her doctor?'

No, there is no doctor. This is no surprise. My mother has little faith in doctors. I ring the local practice. There are no appointments unless it is an emergency. Is this an emergency? I doubt she is in danger so I take an appointment for the following week and then search the cupboards for food. It's eight hours since my last meal. The cupboards are empty and it appears it may have been even longer since my parents have eaten.

Over the next week I realise the problems my father has had. For him too there has been a role reversal. He is older than my mother and has become frail and demanding as he aged. My mother has been his carer, driver, cook and motivator over the past few years; now he must regain those skills. We drive to the supermarket. My mother trembles on the verge of weeping—she doesn't want to get out of the car. My father stays with her while I quickly gather the provisions for a meal that both of them barely touch.

I wash, I clean, I cook; and in all this I try to kid myself that I am being useful but when I walk into the lounge my father has his arms around my mother as tears roll down her face. They both look so lost my heart aches. The house is sombre. We speak in matter-of-fact terms, unsure how to make or continue conversation. To break monotony I suggest a drive to the beach. This will give Dad a chance to practise his driving and Mum a change of scenery. It takes forever to prepare. My mother is cold; the coat, the hat, the gloves, the blanket are not enough. We add a hot water bottle and finally set off. The trip is dismal and I wonder if it was worth the effort. I am angry with my mother, I am angry with myself. I feel guilty that I cannot do more to fix the problem.

At night I retreat to my bedroom, thankful for the space. It occurs to me that my father does not have this respite and I think that I might need to facilitate this. I feel the effects of the pervasive mood of the house and yet it seems impossible to break through the barrier of unresponsiveness in order to lighten it. I also feel a desperate need to know if this is what is to be from now on. I miss my husband and children and I hold doubts that I have the strength to change things.

Waiting to see the doctor has been interminable and when the day arrives I realise I have high expectations. My mother shuffles into the surgery, swamped by her heavy overcoat that hides the dowdy tracksuit she prefers to wear these days. I can see my mother is intimidated. I am unsure whether to go in with her but she seems to want me to. I am surprised to hear my mother answer the doctor's questions but her replies are simple and I feel they hardly paint the picture of what is happening. I wonder if this doctor can have any clue of how far from normal this is when she has never met my mother before. I want to tell her more, but feel it is improper in front of Mum. Later, I suggest Dad book himself an appointment to talk about the problem but he too feels that would breach my mother's confidentiality. We return home, deflated. I think I wanted to know a diagnosis, a prognosis, a magic cure, but it has all been a bit vague. We've been given some tablets that might work and an appointment in a week. A week might as well be an eternity!

Each day we look for improvements. I start a journal to try to document them but it soon becomes clear there is nothing to report. In fact my mother is now becoming distressed by her inability to sleep. I try to get an earlier appointment but the doctor is off for two days.

I am searching for a way of connecting with Mum. She seems so alone in her sadness, so when she complains of cold feet I massage them. This seems to relax her so I begin to give her back massages. This is way beyond the intimacy we had when she was well but I am feeling useful at last. We move a day bed into the lounge so that she can feel our presence as she rests. Over the following weeks her medication is changed and various strengths are tried. The progress is slow. There are bad days and better days. Gradually the better days outnumber the bad. Mum will ask for massages now—up to four a day! She doesn't talk to us about how she feels. That would be out of character anyway but she does see a behaviour modification therapist and it seems to boost her.

I know I can't stay forever and at some point we will have to decide whether Dad can cope if the improvements cease. My mother still does not like to be left alone so I have persuaded Dad to talk to some of the people in their street. They know Mum has been ill and have brought flowers to the door but Dad has been reticent to tell them that Mum is depressed. He holds this tight to his chest as if ashamed that he has somehow failed. The curious thing is that he was once a GP himself, and yet through this whole episode he has been embarrassed and uncertain. After several months, I leave. At the time I felt I was running out on Dad because, although better, Mum was hardly her old self. I felt guilty for leaving them to cope and for my joy to be returning to my own family but the neighbours have been terrific. They drop by frequently and give Dad the freedom to go out.

Two years on, and my father has died. Attending his funeral, I am thrilled to find Mum strong, philosophical about her loss and keen to celebrate my father's life rather than focus on his death. It would seem that the 'old' Mum has finally returned. Interestingly, we don't ask her directly about her illness. It seems that that taboo still exists but we watch her carefully and are glad to see that she is eating and sleeping well and has become active in a number of social groups. I think she still takes her tablets and sees her GP but, again, I don't ask.

Lifelong behavioural patterns are hard to break and now as I write this I realise it would be good to be more open. I make another mental note to do better. Liz

At some point, as people grow older, they usually 'hand over the baton' to their child or children and roles become partially reversed, with the child becoming the carer of the parent. Liz's fiercely independent mum, however, retains her authority, and Liz is faced with the additional difficulties of accessing care in an unfamiliar environment for an illness that her parents will not, through shame and stigma, address directly. Meanwhile Liz has put her own family's life on hold for an unknown amount of time. Her resourcefulness in this situation demonstrates that she has indeed inherited her mother's physical and emotional strength.

SYMPTOMS OF CARER STRESS

Carers are at higher risk of social isolation, reduced interests and reduced employment because of the demands on their time and the associated financial costs of consultations, treatment and ongoing management of their charge.

Carers who go on to develop depression themselves are then also at higher risk of physical morbidity. Risk factors to depression in these circumstances (from studies of those who care for people with dementia) include being a spouse (rather than a child, relative or friend), low marital 'cohesion', low self-rated health and caregiving competence, and high numbers of hours of assistance. Other factors shown to affect carers' levels of depression are the burden of functional limitations, agitation and depression in the care recipient.[4]

Some of the strains of being a carer are outlined by 'Maggie' in the following narrative.

Tom and Maggie's story

Well, here they were: children grown up, all successfully pursuing their careers and living away from home; family business fine; financially comfortable; about to celebrate 40 years of marriage. Life was going well for Tom and

Maggie as they considered retirement. Then Tom started getting really distressing headaches.

The doctor arranged many tests and scans but couldn't find a reason. The headaches got worse and Tom was not sleeping well—horrible nightmares every night. He started losing his confidence, forgetting things, and was generally very miserable and unhappy and venting his irritations on Maggie . . . telling her that she hadn't told him things, though it was him who'd forgotten!

Tom had always been a very practical man who could put his hands to any task with success and had always worked long and hard. Now he was finding even menial tasks difficult. He began losing his temper, particularly with Maggie (who avoided retaliation and tried to ignore what was said). The more frustrated he became, the more he smoked and withdrew.

After further months of frequent visits to doctors and deteriorating health, Tom was diagnosed with endogenous depression. Then began the long hard road for both Tom and Maggie to get his health back to somewhat normal.

He was prescribed antidepressant and anti-anxiety medication, which had side effects and took time to adjust to. The medications did help somewhat but Tom was still having trouble with sleeping, nightmares, loss of self-confidence, feeling a failure and being just generally miserable. He avoided seeing people, and because of the stigma attached to mental illness he felt that he couldn't tell his friends what was really wrong or how he was feeling. Maggie was very tactful about what she said to people out of respect for Tom, usually saying he just had a tired brain from all the strain he'd put on it over his life.

By now Maggie was taking all the responsibility she could with the business, their finances and any family matters. She went with Tom to all his appointments, taking her daily reports on Tom for the doctor to read later so as not to embarrass Tom with speaking about it. Their GP was a great support to them both. Maggie filled dosettes with Tom's medication so they knew whether he'd taken his medication, and both carry a list of Tom's medication in their wallets.

Maggie also learnt not to tell Tom anything of importance later in the day as he was too tired and got irritable about almost anything. She learnt the skill of 'walking on eggshells'. Maggie's way of coping was always to look for positives to focus on in any situation. Her hobbies of knitting, reading, sewing and scrapbooking were of great benefit, as were her phone conversations with her children as they often laughed about things—better than crying, which would have been easy enough to do. Maggie just tried to find humour in the negativity that now surrounded her, though being the carer of a spouse was not easy—it was hard to ignore nasty comments and accusations nearly 24 hours a day.

Maggie and the children felt that the cause of Tom's depression went back to his childhood—his mother passed away when he was only ten. Over the years Tom often commented, 'It would be good if Mum could have shared this with us' when there was some special family event. And he often said that people were lucky to still have their mum. Interestingly, the doctor and the psychiatrist did not feel this was the cause, though they didn't suggest any other.

Feeling the need for it to be recognised that she was a carer, Maggie decided to apply for a carer payment for herself and a disability support pension for Tom. After endless form-filling they were granted a small amount per fortnight each. Their business was firstly leased and then sold. Tom was reluctant to see this happen as he felt he had put so much into it. Maggie felt pleased to not have to think about it all. She had enough to cope with!

In time, after a few more changes of medication there was some improvement for Tom but he wasn't sleeping and was still having horrible nightmares every night. Eventually the doctor referred him to a specialist, feeling that Tom may have been suffering from sleep apnoea. Well! The test showed that Tom was having apnoeas every 30 seconds all night—no wonder he got up exhausted. He was prescribed a CPAP machine to use for sleeping. From the very first night Tom slept so well and with no nightmares; he couldn't believe it. Is that how people always sleep, he thought! Also, he no longer snored, which was great for Maggie. Now he never sleeps without his CPAP machine and his health has certainly improved. Around this time Maggie decided to add some fish oil capsules to Tom's medication. She and the children feel these have also been helpful.

Ten years on, life is much better but Tom has not gone back to all that he was before. He still can't cope with crowds, funerals, dealing with banks or more intense thinking; he does not have a good memory now and still has occasional times of really feeling 'down'. Meanwhile, however, the grandchildren have arrived. Being grandparents is so enjoyable and both love spending as much time as possible with the littlies.

Here are some observations from Maggie, directed to all professional people:

- headaches are a real symptom of depression
- bad sleeping patterns may be a symptom of sleep apnoea as well as of depression
- listen to a patient's spouse, as they may have the best information for the diagnosis.

Maggie also offers the following advice to carers:

- always look for positives—no matter how negative everything may seem there is always a positive
- look after your own health first!

Finally, it has been a privilege to write this story and I hope the information will be useful to many others facing similar situations. Maggie

THE WEB OF SUPPORT

An anchor of stability for most carers is the partnership between care recipient, carer, other service providers and the GP and/or specialist/s. In the case of a carer responsible for the care of an intimate with clinical depression, for instance, the GP can refer both parties to counselling, more structured interventions for personal wellbeing, and community support systems. The GP can also monitor the physical health of both parties and encourage regular review.

Diagnosis of the care recipient's disorder—and sometimes of the carer if their mental health has become compromised—is a crucial step. Next comes therapy and/or medication, the provision of information and an explanation of where to acquire more of it (identified by carers as key to their capability), and support.

A surprising barrier to the use of community self-help groups has been found: carers have not been told about them. An informed carer can be the health professional's ally, able to partner with them in depression management strategies and monitoring the response to interventions. A protective factor for a carer's mental health is such perceived support, especially if it is tailored to the unique circumstances of the carer and care recipient.

WHICH ARE THE MOST EFFECTIVE INTERVENTIONS?

Research into programs that support the mental health of carers looking after people who have dementia indicates that helpful interventions include educating carers about the disease process, providing training to improve coping skills and problem-solving, and support groups and counselling.

Research has also endorsed the effectiveness of individually tailored treatments that are more resource-intensive, such as behaviour management training, multi-component interventions and individual skills training—especially when the care recipient is also involved—in a structured program that teaches the carer problem-solving skills, provides readily available practical support, involves the extended family, and gives access to structured individual counselling and a consistent professional to provide long-term support. Interventions found not to be effective were stand-alone support groups, single interviews to give advice, and brief interventions or courses that were not supplemented with long-term contact.[5]

In a study where carers were instructed in using a pleasurable-events schedule for spouses with early Alzheimer's disease and depression, both the depression levels of the care recipients and of the carers improved.[6] Engagement in activities which previously gave pleasure was in itself reinforcing and helped lift the mood of the depressed charge. It was usual to start with the easiest first and gradually work down the list. As well, teaching carers to use problem-solving approaches and exercise[7] has been shown to provide benefit for depression in this setting.

OUTCOME MEASURES OF CARER PROGRAM SUCCESS

After successful interventions, carers reported:

- fewer feelings of frustration towards care recipients
- fewer sleep problems for both
- better knowledge and ability to manage problematic behaviour in the care recipient

- improved psychosocial outcomes (lower sense of burden, better subjective wellbeing, lower levels of depression, less anxiety, improved self-efficacy and positive experiences of caregiving, more satisfaction with health care and quality of life)
- better health behaviours (diet, exercise)
- improved health (reported health, symptoms, medication use/misuse, service use).

CONTINUITY OF CARE AND THE ROLE OF THE KEY WORKER

An issue often raised by carers and service providers involved in the management of those who are ageing is the lack of continuity of care. Ideally, there should be a key worker to act as a guide, build up a longstanding relationship with the carer and care recipient and provide continuing care.[8]

The key worker best acts to:

- facilitate the carer by encouraging them to record questions as they arise, and to diarise appointments to keep track of them
- encourage the carer to rank problems in order of urgency/importance
- provide information to carers about the nature of depression (such as types, therapies, resources, recovery and relapse, precipitating and perpetuating factors)
- discuss the carer's role, validate the stress associated with being a carer and outline the adverse effects of stress and techniques for alleviating it
- arrange and keep track of home care services, and notify of other facilities and supports available
- offer understanding to the carer about his or her difficult role—a high level of perceived support can help address carer anxiety and reduce stress

- be flexible when there is more than one carer in the family, and strive to facilitate and to meet with all carers concurrently.

A HEALTH PASSPORT

The National Association of Chronic Disease Directors in Atlanta suggests the idea of a 'health passport' for carers. This is designed to collate and keep together:

- educational topics and advice
- details of relevant local services and support groups
- contact details for various official agencies on ageing
- medications, safety procedures and emergency numbers
- the carer and care recipient's health records and health history
- other important records such as health screenings, tests and immunisations
- medical insurance contact details
- medication records and allergies
- future appointments.[9]

IMPROVEMENTS IN PSYCHIATRIC CARE FOR OLDER PEOPLE AND CARERS

As we grow older, health care will be required to stretch further and service our needs more efficiently.

Future models of care might include some of the following approaches:

- preventive programs—encouraging active engagement with the community, exercise, mental stimulation, volunteering
- integration of mental health and general medical services, to enable collaboration between primary care, aged care and psychogeriatrics

- integration of hospital and community care to form a comprehensive model of acute and long-term care
- 'capitated' care arrangements to contain costs and to encourage use of cost-effective services
- reallocation of funding to support home- and community-based alternatives to long-term care
- risk-adjustment strategies that factor in the huge costs associated with comorbid physical and mental disorders in older age, ensuring accountability, advocacy and outcomes
- offering GPs special training courses in aged care, with an added rebate for GPs qualified in aged care; allowing specially trained GPs special rights for prescribing medications for mood disorders and dementia (currently restricted and requiring a specialist confirmation of diagnosis); and additional rebates for attending for nursing home care, so that nursing home approved (or aged care trained) GPs would have a specialist interest in elder care within resident aged care facilities (RACFs)
- training practice nurses in assessment of older people with cognitive impairment and mood disorders, and supporting them to work with GPs
- training and credentialling clinical nurse consultants or nurse practitioners to work towards making a diagnosis and arranging referral for a plan of management for older people.[10]

NOTEWORTHY

Tips from a carer to other carers
Always look after your own health first! Beware of burnout—many carers develop depression; headaches can be a symptom of depression; bad sleeping patterns could signal sleep apnoea or the beginnings of depression in yourself.

Look for positives, no matter how negative everything may seem—there is always a positive, or you can turn a negative into one! Talk to a clinical professional if you feel down and join a carer's support group.

The person you are caring for may refuse to seek help for depression or cognitive decline. You can only assist up to the point when your charge will let you help. Discussion—within the family, with health care professionals and support organis-ations—can shape the way forward. Family support/pressure can persuade your charge to accept assessment and manage-ment for his or her disorder.

As a carer, you need to look after your own wellbeing. Maintain parts of your life that do not include the person you care for, just as you would if that person was healthy.

It is important that the person with the disorder develops his or her own strategies. You must realise your own limits as a carer—you are not responsible for curing your charge, but you can lessen his or her distress and be emotionally available.

You will benefit from widening your circle of support. When others offer help, take them up on their offer. This builds a network for both you and your charge. Friends might help with housework, post letters, pay bills, collect groceries, cook a meal or tend the garden. They will follow your suggestions for how they can help. It works best if you are organised, specific and realistic about what you can expect help with and how often.

Carers' support groups are important anchors and offer education, strategies and advice on identifying early warning signs; they also promote advocacy, help with coping with the consequences of the disorder, and link you to health care profes-sionals. Join one!

As a carer, you can proactively encourage your charge to develop a management plan while they are well that can then be used in coordination with health care professionals in the event of further depressive episodes. When ill, your charge may be too unwell or unmotivated to pursue his or her own treatment.

One sign of burnout is when you, the carer, feel numb or increasingly unsympathetic or angry towards your charge, or you continuously experience feelings of failure and powerlessness. Seek help! Use support services/groups, service providers and respite programs to assist you to regain your emotional stamina.

Darren

Appendix I
Risk factors for self-harm

If you can get someone at risk to talk about it, you can significantly reduce the chance of them taking their life.

www.ruokday.com.au

Aside from the psychological pain for the individual, depression makes it more difficult to cope with chronic health problems and is associated with overuse of medications, substance abuse, premature retirement, interruption and permanent loss of family and community roles, alienation of family and friends, overuse of social and medical services, reduced self-care and consequent malnutrition and premature death—including by suicide.

Assessment of suicide risk is an important part of the evaluation of depression in later life. Suicide rates in older people have always been relatively high, especially in older men. There is usually a strong intent to die and so methods used are more lethal.

A guide to depression in older age for patients and family outlines symptoms, causes and risk factors, and nominates depression—treated and untreated—as the most common psychiatric diagnosis and the number-one cause of suicide in older adults. Their suicide risk is almost twice that of the younger adult population.[1]

Situations in which an older person becomes preoccupied with changing their will, gives away personal possessions, talks about death,'stockpiles'medications or takes an unprecedented interest in firearms should not only alert friends and family to the possibility of depression but also to suicide risk. Another potential sign is when an older depressed person at risk for suicide becomes uncharacteristically calm and appears—paradoxically—more content and at ease than they have been for months. This may be because they have made the decision to end their life.

Evaluating suicide risk

An older person may have expressed suicidal ideation (thoughts), or stated their intent—or made plans—to attempt suicide, or expressed severe hopelessness about their situation.

In order to evaluate suicide risk it is necessary to talk to the person alone, allow sufficient time and establish rapport.

It can be helpful to:

- acknowledge the difficulty of talking about such sensitive issues
- explore the problem that led to the current crisis
- ask the person about his or her arguments for/against suicide
- evaluate access to any means for attempting suicide
- ask directly about suicidal thoughts, behaviours or plans, and their frequency and persistence
- ask what has stopped him/her from acting on such thoughts so far
- check whether there have been previous suicide attempts, the relevance of past occupation (for instance, police force, nursing), and access to means
- check whether any family member or friend has suicided
- obtain collateral history from those in closest contact, including family, friends and/or carers. The person may have more openly expressed suicidal ideas or plans to them.

High suicide-risk patients requiring urgent psychiatric review include those who:

- spontaneously express suicidal ideation
- state an intent to suicide, or have made definite plans
- have planned suicide or attempted it previously—assess the circumstances and similarities to the present situation, and how planned and 'lethal' any previous attempt was
- express severe hopelessness about their situation.[2]

Better understanding of why older people kill themselves could help prevent suicide. Prevention can depend on recognising the relevant biological and psychosocial components, and intervening to diminish their risk. There is some opportunity to do this, in that older suicide victims have usually been in contact with health professionals, particularly GPs, in the month before death.[3]

Psychological autopsy (in-depth analysis of everyone connected to the person who has suicided) and pathological autopsy helps researchers to determine more accurately the causes of depression and self-harm in late life. Research is focused on improving screening and management of depression and suicidal ideation in older people who are in contact with their GP.

The risk of suicide and self-harm
An individual with a mood disorder may find it difficult to keep going.

Risk of self-harm can arise as:

- the direct result of the mental illness and the thoughts and drives that result from it—which can sometimes be a wish to 'stop the pain' rather than necessarily to die
- an attempt to end unmanageable physical pain and despair
- an attempt to send a message or leave a particular legacy
- a result of delusions or hallucinations driving the suicidal behaviour

- an altruistic act, in the mistaken belief of relieving others of a burden.

The risk is difficult to estimate as, for some individuals, self-harm can be impulsive and occur apparently without warning. Previous suicide attempt/s are indicators of especially high risk.

Early warning signs of suicidality may include:
- expressing feelings of hopelessness and helplessness
- giving away personal possessions
- talking about suicide, saying things such as, 'I wish I were dead' or 'What's the point of going on?'
- mentioning ways of suiciding, and a plan
- talking about letting others down
- talking about feeling trapped
- leaving organised activities
- expressions of rage, anger, revenge
- abnormal sleep patterns
- dramatic changes in mood
- withdrawing from friends
- self-neglect
- engaging in risky self-destructive behaviour
- a sudden bout of unexplained calm or cheerfulness following a long period of sadness or anger.

These signs can vary across culture, age group and gender.

Other associated suicide characteristics include:[4]
- individuals with more rigid, emotionally restricted personality traits; this contrasts with the high impulsivity scores reported in younger suicide victims
- those with obsessive and compulsive, anxious and dependent personality traits

- those who consult GPs more frequently
- risky levels of alcohol consumption
- complaints of pain
- the presence of certain physical illnesses, such as renal failure, chronic breathing difficulties, stroke or early dementia
- the experience of major life events causing guilt, shame, humiliation or financial ruin.

Critical information that might have altered the management is often not accessed from family members.

While self-harming may be an attempt to self-soothe rather than an attempt to die, people who self-harm are demonstrating their limited ability to develop effective coping strategies and do sometimes attempt suicide. In later life, the ratio of completed-to-attempted suicide increases; in other words, the older the person, the more likely it is that a suicidal attempt will succeed.

Some factors that can exacerbate the risk of self-harm:
- vulnerability caused by inner distress or psychosis
- inability to communicate distress in a less harmful manner
- recent stressful life events such as a diagnosis of physical or mental illness
- the recent loss of a loved one or a pet, or the suicide of a friend or role model
- a relationship breakdown or separation from a loved one
- a major disappointment
- access to means of self-harm.

Impulsiveness is increased if there is involvement with intoxicants, particularly alcohol.

Factors that may protect a person from suicide include:[5]
- strong perceived social supports
- family cohesion
- peer group affiliation
- good coping and problem-solving skills
- positive values and beliefs
- ability to seek and access help.

Special advice for carers:
If there have been threats or changed behaviours, seek professional advice immediately. Though some behaviours are more obvious high-risk ones—such as giving away possessions, or the older person shows a mood of relief, resolution and calm after a particularly bad patch—there are no absolute predictable signs.

An excellent resource providing further information about aspects of suicide and self-harm is the Australian Government's Living Is For Everyone (LIFE) website: www.livingisforeveryone.com.[6]

Appendix II
Further information
for older people and carers

If finding out information seems a little challenging, or you are not sure which websites are the official ones with expert information, ask for assistance from the librarian at your local library.

Further information about ageing well can be found under the following subject areas.

WEBSITES

Search for national and local government, hospital and university websites, and websites affiliated with older people or which lobby for them. As a guide, search under the following topics:

- older age
- positive ageing
- maintaining health in older age
  —sub-topics: exercise and diet
- services for older people
- gerontechnology
- leisure groups and interests
- problems of older age

- medications in older age
- coping strategies
- mental health
- fact sheets from national coalitions for older people
- healthy ageing
- depression in older age.

You can also access websites from professional groups such as psychologists for strategies, therapies and treatments for:

- better mental health in older age
- managing depression
- managing bipolar disorder (older term: manic depression).

There are also websites that discuss financial security in older age. Ensure, however, that they are websites of accredited professional bodies.

OTHER IMPORTANT RESOURCES

- Your general practitioner (GP) should be your first port of call if you, or someone you know, is aged 60 or older and is experiencing problems with depression.
- You can obtain a referral from your GP to a psychiatrist, or a psychiatrist who specialises in geriatric care (a psychogeriatrician), for more detailed assessment.
- There are information phone lines that you can ring to get advice about resources relevant to older age. A community resource centre, mental health advisory service and/or your library should be able to assist you to track down further information.

A NOTE ON THE ORIGINS OF THIS BOOK

This book had its origins in the Black Dog Institute's annual Writing Competition. In 2010, older people, their children and people who care for them told their personal stories in an insightful look at how depression impacts on the over-60s. The editors also approached world-ranking psychogeriatricians, geriatricians and other clinicians in this field, who generously shared their insights and accounts. This book therefore offers both a 'top down' professional-based framework, and a 'bottom up' perspective. Because mood disorders vary in type and severity, in degree of impairment and disability, across time, and in response to the environment, we hope that readers can select pieces of wisdom and advice to shape their own approach to such issues. All views add to the 'democracy of knowledge'.

This book joins four earlier companion books—Journeys with the Black Dog, Mastering Bipolar Disorder, Navigating Teenage Depression and Tackling Depression at Work—which detail the views of those who have learnt to manage their mood, and seek to inform about mood disorders and the Black Dog Institute approach.

THE BLACK DOG INSTITUTE'S WEBSITE

The Institute's website—www.blackdoginstitute.org.au—provides further information on mood disorders. It also features:

- self-tests for depression, postnatal depression and bipolar disorder
- fact sheets covering signs and symptoms of mood disorders
- a free Mood Assessment Program (MAP), where a computer algorithm weighs up patient data collected at assessment at the Institute's clinic to compute the individual's likely mood disorder diagnosis, with the MAP report sent to the referring doctor
- further data on 'older age' (enter this term into the 'search' option).

Appendix III
Clinician contributors' short biographies

Professor Osvaldo P. ALMEIDA completed Medicine and specialist training at the University of São Paulo, Brazil, and postgraduate education at the Maudsley Hospital, UK. His PhD investigations assisted in the better diagnosis of late-life psychotic states. He is Professor and Winthrop Chair of Geriatric Psychiatry at the School of Psychiatry and Clinical Neurosciences, University of Western Australia; Consultant Geriatric Psychiatrist at the Royal Perth Hospital; and the Director of Research at the Western Australian Centre for Health and Ageing. He contributes substantially to training in older age psychiatry. His research group identifies and modifies factors associated with poor mental health outcomes in later life, most recently physiological and lifestyle risk factors associated with depression. He is an Associate Editor of International Psychogeriatrics.

Professor David AMES graduated in Medicine from the University of Melbourne, Australia, and trained in psychiatry at the Royal Melbourne Hospital and Friern and Royal Free Hospitals in London. He took up the Chair of Psychiatry of Old Age for the University of Melbourne at St Vincent's Health–St George's Hospital, Kew, and then became Director of the National Ageing Research Institute in Melbourne, and the University of Melbourne Foundation Professor of Ageing and Health. As the Editor of International Psychogeriatrics, he oversaw its impact factor more than double. He co-founded Victoria's first memory clinic, and currently his main clinical and research interests include the detection and management of Alzheimer's disease and new drug therapies, and the care of the depressed elderly.

E/Professor Tom ARIE CBE studied at Oxford University, and trained in psychiatry there and at the Maudsley and London Hospitals. He is widely recognised for establishing the foundation principles and practices of a comprehensive, integrated, multidisciplinary service system of psychogeriatric care. He established, at Goodmayes Hospital in London, one of the first psychiatric units for old people. He became Foundation Professor of Health Care of the Elderly at Nottingham University, establishing a joint department of physicians, psychiatrists and gerontologists, and where he is now Emeritus Professor. He has been Vice-President of the Royal College of Psychiatrists, Chairman of its Old Age Section, is an Honorary Fellow of the Royal College of Psychiatrists, and Chairman of the World Psychiatric Association Old Age Section.

Professor Dan BLAZER practises at Duke University Medical Center in North Carolina, where he is the JP Gibbons Professor of Psychiatry and Behavioral Sciences, Vice Chair for Faculty Development, and Head of the University Council on Aging and Human Development. Recognition includes listings in Who's Who in America and The Best Doctors in America; Honored Teaching Professor in the Department of Psychiatry; Fellowships in the American College of Psychiatry and the Gerontological Society of America; Distinguished Life Fellowship in the American Psychiatric Association;

and Institute of Medicine membership. He is the editor of Duke Medicine Health News and on the Editorial Board of the Archives of General Psychiatry. His extensive publications focus on the areas of depression, epidemiology, and psychiatry and religion, especially in the elderly.

Professor Henry BRODATY AO is Scientia Professor of Ageing and Mental Health, University of New South Wales; Director, Aged Care Psychiatry and Head of the Memory Disorders Clinic, Prince of Wales Hospital, Sydney; and Director of the Primary Dementia Collaborative Research Centre. He has served on New South Wales and Commonwealth committees related to ageing and dementia. He is the past Chairman of Alzheimer's Disease International and past President of Alzheimer's Australia and Alzheimer's Australia (NSW), and President-Elect of the International Psychogeriatric Association. He is on the editorial board of several journals. His research interests include all aspects of dementia—particularly Alzheimer's disease—and new drug therapies; support of carers; mild cognitive impairment; psychiatric sequelae of stroke; quality of life in nursing homes; and late-life depression.

Professor Brian DRAPER is Conjoint Professor in the School of Psychiatry, University of New South Wales (UNSW); Assistant Director, Academic Department for Old Age Psychiatry, Prince of Wales Hospital, Sydney; and Senior Old Age Psychiatrist, South Eastern Sydney Local Health Network. He is Chair of the Australian Government's Psychogeriatric Care Expert Reference Group and of the International Psychogeriatric Association's (IPA) Behavioral and Psychological Symptoms of Dementia Taskforce; and Immediate Past Chair of the Faculty of Psychiatry of Old Age (FPOA), RANZCP. He is on the management committee of the Primary Dementia Collaborative Research Centre at UNSW. He is Deputy Editor of the IPA online website and a board member. His interests include psychogeriatric service delivery, suicidal behaviour in old age, dementia care, carer stress, depression and professional development.

E/Professor Robin JACOBY studied modern languages at Oxford, and Medicine at Oxford and Guy's Hospital. He undertook post-graduate training in internal medicine at Southampton University Hospitals and psychiatric training at the Bethlem Royal and Maudsley Hospitals, where he was a consultant for ten years. Currently, he is Professor Emeritus of Old Age Psychiatry at the University of Oxford. With Drs Oppenheimer, Dening and Thomas, he edits The Oxford Textbook of Old Age Psychiatry—now in its fourth edition. Until recently he was Chairman of the Global Initiative on Psychiatry (an international charity dedicated to reform of psychiatry, especially in countries of the former Soviet bloc). He has a particular interest in testamentary capacity, and has considerable experience in contentious probate cases.

E/Professor Max KAMIEN AM graduated from the University of Western Australia (UWA). Postgraduate qualifications include Internal Medicine, Child Health, Psychiatry and General Practice. He was Foundation Professor of General Practice at UWA. He prefers primary care settings and has worked in many Third World countries and in Fourth World situations in Australia. The 'Kamien Report' he chaired led to more effective recruitment and support of doctors in rural areas. Currently, he maintains a part-time general practice and also works at the Kununurra Aboriginal Medical Service. He provides support for international medical graduates in rural and remote Western Australia. He is an honorary research fellow at UWA, an RACGP Corlis Travelling Fellow and Provost of the WA Faculty of the RACGP.

Dr Lana KOSSOFF graduated from the University of New South Wales and did specialist training at Royal Prince Alfred Hospital,

Northside Clinic and Macquarie Hospitals in Sydney. She is a Member of the Faculty of Psychiatry of Old Age, RANZCP. She was Unit Director of the Psychogeriatric Admission Unit at Macquarie Hospital, became Director of Clinical Services and then Executive Director. Subsequently, she returned to clinical work in aged care psychiatry, involving inpatient, consultation-liaison and outpatient settings, and provided a fly-in service for three cities in rural New South Wales. She also maintains a private medico-legal practice and is a member of the RANZCP's Forensic Section. Clinical interests include the diagnosis and treatment of complex cases and the assessment of testamentary capacity.

Professor Nicola LAUTENSCHLAGER received undergraduate and postgraduate training at the Technical University in Munich, Germany, and as a postdoctoral fellow at Boston University, USA. She moved to the University of Western Australia, Perth, ultimately to the position of Professor in Old Age Psychiatry and Deputy Head of School. Currently at the University of Melbourne, she is Professor and Chair of Old Age Psychiatry at the Department of Psychiatry, and Head of the Academic Unit for Psychiatry of Old Age. She is also Director of the St Vincent's Health Aged Mental Health Service and Honorary Professorial Fellow, National Ageing Research Institute (NARI). Her research focus includes dementia, early diagnosis of cognitive impairment and intervention trials for older adults to improve mental health outcomes.

Dr Jan ORMAN is a Sydney general practitioner and a past president of the Australian College of Psychological Medicine. She has a particular interest in mental health, especially that of adolescents and young adults. She practises as a GP at the University Health Service at the University of Sydney and as a psychotherapist in the inner west of Sydney. Other roles include work for the Black Dog Institute as a facilitator of General Practice education programs—which shealsoassistedindeveloping—andastheGeneralPracticeServices Consultant, helping to tailor the Institute's initiatives to the general practice environment. Clinically her areas of special interest include mood disorders and eating disorders. She has a personal and professional interest in writing as therapy.

Professor Gordon PARKER AO is Scientia Professor of Psychiatry, University of New South Wales and Executive Director, Black Dog Institute, Sydney. He was, for two decades, Head of the School of Psychiatry at UNSW and Director of the Division of Psychiatry at Sydney's Prince of Wales and Prince Henry Hospitals. He has held a number of positions with legal organisations, including the NSW Guardianship Board and the NSW Administrative Appeals Tribunal. Responsibilities for the College of Psychiatrists have included Editor of the Journal and Chair of the Quality Assurance Committee. In 2004, he received a Citation Laureate as the Australian scientist most highly cited in the field of psychiatry/psychology. Research focuses include modelling psychiatric conditions, and causes, mechanisms and treatments for mood disorders.

Professor Peter V. RABINS is the Richman Family Professor for Alzheimer's and Related Disease in the Department of Psychiatry and Behavioral Sciences at The Johns Hopkins University School of Medicine in Baltimore, USA. He directs the Division of Geriatric Psychiatry and Neuropsychiatry, and is director of a clinical program that includes an inpatient unit, partial day hospital program, an outpatient clinic and the PATCH Program (Psychogeriatric Assessment and Treatment in City Housing). The latter service delivers mobile treatment services to elderly people with serious and persistent mental illness who live in city housing. Research interests include depression and bipolar disorder in the elderly; effectiveness of treatment and development of measures of quality of life in persons with Alzheimer's disease; and best care of patients with late-stage dementia.

Professor Joel SADAVOY is Professor of Psychiatry and former head of the divisions of geriatric and general psychiatry at the University of Toronto, immediate past psychiatrist in chief and head of the Geriatric and Community Psychiatry Programs at Mount Sinai Hospital, holds the Sam and Judy Pencer and Family Chair in Applied General Psychiatry and is also Director of the Cyril & Dorothy, Joel & Jill Reitman Centre for Alzheimer's Support and Training. He is a past president of the International Psychogeriatric Association and was founding President of the Canadian Academy of Geriatric Psychiatry. Most recent awards include the International Psychogeriatric Association Distinguished Service Award and the President's Award of the International Federation on Aging. His interests include services for family carers of those with dementia, psychotherapy, personality disorders in the elderly, and access to mental health care for ethnocultural seniors.

Professor Kenneth I. SHULMAN completed Medicine and post-graduate training in psychiatry from the University of Toronto, then specialty training in geriatric psychiatry in London, England. He obtained a Master of Science in Health Policy and Management at the Harvard School of Public Health. Formerly the Director of the Division of Geriatric Psychiatry at the University of Toronto, he served for a decade as Psychiatrist-in-Chief at Sunnybrook, and Vice-Chair, Clinical Affairs of the University of Toronto, Department of Psychiatry. He is now Chief of the Brain Sciences Program at Sunnybrook and inaugural recipient of the Richard Lewar Chair in Geriatric Psychiatry, University of Toronto. His research interests include cognitive screening; bipolarity in old age; and the pharmaco-epidemiology of mood stabilisers in late life.

Professor John SNOWDON AM trained at Clare College, Cambridge and St Thomas' Hospital, London. His MD explored the typology of depression in old age. Previously at Sydney's Prince of

Wales and Prince Henry Hospitals, he is currently a Clinical Professor in Psychiatry, University of Sydney Medical School. His inpatient team at Concord Hospital links with the Royal Prince Alfred Hospital-based community mental health service for older people. He was the first Chair of the RANZCP's Faculty of Psychiatry of Old Age and is currently Chair of the International Psychogeriatric Association's Task Force on mental health in long-term care homes. His research interests include severe domestic squalor, prevalence and treatment of late-life depression, suicide risk in the elderly, and mental health in nursing homes.

Professor Sergio E. STARKSTEIN qualified at the University of Buenos Aires, Argentina, then specialised in internal medicine, neurology and psychiatry. He was Post-Doctoral Fellow and subsequently Assistant Professor at the Department of Psychiatry, The Johns Hopkins University School of Medicine, Baltimore, USA; then Head of the Department of Neuropsychiatry at the Raul Carrea Institute of Neurological Research, Buenos Aires. He is now Professor at the School of Psychiatry and Clinical Neurosciences, University of Western Australia. He is involved in many internationally and locally funded research projects and his research—using laboratory methods that range from neuropsychological testing to volumetric MRI, quantified EEG, SPECT, and PET scans—covers the psychiatric disorders in neurological diseases such as stroke, dementia and Parkinson's disease.

Doctor Chanaka WIJERATNE graduated in Medicine at the University of New South Wales (UNSW). He is a psychiatrist in the Academic Department for Old Age Psychiatry at Sydney's Prince of Wales Hospital, and a Conjoint Senior Lecturer in the School of Psychiatry, UNSW. He also has a private practice that incorporates general adult and forensic psychiatry, in particular mood disorders, and old-age forensic psychiatry, including assessment of testamentary capacity. He has contributed to the Black Dog Institute's Developing Countries Project, is a Consultant to the NSW Medical Board's Impaired Registrant's Panel, and has a longstanding commitment to improve the quality of electroconvulsive therapy service provision in the public sector. Research interests include late-life bipolar disorder, and the effectiveness of exercise groups in late-life depression.

Professor Sid WILLIAMS is a medical graduate of the University of Sydney, and Fellow of the Australian and New Zealand College of Psychiatrists. While working at Lidcombe Hospital, he was appointed Associate Professor of Psychiatry at the University of Sydney. He developed the first Australian carer-oriented, multidisciplinary outpatient dementia clinic; Psychiatry of Old Age Services at Lidcombe and Braeside Hospitals; and a multidisciplinary course ('Older Person Mental Health') at the NSW Institute of Psychiatry. He has had a prominent role in the renaissance of the discipline of Psychiatry of Old Age in Australia, raising public and health professional awareness of dementia, and facilitating education for health professionals, students and carers. He continues to provide an old-age psychiatry service to rural and regional New South Wales.

Notes

Cover

1   L. Wolpert, Malignant Sadness: The anatomy of depression, Faber & Faber, London, 2001.

Chapter 1

1   Y. Zhan, M. Wang, S. Lui and K.S. Shultz, 'Bridge employment and retirees' health: A longitudinal investigation', Journal of Occupational Health Psychology, vol. 14, 2009, pp. 374–89.

2   Wikipedia, 2011, 'Positive Psychology', <http://en.wikipedia.org/wiki/Positive_psychology> [14 August 2011].

3   C. Peterson and M. Seligman (eds), The Character Strengths and Virtues: A handbook and classification, Washington, DC, and American Psychological Association, Oxford University Press, New York, 2004.

Chapter 2

1   E.H. Erikson, Childhood and Society (2nd edn), Norton, New York, 1963; and E.H. Erikson, The Life Cycle Completed. Extended version with new chapters on the ninth stage by Joan M. Erikson, Norton, New York, 1998.

2   J.A. Herce, N. Ahn, R. Génova and J. Pereira, Bio-demographic and Health Aspects of Ageing in the EU, CESIFO working paper no. 1027; Category 3: Social Protection, 2003, presented at the CESIFO Conference on Health and Economic Policy, June 2003.

3   Ibid.

4   Agency for Health Care Administration (AHCA), 'Nursing Home Statistics', 1998, <www.efmoody.com/longterm/nursingstatistics.html> [14 August 2011].

5   H. Brodaty and A. Withall, 'Positive Ageing: A good news story', Seminar, South Sydney Juniors Rugby League Club, Kingsford, 8 November 2010.

6   The Elderly Suicide Prevention Network (NSW), 'Depression', <www.livingisforeveryone.com.au/IgnitionSuite/uploads/docs/Depression.pdf> [14 August 2011].

7   D. Gibson, P. Braun, C. Benham and F. Mason, Projections of Older Immigrants: People from culturally and linguistically diverse backgrounds, 1996–2026, Australia, Aged Care Series no. 6, Australian Institute of Health and Welfare, Canberra, 2001.

8   The Hon. K. Andrews MP, Work and Family: The importance of workplace flexibility in promoting balance between work and family, Australian Government

Issues Paper, 2006, <www.workplace.gov.au/NR/rdonlyres/B2C64166-2538-4892-BE1E-10112F798C8D/0/IssuesPaperFINALPDF.pdf> [14 August 2011].

9 Ibid.

10 House of Lords Science and Technology Committee, Ageing: Scientific aspects, First Report of Session 2005–06, vol. 1, UK Parliament publications, p. 26.

11 Sherwin B. Nuland, The Art of Ageing, Scribe, Melbourne, 2007, p. 8.

12 Access Economics, 'Population Ageing and the Economy', 2001, pp. 13–14.

13 Australian Institute of Health and Welfare, 'Dementia in Australia', AIHW, Canberra, 2007, p. 26.

14 Adapted from W.J. McG. Tegart, 'Ageing-in-Place', Smart Technology for Healthy Longevity, Australian Academy of Technological Sciences and Engineering, Melbourne, 2010, <www.atse.org.au/resource-centre/func-startdown/220/> [14 August 2011].

Chapter 3

1 US National Institute of Mental Health, 'Older Adults: Depression and suicide facts (fact sheet)', <www.nimh.nih.gov/health/publications/older-adults-depression-and-suicide-facts-fact-sheet/index.shtml#part-of-aging>[14 August 2011].

2 Ibid.

3 Ibid.

4 G. Parker, T. Hilton, W. Walsh, C. Owen, G. Heruc, A. Olley, H. Brotchie and D. Hadzi-Pavlovic, 'Timing is everything: The onset of depression and acute coronary syndrome outcome', Biological Psychiatry, vol. 64, 2008, pp. 660–6.

5 Black Dog Institute, 'Depression in Older People' (fact sheet), <www.blackdoginstitute.org.au/docs/DepressioninOlderPeople.pdf> [14 August 2011].

Chapter 4

1 Adapted from 'Talking Therapies for Older Adults', RANZCP project team, Mental Health Programmes Ltd, 2010, Auckland, New Zealand, <www.tepou.co.nz/page/120–publications> [14 August 2011].

2 A.V. Horwitz and J.C. Wakefield, The Loss of Sadness, Oxford University Press, New York, 2007.

Chapter 5

1 J. Damián, R. Pastor-Barriuso and E. Valderrama-Gama, 'Descriptive epidemiology of undetected depression in institutionalized older people', Journal of the American Medical Directors Association, vol. 11, 2010, pp. 312–19.

2 D. Seitz, N. Purandare and D. Conn, 'Prevalence of psychiatric disorders among older adults in long-term care homes: A systematic review', International Psychogeriatrics, vol. 22, 2010, pp. 1025–39.

3 W. Styron, Darkness Visible: A memoir of madness, Vintage Press, New York, 1992.

4 Academic Department for Old Age Psychiatry, Prince of Wales Hospital and University of New South Wales, Sydney, Research Report 2007–2009, p. 18.

5 Ibid.

Chapter 6

1 P. O'Connor, 'Rite of passage', ch. 3 in Facing the Fifties: From denial to reflection, Allen & Unwin, Sydney, 2001, p. 69.

2 W. Styron, op. cit.

3 D.L. Segal, J.N. Hook and F.L. Coolidge, 'Personality dysfunction, coping styles and clinical symptoms in younger and older adults', Journal of Clinical Geropsychology, vol. 7, 2001, pp. 201–12.

4 Ibid.

5 H. Brodaty, C. Joffe and G. Luscombe, 'Vulnerability to post-traumatic stress disorder and psychological morbidity in aged Holocaust survivors', International Journal of Geriatric Psychiatry, vol. 19, 2004, pp. 968–79.

Chapter 7

1 H. Variend and Y. Vishnu Gopal, 'Late-onset depression: Issues affecting clinical care', Advances in Psychiatric Treatment, vol. 14, 2008, pp. 152–8.

2 B. Draper, 'Depression in the elderly', Medical Observer, Clinical Review Update, 29 January 2010, pp. 21–4.

3 US National Institute of Mental Health, op. cit.

4 B. Draper, op. cit.

5 Ibid.

6 Adapted from H. Brodaty, K. Burns and K. Berman, 'Apathy in dementia', Dementia Collaborative Research Centre Forum, 24 September 2010, Gold Coast, Australia.

Chapter 8

1 B.M. Draper and A. Koshera, 'Do older people receive equitable private psychiatric service provision under Medicare?', Australian and New Zealand Journal of Psychiatry, vol. 35, 2001, pp. 626–30.

2 D-A. Koder, H. Brodaty and K. Anstey, 'Review, Cognitive Therapy for depression in the elderly', International Journal of Geriatric Psychiatry, vol. 11, 1996, pp. 97–107.

3 Ibid.

4 Ibid.

5 G. Parker and K. Eyers, Navigating Teenage Depression: A guide for parents and professionals, Allen & Unwin, Sydney, 2009.

6   C. Strenger, The Designed Self: Psychoanalysis and contemporary identities, The Analytic Press Publishers, New York, 2005.

7   J.T. Little, C.F. Reynolds III, M.A. Dew, E. Frank, A.E. Begley, M.D. Miller, C. Cornes, S. Mazumdar, J.M. Perel and D.J. Kupfer, 'How common is resistance to treatment in recurrent, nonpsychotic geriatric depression?', American Journal of Psychiatry, vol. 155, 1998, pp. 1035–8.

8   C.J. Frazer, H. Christensen and K.M. Griffiths, 'Effectiveness of treatments for depression in older people: A review', Medical Journal of Australia, vol. 182, 2005, pp. 627–32.

9   R. Lieverse, E.J. Van Someren, M.M. Nielen, B.M Uitdehaag, J.H. Smit and W.J. Hoogendijk, 'Bright Light Treatment in elderly patients with non-seasonal Major Depressive Disorder: A randomized placebo-controlled trial', Archives of General Psychiatry, vol. 68, 2011, pp. 61–70.

10 D-A. Koder et al., op. cit.

Chapter 9

1   Trinity University, Academic Programs in Gerontology, 'Social gerontology and the aging revolution', San Antonio, Texas, <www.trinity.edu/~mkearl/geron. html> [14 August 2011].

2   Chair of Positive Ageing and Care, University of New South Wales, News Release, 2010.

3   J. Tinney, 'What purpose do I serve? Finding meaning in being old and in care', survey, National Ageing Research Institute, 40th National Australian Association of Gerontology Conference, Adelaide, Australia, November 2007.

4   J. McCredie, 'Aged care: The depressing reality', 2009, ABC Health and Wellbeing, article including material from Dr Dimity Pond and psycho-geriatrician Professor John Snowdon, 20 August 2009, <www.abc.net.au/health/features/stories/2009/08/20/2661451.htm> [14 August 2011].

5   J. Tinney, op. cit.

6   T. Knight and D. Mellor, 'Social inclusion of older adults in care: Is it just a question of providing activities?', International Journal of Qualitative Studies on Health and Well-Being, vol. 2, 2007, pp. 76–85.

7   J. McCredie, op. cit.

8   T. Knight and D. Mellor, op. cit.

Chapter 10

1   B. Draper, op. cit.

2   M. Petrovic, P. De Paepe and L. Van Bortel, 'Pharmacotherapy of depression in old age', Acta Clinica Belgica, vol. 60, 2005, pp. 150–6.

3   G. Parker and K. Eyers, op. cit., p. 114 ff.

4   R. Burton, The Anatomy of Melancholy, New York Review of Books, New York, 2001. (First published 1621.)

5 S.W. Jackson, Melancholia and Depression: From Hippocratic times to modern times, Yale University Press, New Haven, 1986.

Chapter 11

1 Centers for Disease Control and Prevention, 'Healthy Aging', <www.cdc.gov/aging/index.htm> [14 August 2011].

2 R. Cooper, D. Kuh and R. Hardy, 'Objectively measured physical capability levels and mortality: Systematic review and meta-analysis', British Medical Journal, vol. 341, 2010, c4467.

3 T. Kasser, 'Happiness', ch. 12 in R. Gittins, Gittinomics, Allen & Unwin, Sydney, 2007.

4 D. Blazer and E. Palmore, 'Religion and aging in a longitudinal panel', The Gerontologist, vol. 16, 1976, pp. 82–5.

5 H.G. Koenig, 'Religion, spirituality and medicine in Australia: Research and clinical practice', editorial, Medical Journal of Australia, vol. 186, 2007, p. S46.

6 J. Onedera and F. Stickle, 'Healthy aging in later life', The Family Journal, vol. 16, 2008, pp. 73–7.

7 S. Scott, Roadtesting Happiness, HarperCollins, Sydney, 2010.

Chapter 12

1 P. Span, 2009, 'Who are we now', the New Old Age blog, The New York Times, <newoldage.blogs.nytimes.com/2009/12/09/who-we-are-now/> [14 August 2011].

2 R. Yeatman, K. Bennetts, N. Allen, D. Ames, L. Flicker and W. Waltrowicz, 'Is caring for elderly relatives with depression as stressful as caring for those with dementia? A pilot study in Melbourne', International Journal of Geriatric Psychiatry, vol. 8, 1993, pp. 339–42.

3 H. Brodaty, A. Green and A. Koschera, 'Meta-analysis of psychosocial interventions for caregivers of people with dementia', Journal of the American Geriatrics Society, vol. 51, 2003, pp. 1–8.

4 H. Brodaty and A. Green, 'Who cares for the carer? The often forgotten patient', Australian Family Physician, vol. 31, 2002, pp. 1–4.

5 E. Goy, D. Kansagara and M. Freeman, 2010, 'A Systematic Evidence Review of Interventions for Non-Professional Caregivers of Individuals with Dementia', Department of Veterans Affairs, Washington, DC, <www.ncbi.nlm.nih.gov/books/NBK49200/> [14 August 2011].

6 L. Teri, R.G. Logsdon, J. Uomoto and S.M. McCurry, 'Behavioral treatment of depression in dementia patients: A controlled clinical trial', The Journals of Gerontology, Series B: Psychological Sciences and Social Sciences, vol. 52, 1997, pp. 159–66.

7 L. Teri, L.E. Gibbons, S.M. McCurry, R.G. Logsdon, D.M. Buchner, W.E. Barlow, W.A. Kukull, A.Z. LaCroix, W. McCormick and E.B. Larson, 'Exercise plus behavioral management in patients with Alzheimer Disease: A randomized

controlled trial', The Journal of the American Medical Association, vol. 290, 2003, pp. 2015–22.

8 H. Brodaty, 'Caring for Older Australians', submission to the Productivity Commission, July 2010, <www.pc.gov.au/__data/assets/pdf_file/0012/99867/sub045.pdf> [14 August 2011].

9 University of Michigan's Institute of Gerontology and the National Association of Chronic Disease Directors, 2001, 'Implementing a community-based program for dementia caregivers: An action guide using REACH OUT', <www.diseasechronic.org/files/public/HA_Reach_Out_Action_Guide_09.pdf> [14 August 2011].

10 B. Draper, P. Melding and H. Brodaty, 'Psychogeriatric services: Current trends in Australia and New Zealand', ch. 10 in Psychogeriatric Service Delivery: An international perspective, Oxford University Press, New York, 2005.

Appendix I

1 A. Alexopoulis, I.R. Katz, C.F. Reynolds III and R. Ross, 'Depression in older adults: A guide for patients and families', The Expert Consensus Guideline Series, Expert Knowledge Systems, L.L.C. and Comprehensive NeuroScience Inc., 2001.

2 B. Draper, op. cit.

3 J.B. Luoma, C.E. Martin and J.L. Pearson, 'Contact with mental health and primary care providers before suicide: A review of the evidence', American Journal of Psychiatry, vol. 159, 2002, pp. 909–16.

4 J. Snowdon, 'Review: Suicide in late life', Reviews in Clinical Gerontology, vol. 11, 2001, pp. 353–60.

5 Suicide Risk Assessment and Management Protocols: Mental Health In-patient Unit, NSW Health, NSW Department of Health, 2004.

6 Commonwealth Department of Health and Ageing, 2011, 'Living is for Everyone', <www.livingisforeveryone.com/> [14 August 2011].

Index